SG13
6

THE BRITISH SOLDIER
A SOCIAL HISTORY
FROM 1661 TO THE PRESENT DAY

THE BRITISH SOLDIER

A SOCIAL HISTORY

FROM 1661 TO THE PRESENT DAY

J. M. BRERETON

THE BODLEY HEAD
LONDON

British Library Cataloguing
in Publication Data

Brereton, J.M.
The British soldier: a social history from
1661 to the present day.
1. Great Britain, Army — History — Military
life
I. Title
355.1'0941   U767

ISBN 0-370-30551-5

© J.M. Brereton 1986
Printed in Great Britain for
The Bodley Head Ltd
30 Bedford Square, London WC1B 3RP
by The Bath Press, Avon
Set in Linotron Electra
by Wyvern Typesetting Ltd, Bristol
First published 1986

CONTENTS

NOTE

In the text, numerals printed in a bracket, as (1), refer to the source references printed at the end of the book, pp. 192 ff. Numerals printed above the line, as[1], refer to footnotes on the same page.

PREFACE

There is a voluminous and constantly expanding literature on the British Army, its development, organisation, weaponry and its campaigns. But relatively little study has been devoted exclusively to the 'social' story of the soldier himself. In order to discover how, over the centuries, the rank-and-file were cared for (or not) in peace and war, how disciplined, fed, housed and paid, the student must cast his net wide. He must pore through the indexes to Fortescue's classic thirteen-volume *History of the British Army*; delve into other lesser works; consult the vast body of individual regimental histories, sometimes with profit, often not. He will have to seek out numerous contributions to military and other periodicals.

In this book I have attempted to collate and present in a readily accessible form the many facets of the soldier's social history, from the creation of Britain's Standing Army down to the present day. Since the emphasis is on 'care and maintenance' and welfare, the reader must look elsewhere for accounts of wars and campaigns, though I have not omitted to deal with conditions of active service. And since the soldier's way of life is inevitably interlinked with such broader aspects as army organisation and administration, developments in weapons technology and methods of warfare, these are also touched on where appropriate.

I must stress that the term 'soldier' in title and text conforms to modern usage, as referring to the non-commissioned ranks, or what until latterly were called 'Other Ranks'. Nevertheless, the soldier has always been dependent on his officers for his wellbeing, besides discipline and leadership: it is a venerable truism that there are no bad regiments, only bad officers — or, in today's jargon, bad man-management. Thus where relevant I have made due reference to the officer corps.

While my sources are acknowledged in the notes at the end of the volume, I owe much to individuals and public bodies who have responded to my queries or provided essential reading. I especially thank the following: General Sir Patrick Howard-Dobson, GCB; Lieutenant-General Sir Rollo Pain, KCB, MC; Colonel C. T. J. Wright; Major R. J. Jeffreys, MBE; Major R. P. Smith; Mr Boris Mollo (Deputy Director, National Army Museum); The Librarians and staff of The London Library, Powys County Library, MOD/RUSI Library.

I must also thank Miss Ann Hoffmann of the Authors' Research Service for unpublished material from the Public Record Office and other sources in London. And as always, I pay tribute to my typist, Mrs Trevor Harris of Clyro near Hay-on-Wye, for her transformation of a chaotic manuscript into an immaculate typescript.

Finally, I am grateful to Mr David Machin of The Bodley Head, who first gave me the idea for this book.

J. M. BRERETON

1985

1

EMERGENCE OF
THE REDCOAT

The British Army traces its origins to February 14th, 1661, when on Tower Hill, London, the last two surviving units of Cromwell's New Model Army laid down their arms in token disbandment, then took them up again as loyal soldiers of King Charles II. These two units had served the Commonwealth as the Lord-General's Regiment of Foot and the Lord-General's Life-Guard of Horse. In due course the former became the Coldstream Guards and the latter was merged into the Life Guards. The Lord-General himself was General George Monck who, marching from the Border town of Coldstream with his own regiment the previous year, had been instrumental in securing the restoration of the King.

A little later King Charles brought over from France the troops who had been guarding his royal person in exile, and these were augmented into a regiment of Foot Guards and two Troops of Horse Guards, which eventually emerged as the 1st or Grenadier Guards and the Life Guards.[1] Finally, the King ordered the raising of a regiment of Horse formed largely from a disbanded regiment of Cromwell's army. This was styled the 1st or Royal Regiment of Horse, but as command was given to the Earl of Oxford, who clad them in his own livery of blue instead of scarlet, they quickly became known as 'Oxford Blues'. By 1788 they had become, officially, the Royal Horse Guards.

By the end of 1661 the King's forces had been increased by a regiment of Scottish mercenaries returned from service with the French monarchs. This has ever since been the senior Line regiment of Foot in the British Army, with the present title of The Royal Scots (The Royal Regiment). In the same period another regiment of Foot and a strong Troop of Horse were freshly raised to garrison the King's newly-acquired

---

1. Until the cavalry reorganisations of 1788 the Life Guards were officially designated 'Horse Guards'. They are not to be confused with the Royal Horse Guards (the Blues).

possession of Tangier. 'The Tangier Regiment of Horse' and 'Tangier Regiment of Foot' were to become more familiar as The Royal Dragoons and The Queen's Royal Regiment (2nd Foot).

Embodying elements and traditions of former opposing factions, Parliamentary and Royalist, this modest force of King Charles II's 'Guards and Garrisons' was the true nucleus of the modern British Army.(1)

Since this book is a history of the British soldier, and not of the Army, the subsequent development of those Guards and Garrisons with the creation of new regiments need not concern us. But a word must be said about the status and structure of the embryonic Army.

First it must be stressed that the King's body of troops was in no sense a Regular Army, for there was as yet no constitutional provision for a permanent force of regular soldiers in peacetime. The very notion of such was repugnant both to Parliament and to people who, with memories of Cromwell's Major-Generals, abhorred the red coat as symbolic of military dictatorship. The only armed force recognised by Parliament was the part-time Militia which, although nominally under the King as Captain-General, was actually organised and controlled by the Lord-Lieutenants of Counties.

However, Parliament conceded that the Sovereign was traditionally entitled to maintain sufficient soldiers to guard his royal palaces, to escort him on his journeyings and to garrison the few royal fortresses, such as those of Dover and the Tower of London. Thus the King's forces were referred to not as the Army, but as 'Guards and Garrisons'. Exactly what strength should be deemed adequate for them, in time of peace, was to remain a matter of controversy throughout Charles's reign, and his successors'.

The absolute command of the troops was vested in the King but the *de facto* command was delegated to a Captain-General, or Commander-in-Chief.[2] In addition to his responsibilities for discipline and training, the Captain-General issued commissions to officers, with the King's authority, and was empowered to raise such additional forces as were sanctioned by Parliament. All war *matériel* and military stores were handled by the ancient Department (later Board) of Ordnance under its Master-General, while a Paymaster-General supervised financial matters, including the payment of the troops. A civilian Secretary-at-War

2. General George Monck, created Duke of Albemarle by Charles II, was the first Captain-General and held supreme command until his death in 1670.

existed, but in the days of the Stuarts he was totally subservient to the Captain-General, had no powers over the military, and was little more than a superior form of clerk. It was not until William III's reign that the post began to acquire the influence and authority that distinguished it in the eighteenth and nineteenth centuries. Later, the offices of Adjutant-General and Quartermaster-General were established (1673 and 1686 respectively), the former being responsible for personnel, the latter for quarters and supplies.

Except for some modification in duties, the above hierarchy of the Army remained virtually unchanged for nearly two hundred years. However, although on paper it seems a logical and workmanlike organisation, the machinery of administration was by no means smooth running. As will be seen, corruption, jobbery and sheer inefficiency throughout the chain of command resulted in breakdowns, to the inevitable detriment of the soldier.

The Army itself (or 'Guards and Garrisons') comprised Horse (or cavalry), Dragoons and Foot. There were no permanent organised ancillaries or services. In time of war the Ordnance Department raised 'trains' of artillery with hired horses and civilian drivers, and engineer specialists were likewise co-opted, all these being disbanded when no longer required, as were the *ad hoc* commissariat services.

The structure of the regiments themselves was one which, except for fluctuations in strength, was to remain constant almost down to modern times. A regiment of Horse deployed from six to eight Troops, each of about fifty men and horses, commanded by a Captain with two subalterns under him. In war two, or sometimes three, Troops could be combined to form a Squadron, but this was purely a hostilities-only arrangement for tactical convenience, and the Squadron did not become a permanent sub-unit of a cavalry regiment until the 1880s.

A regiment of Dragoons was structured similarly to that of the Horse, but in the seventeenth century dragoons were not classed as cavalry: they were essentially mounted infantrymen. It was only in the early part of the next century that they became recognised as cavalrymen, capable of shock action with the sword.

The Foot were organised in battalions, or regiments, these terms being practically synonymous, for very few Foot regiments had more than a single battalion in the first decade of the Army's existence. The battalion usually consisted of ten or twelve companies, each company (like the Roman Century) being nominally one hundred men strong, with one

Captain and two subalterns. These strengths fluctuated widely in peace and war, and in the recurring Government defence cuts a company might be pared to only fifty men.

All regiments were commanded by a Colonel, with a Lieutenant-Colonel, a Major and an adjutant on his headquarters staff. Unlike the modern Regimental Colonel who holds an honorary, unpaid appointment and is more often than not a retired General, the early Colonel was the active Commanding Officer with all the responsibilities and duties of that post, and was expected to lead his regiment in the field. Moreover, not only were his powers far greater than those of a modern Commanding Officer, but he could be described as the proprietor of his regiment, for expenditure of the funds allotted by Government (or the King) for the clothing, equipping and pay of his men was left to him. The soldier in the ranks was entirely at the mercy of his Colonel for his wellbeing, even for the due amount of his pay. While there were of course good Colonels as well as bad, the almost despotic power enjoyed by all of them led to notorious malpractices. 'To bad Colonels were due the crying abuses of the pay system as well as those of the clothing system — the systematic robbery of the soldier, the mean frauds by which an income was literally swindled out of Government or sweated off the backs of the men.'(2) That such strictures were no exaggeration will become apparent later.

As noted above, the army was at first unconstitutional: it was tolerated rather than sanctioned by Parliament, and only grudgingly acknowledged to exist. This curious state of affairs persisted until April 1689 when the first Mutiny Act was passed by Parliament and received the assent of King William III. Hitherto there was no military law as such. The soldier was subject only to the Common Law of the land like any civilian; for desertion in time of war he might be convicted by a civil court as a felon and sentenced to death, but such military offences as desertion in peacetime, insubordination, even striking a superior officer, were unprovided for. Thus discipline suffered. Matters came to a head in March 1689 when Colonel Dumbarton's Regiment of Scots Foot, ordered to embark for the Netherlands, broke into open mutiny and set off for Scotland, declaring that the deposed Stuart, James II, was their rightful King, not Dutch William.

The resultant Mutiny Act declared that any officer or soldier mustered in Their Majesties' service who should join in any mutiny or sedition, or desert the service, 'shall suffer Death or such other Punishment as by a Court-Martial shall be inflicted.' Other provisions of this far-reaching

Act dealt with offences relating to false mustering, the billeting of troops, and their pay, but the all-important effect was that Parliament now recognised the existence of a regular Army. However, the preamble was careful to emphasise that 'the raising or keeping a Standing Army in time of Peace, unless it be with Consent of Parliament, is against Law.'(3)

With a few lapses between 1698 and 1702, successive Mutiny Acts with additional provisions were passed annually until 1879 when a revised Act entitled the Army Discipline and Regulation Act came into force. Having been entitled the Army Act in 1881, this became the Army and Air Force Act in 1920. Finally in 1966 the title was changed to the Armed Services Act, and this is still the statutory authority for the maintenance of the British Regular Army.

The total strength of the regular or 'standing' forces of Charles II's army in 1663 was only 3,570. By 1693 the number had risen to 87,440, but Parliament's inevitable clamour for reductions after the Peace of Ryswick in 1697 resulted in a minimal force of only 7,000 Horse and Foot in England, with another 12,000 in Ireland. Reflecting Parliament's rooted hostility to, if not fear of, a powerful military force in peacetime, the Army was to suffer such drastic pruning almost down to the twentieth century.

'An Army is the mirror of the people from which it is drawn,' wrote Clausewitz, and this was probably as true of the seventeenth-century British Army as of the nineteenth-century Prussian. In the England of the late seventeenth century nearly two-thirds of the 5½ million inhabitants were illiterate labouring classes, of whom some four-fifths were employed on the land as 'husbandmen', a term which could embrace yeoman farmers, tenants, or humble peasants. Although there are no firm statistics, individual regimental histories indicate that the majority of the rank-and-file during this period were country men. 'Our armies have been raised by Gentlemen of Figure and Estate,' wrote Daniel Defoe, 'among their Tenants, among their Husbandmen and the farmers' sons, the cottagers and the poor Plebi of the Country...'(4) As might be expected, this was particularly true of the cavalry, whose recruits were obliged to bring their own horses with them on joining (but if they could not, the price of a horse was stopped out of their pay). This very fact adds weight to cavalry regiments' claims that their early soldiers were a cut above those of the infantry, who produced only their own bodies. Few soldiers were literate. A nominal roll of a Troop of Cunningham's Dragoons for 1694 showed that out of sixty men only five could sign their names, and three of these were NCOs.

The British Army prides itself that it has always been a volunteer force, conscription only being resorted to in time of emergency. In the seventeenth century recruits were voluntarily enlisted 'by beat of Drum'. Recruiting parties toured the towns and villages, enrolling men at the local inns. After accepting 'the King's shilling', or a day's pay, the recruit was deemed to have enlisted, and he would then take the Oath of Allegiance by which he swore

> to be true to our Sovereign [name] and to serve him honestly and faithfully in the defence of his person, crown and dignity against his enemies and opposers whatsoever, and to observe and obey the orders of the Generals and Officers set over me by His Majesty. [3]

'The King's shilling' did not in fact imply that the recruit was put on the King's personal payroll and was paid out of the Civil List; in peace as in war, Parliament voted funds for the support of the troops. Enlistment was 'for life', that is, a soldier was committed to serve until he was either disabled by wounds or too old and infirm to be of further use to the Army. It was not until 1806 that the first limited-service terms were introduced.

Although the seventeenth-century Army was theoretically a voluntary force, in times of emergency conscription or 'pressing' could be resorted to. (Once conscripted, the new soldier was required to serve for life and not simply till the conclusion of the emergency which had led to his being pressed into service.) Thus in 1695 an Act was passed granting the King a levy of 1,000 men annually in Scotland, the Sheriffs being empowered to seize 'all idle, loose and vagabond persons' and 'those who have not wife or children', and to select among them 'which of them shall go forth to serve as soldiers'. Walton quotes this as the earliest record of legalised conscription, and similar methods of 'pressing' continued down to Wellington's day.(5) Another Act of 1696 enabled gaolers to release men imprisoned for debt on condition that they enlisted in the Army or the Navy. For the first thirty-odd years of the Standing Army's existence there were no age limits, but in 1696 William III issued a Royal Warrant stipulating that no man was to be enlisted above the age of forty or below the age of seventeen.

3. The wording of the Oath varied from time to time. The above was the form prescribed in the *Articles of War*, 1686.

The Regimental Colonels were entirely responsible for recruiting their own men, and their problems in obtaining the right material are illustrated in a letter dated December 3rd, 1688 from a regimental Agent commenting on recruits for the Earl of Devonshire's Regiment of Horse (10th Horse, later 7th Dragoon Guards) which had just been raised. It was addressed to the Lieutenant-Colonel.

I send here a note of the soldiers and of every horse they ride upon. They are all willing enough to follow your Worship... but I doubt some of them do not deserve to be maintained, being very careless about their horses and duty, uncivil in their quarters and saucy to their officers. Doncaster hath given himself very much to swear and drink, so that his landlord saith that he is not fit to be among Christians... Our trumpeter John Cock was so simple a man and so bad trumpeter that Mr. Millward and I thought not fit to keep him for 3 shillings a day.(6)

The system of recruiting which remained virtually unchanged until the nineteenth century, lent itself to so much sharp practice and jobbery that it became almost a national scandal. Recruiting parties usually set up business in taverns, and having lured in their prey would besot him with ale, so that when the luckless dupe came round it was not only with a hangover, but with the King's shilling in his pocket as a duly enlisted soldier. Then there were the crimps such as the notorious Charles Tooley who in 1693 was exposed in the House of Commons as running a flourishing establishment in Holborn where men were enticed by drink, or even physical force, and then disposed of to recruiters at a profit.

Theoretically, on attestation a recruit was entitled to 'bounty money', fixed at twenty shillings in 1678 and raised to forty shillings in 1690. This was yet another source of abuse. A large portion of the sum due often found its way into the pocket of the Troop or Company Captain 'to defray expenses', the simple, illiterate recruit being too ignorant to query the trifle he himself received. But not all recruits were simple-minded. Many wily rogues would enlist, take what bounty was forthcoming and then disappear, to turn up again under false names in successive units, with successive bounties. This trickery of 'fraudulent enlistment' became so prevalent that in 1692 a Royal Warrant was issued, making it a penal offence to re-enlist in a second regiment without having been legally discharged from the first.

Once attested, soldiers were entitled to rates of pay fixed by successive Royal Warrants. One of the earliest of these, still extant, is that signed by

King James II on January 1st, 1685, from which the following figures for rank-and-file are extracted.(7)

DAILY RATES OF PAY 1685

	HORSE	DRAGOONS	FOOT
Sergeant[4]	—	2s 6d	1s 6d
Corporal[4]	3s	2s	1s
Trumpeter	2s 8d	—	—
Drummer	3s (Kettledrummer)	2s	1s
Private	2s 6d	1s 6d	8d

Compared with average earnings of labouring classes in the same period, the above rates might seem reasonably adequate. For instance, Trevelyan records that an agricultural labourer in the Midlands could not expect more than four shillings per week, out of which he had to pay all expenses for himself and family, while unlike the soldier, he enjoyed no security of employment, and his earnings could fluctuate widely. Of course the soldier was deemed to have no family to support — no allowance was made for dependants.

But, as with so much else that was held out to lure recruits, the pay scales laid down by no means represented the sums actually received by the soldier. Until well into the nineteenth century the pay system was so complex and the rates were subject to so many deductions, authorised and unauthorised that, as Walton remarks, the soldier 'may without exaggeration be said to have been robbed wholesale both by the Government and by his own officers.'

Pay was divided into three parts. First there was what was aptly termed 'subsistence money', out of which the soldier had to pay for his food, lodging and, if in a mounted unit, stabling and forage for his horse. The second division was 'Gross Off-reckonings', representing the difference between total pay and subsistence money. Out of this sum numerous stoppages were made, such as one shilling in the pound for the support of the newly-founded pensioners' Hospital at Chelsea, medical supplies, and fees payable by regiments to their agents and civilian bureaucrats such as auditors, even the Paymaster-General himself. What, if any-

---

4. Until 1788 regiments of Horse had no sergeants, the equivalent rank being that of corporal.

thing, was left after all this was styled 'Net Off-reckonings', and was supposed to be the soldier's spending money.

To take the example of a private of Foot on 8d per day, his subsistence money was fixed at 6d, leaving Gross Off-reckonings of 2d. When the above stoppages had been accounted for, he was lucky if he had anything left to spend on himself.

In theory the subsistence money was inviolate, supposed to be paid in full to the soldier for his living expenses. But dishonest Colonels or their officers constantly found means of withholding large sums, ostensibly for clothing and 'contingencies', but in reality for their own pockets. To quote Walton again: 'The whole system of military finance in the seventeenth century was one vast entanglement of fraud. Not only did the officers defraud the soldiers, but they defrauded the government also, while the government in turn defrauded both officers and soldiers.' In the next century the defrauded soldiers were to find an outspoken but, alas, unavailing champion in William Cobbett, who served in the Army before going into Parliament.

Despite constant inflation in living costs, the rates of pay quoted above remained unaltered for more than one hundred years. It was only in 1783 that some niggardly increases were authorised.

Apart from the few royal fortresses, there were no permanent barracks in England until the end of Queen Anne's reign, and this resulted in the contentious billeting system. Dispersed in detachments throughout the Kingdom, the soldiers (and cavalrymen's horses) were quartered on a reluctant civilian populace. During the Civil War private householders had been forced to provide free quarters to troops, but after the first Mutiny Act of 1689 the billeting of soldiers in private houses, except in emergency, was expressly forbidden. Instead, ran the Act, they were to be accommodated in 'Inns, Livery Stables, Ale-houses, Victualling-houses, and all Houses selling Brandy, Strong-Waters, Sider, or Metheglin by retail.... and in no Private Houses whatsoever'.

Since drunkenness was always one of the most prevalent crimes in the Army, such deliberate exposure of the soldier to the temptation of 'strong-waters' seems curiously perverse. But it was a case of sheer necessity, for in the absence of barracks there was nowhere else to shelter him. The innkeepers were only obliged to supply 'dry lodgings, stable-room for horses, and Fire and Water, and necessary Utensils to dress their Meat', the 'meat' itself and all other provisions to be paid for by the soldier out of his subsistence money.

The billeting system remained as unpopular with the troops as with their unwelcoming hosts until well into the nineteenth century. 'Go where we would,' wrote Gunner Alexander, 'as soldiers we were hated and despised, insulted and loaded with the foulest epithets — in our billets looked upon and received as if we had carried pestilence, robbery and pillage with us.'(8) Instances are recorded of innkeepers taking down their signs and relinquishing their licences as soon as it was learned that troops were being posted to the neighbourhood. Naturally, the landlords begrudged anything but the barest minimum in accommodation. A letter of March 1698 from a young soldier to his brother at home, describes conditions which were probably typical:

> We was 8 of us and Corprl set in a hut backside of Aylhowse. Scarse room to lay our Kit. Ther was no fyre and we got tow truss of Strawe for bed. When we wode boyl our Meate and taters in the Kichen, the wyfe sayd we must wait till all the rest had eaten. Ther was naut but won Potte. In the nite it raynd and we was all very wet. Josh Carter kilt a rat with his baynit.(9)

If the orthography is rather eccentric, we must remember that at this period it was unusual for a private soldier to be able to sign his name, let alone compose a letter. 'An army is the mirror of the people...' and in the seventeenth century very few of the class from which recruits were drawn could read or write. In the Army little or no attention was given to the three Rs for the soldier: so long as he could understand verbal orders, handle his weapons and clean his kit, nothing more was necessary. The theory of 'thinking bayonets' was still far off.

Over in Ireland, which had its separate military establishment, the first barracks had been built as early as 1697 and the process continued year by year. But the contemporary term 'barracks' bore no relation to its modern connotation. The type of accommodation may be gauged from the definition in the *English Military Dictionary* of 1702:

> Barrack. A hut, like a little Cottage, for Soldiers to lie in... those of the Horse were called Barracks, and those of the Foot Huts; but now the name is indifferently given to both.... They are generally made by fixing four strong forked Poles in the ground, and laying four others across them; then they build the Walls with Wattles, or Sods, or such as the Place affords. The Top is either thatch'd, if there be straw to spare, or covered with Planks, or sometimes Turf.(10)

The clothing of the soldier was organised on a curiously complex system which itself led to abuses by the Colonels. There was no central Clothing Board, no 'sealed pattern' for uniform, and the Colonel was entirely responsible for supplying his men with every article of apparel (and saddlery in mounted units). The cost was supposed to be met from the Net Off-reckonings of each man's pay, which in the case of a private of Foot amounted in the late seventeenth century to 8s per year. Walton states that the average cost of clothing a Foot soldier was about £2 9s, so that unless the Colonel were to put himself out of pocket, he had to find the money from other sources. Consequently the soldier's supposedly sacrosanct subsistence money was robbed. The Colonel was responsible for engaging his own clothing contractor, and of course jobbery was rife. Sometimes a clothier would offer a direct bribe of several £100 for the contract, or he might quote nominal prices considerably higher than the sums actually to be paid. The difference went into the Colonel's pocket.

Such peculations on the part of officers entrusted by their King with the proper care of their soldiers seem to have been tacitly accepted. Writing from Dublin Castle in April 1686, General the Earl of Clarendon revealed to his brother:

> Some of the Colonels told me they were offered £600 by tradesmen to have the clothing of their regiments, which they thought a very unconscionable thing, to get so much money into their own pocket out of the poor soldiers' bellies.(11)

The actual scale of clothing for the soldier varied at various dates, and among the different arms, but in 1697 a private of Foot was entitled to receive out of the Off-reckonings: one cloth coat, one pair of kersey breeches, two shirts, two cravats, two pairs of shoes, one pair of yarn stockings, one hat with band, one sash and one sword with belt. Nowhere is there any mention of underwear, so presumably the soldier had to provide his own. The sword, and later the bayonet, were known as the 'small armament' (origin of the modern term 'small arms'), and it was optional for the Colonel to bargain with contractors for their supply. The 'greater armament', i.e., muskets, carbines, horse pistols and ammunition, were issued from the Government arsenals.(12)

The prerequisite in any body of troops had always been discipline, implying total submission to authority and unhesitating obedience to orders. In the early days of the British Army, and almost down to the present century, discipline was enforced by deterrent in the form of harsh punishments for offenders. The types of punishment inflicted on the soldiers seem to us brutal, if not barbaric. But we must remember life itself was raw and cruel; society was callous and the term 'human rights' had not yet been coined. If punishment was severe in the Army, so it was in civilian life. The death penalty could be inflicted for more than fifty crimes in 1689, among them stealing a horse, or picking a pocket to the value of one shilling. And a popular entertainment among the populace was the frequent public execution. Corporal punishment, for lesser offences, is often imagined to be the prerogative of the military, but not so. Whipping, as it was then termed, had been a common legal punishment since Tudor times, and in 1691 an Act directed that a poor vagrant caught begging without a licence should be stripped from the waist up and 'whipped till his or her body be bloody'.

In the Army, discipline in peacetime was governed by the Mutiny Act of 1689 and its subsequent renewals. This was not very specific regarding sentences, being chiefly concerned with mutiny, desertion and fraudulent enlistment, all of which carried the death penalty. However there existed another ordinance, commonly known as the Articles of War[5] which had first been published in 1640. As the title implies, these articles were theoretically only applicable in time of war, or to any body of troops on active service, but their detailed precepts formed the basis of military law and discipline until 1879 when the Articles were merged with the Mutiny Act to form the Army Discipline and Regulation Act.

The Articles of War specified twenty-five distinct offences for which the death penalty could be imposed. Among them were serious crimes such as murder, mutiny, sedition, striking a superior officer, cowardice in the face of the enemy. But there were some offences for which forfeiture of life seems to us unduly harsh. For instance, robbery was one of them; so was offering violence 'to any who shall bring victuals to the Camp or Garrison, or shall take his Horse or Goods'. Hindering a Provost-Marshal or his deputies in the performance of their duties was a capital offence and so was rape ('whether she belong to the Enemy or not').

For lesser offences there were correspondingly lesser punishments, such as boring the tongue with a red hot iron for blasphemy 'or to speak against any known article of the Christian Faith'; riding the wooden horse

5. The full title was (with slight variations) *Rules and Articles for the better Government of his Majesty's Land Forces*. The complete Articles for 1692 are printed in Walton, *History of the British Standing Army*.

or imprisonment in irons for absence from parade. A ride on the wooden horse was a painful (and often injurious) experience. The victim was mounted astride two planks joined like an inverted 'V' and standing on four legs, with a crude imitation of a horse's head at the front (hence it was known as the 'mare foaled of an acorn'). Weights in the form of muskets and/or round shot were attached to the 'rider's' heels, thus exerting increased pressure on his crutch. Oddly enough, riding the wooden horse was reserved for infantrymen; cavalry offenders were subjected instead to the Piquet (or Picket), which could be even more painful. The man, barefooted, was suspended from a post by a rope attached to his wrists, his feet just touching pointed wooden stumps driven into the ground. If he attempted to relieve the strain on his wrists by resting his feet on the stumps, the sharp points punctured them.

Today, such legally approved deterrents seem more reminiscent of the Gestapo than of the British Army. But in the age of Bunyan and Milton it was accepted, and expected, that those who offended against the laws should suffer, *pour encourager les autres*. The soldier was no exception. While we lack first-hand accounts of the moral or physical effects of these barbaric tortures, we know from personal reminiscences that the later savage flogging with the cat-o'-nine-tails was endured with remarkable stoicism and fortitude, and no doubt the sufferers on the wooden horse and the Piquet accepted their punishment likewise. There were no anaesthetics or analgesics in the seventeenth century, and the endurance of pain was a necessary evil of life, for the innocent as well as the guilty. (It may at least be claimed for the Army that, however ill-considered was the soldier at this time, he was not handed over for punishment until a quite rigorous process of law had fairly established his guilt.)

Although corporal punishment was a common sentence for minor offences, this was not flogging with the 'cat', which was only introduced in the early eighteenth century. The earlier term was 'whipping', carried out as on civilian offenders, with either the stick or birch — a much milder form of correction. The Articles of War do not specify the number of strokes, but as Walton observes, the maximum was nowhere near the appalling thousand and more inflicted in the flogging days, and was usually limited to fifty. In more modern times it became an offence for an officer or NCO to strike a soldier, but in the early days of the Army 'summary correction', or a swipe with cane or flat of sword was perfectly legitimate, provided it was not carried to excess. At Tangier in 1669 a sergeant was court-martialled for 'excessive beating' of a private soldier, but was acquitted when it was proved that he had only used a hollow bamboo cane.(13)

Although the great majority of the Articles of War were concerned with punitive measures for the maintenance of discipline, there was some acknowledgement that even the humble private soldier had certain rights. Thus, the Articles of 1692 declared that if a soldier considered himself wronged by his officer, he could complain direct to his Colonel or Commanding Office for redress; if this failed, he could then take his complaint to a General Officer. And if any Colonel or Captain should 'force or take anything away from a private soldier', such officers were to be court-martialled. But if this was aimed at the notorious embezzlement and swindling perpetrated by many of the Colonels, it obviously had little effect.

If a soldier fell sick or was wounded on service, he was to be evacuated 'to some fit place for his recovery, where he shall be provided for.... and his wages or pay shall go on and be duly paid, till it does appear that he can be no longer serviceable in the Army....' He was then to be given a free pass home, with sufficient funds for the journey. The same issue of the Articles, moreover, stated that one-tenth of the total spoils of war on a campaign should be set aside for the relief of sick and wounded soldiers.

And this brings us to the 'care and maintenance' aspect of military service. The tending of sick and wounded men was essentially a regimental matter, for many generations of soldiers were to suffer before the emergence of an organised, professional Army medical service. The Regimental Colonel was responsible for engaging a doctor, or 'Chirurgeon', who was a civilian, paid out of regimental funds and hired by contract like the clothiers and sutlers. This man, whose skills were limited to little more than bloodletting, cauterising and amputation, had a 'surgeon's mate' to assist him. There was no permanent hospital accommodation, and regiments had to make their own *ad hoc* arrangements for the housing of their sick. However, better facilities were sometimes made available, as on active service, or when a large body of troops was assembled in one place. King James II indulged a passion for military ceremonial and drill, and in the summer of 1686 he ordered a grand 'Camp of Exercise' on Hounslow Heath, attended by 16,000 Horse and Foot and lasting for two months. Among the instructions for the

Camp issued by the Captain-General were detailed 'Rules and Orders for Our Hospitale on Hounslow-Heath'. There was to be a Matron 'or Chief Nurse' in charge, who should have 'a Maid Servant or Cook to dress the Sick Soldiers Diett'. Each Division of the Hospital should have three nurses, or 'Tenders', to assist the Matron in tending the sick and washing their linen. The Regimental physicians were to visit their own sick in the hospital every day, and an apothecary was to be in attendance to provide the necessary drugs. The patients' subsistence money was to be paid to the Matron to defray the cost of diet, 'and such fire, soap and candles that be necessary'.(14)

When William III was campaigning against ex-King James in Ireland in 1689–91, his Army was accompanied by a 'Marching Hospital', including four physicians and 'Chirurgeons', six apothecaries, numerous clerks and purveyors and twenty nurses.

However, such properly organised military hospitals were exceptions, and as we have seen above, in normal times the medical care of a regiment's soldiers was entirely the responsibility of the regiment itself.

So long as the soldier remained serving, on the strength, the Army accepted some responsibility for him. But what was his lot when he completed his 'life' engagement or became so maimed or infirm that he was 'unserviceable ', as the term had it?

Acts passed in the reign of Queen Elizabeth, and subsequently, enjoined every County to raise funds for the relief of discharged soldiers, each man to receive no more than £10 per year. But with the upheaval of the Civil War, and the phobia against a Standing Army after the Restoration, many County authorities became laggard, and the most that an old soldier could hope for was a grudging allowance of some victuals and lodging from the parish according to the Poor Law, or more often, a licence to become a vagrant beggar.

To their lasting credit, however, certain charitably-minded gentlemen of means had taken matters into their own hands and founded alms-houses or 'hospitals' for the relief of deserving old soldiers. The earliest of these was established at Warwick in 1571, by Robert Dudley Earl of Leicester, for the care of twelve infirm or disabled soldiers. It still flourishes, and still bears the name, Lord Leycester's Hospital.[6]

6. The splendid half-timbered building in Warwick's High Street also houses the Regimental Museum of The Queen's Own Hussars.

In 1614 Sir Thomas Coningsby of Hampton Court, Herefordshire (himself a veteran campaigner) founded an almshouse in Hereford for eleven 'servitors', at least six of whom were to be deserving ex-soldiers. Each received £13 per year, with clothing.

But these were rare, private institutions, and for many years after the establishment of the Standing Army there was no properly organised system of relief or pension for the ex-soldier, whether infirm or able-bodied.

It was King Charles II who initiated the care and sustenance of old soldiers on a national scale. Today his name is honoured as the founder of the Royal Hospital Chelsea, in 1682, but few now know that this noble act was preceded by his foundation of a similar hospital for 'antient maimed and infirm soldiers of the Army of Ireland' at Kilmainham, Dublin. The plans were approved in 1679, and the Hospital commenced business in 1684. The inmates were limited to ten officers and 100 soldiers who were disabled, or who after at least seven years in the Army had become incapable of further service through sickness or wounds. At that time, and until the union of 1800, the troops serving in Ireland were administered quite separately from those in England. The Irish Establishment was governed by its own Commander-in-Chief, had its own Ordnance officials and other functionaries, and its own rates of pay, which were lower than those of England. All pensioners, whether officers or other ranks, were given a common diet, which few In-Pensioners of the present Chelsea Hospital would consider either adequate or appetising. Breakfast was one pint of gruel; dinner 1 lb boiled beef or mutton; supper one quart of broth. On Wednesdays ½ lb of cheese or 3 pints of pease-porridge was served, and on Fridays there was also fish and butter. In addition each pensioner received 1 lb bread and three pints of beer daily. Uniform was provided, and a money allowance was paid out weekly: officers got eighteen pence, sergeants twelve pence and other ranks sixpence.

The Royal Kilmainham Hospital continued to function until the formation of the Irish Free State in 1922, after which it closed down.

There is a fanciful story to the effect that the Royal Hospital Chelsea owed its inception to King Charles's mistress Nell Gwyn, who is alleged to have been moved by the pitiful tale of a one-legged old soldier who came begging at her coach window. Historians have proved that this is pure fancy. As related by John Evelyn in 1682, it was King Charles himself who resolved on 'the erection of a Royal Hospital for emerited soldiers on the spot of ground which the Royal Society had sold to his Majesty for 1300 l....'(15) Plans were drawn up by the former Paymaster-General, Sir Stephen Fox, in collaboration with Evelyn, and Sir Christopher Wren was commissioned as architect. The King himself promised £20,000 towards the building costs and Fox contributed £12,000. However, the 'Hospitale at Chelsey' was not entirely a free gift to the Army, for all ranks were obliged to contribute to its erection and maintenance. In 1684 a tax of ten per cent of the purchase price of officers' commissions was levied, five per cent to be paid by the seller and five by the purchaser, the proceeds to be devoted to the Hospital. A little later a deduction of five per cent of all Army pay was authorised, two-thirds of it for the same purpose. Finally, in June 1684 a Royal Warrant authorised the stoppage of one day's pay per year. Thus a private soldier of Foot contributed 9s 4d as the annual premium on his possible pension, or admission to the Hospital, while the Army as a whole was taxed to the yearly amount of £23,000. The royal generosity seems to pale a little, particularly as His Majesty defaulted on the full £20,000 he had promised. The foundation stone of the Royal Hospital was laid by the King in February 1682, but he did not live to see its completion, for he died in 1685 and the Hospital was not ready for occupancy until 1692.(16)

By 1694 Chelsea was accommodating thirty officers (ranked as Ensigns, irrespective of their substantive rank in the Army) and 416 other ranks as In-Pensioners. In addition to their quarters, food and clothing (the still-familiar scarlet coat and cocked hat), officers were allowed 3s 6d per week pension, sergeants got 2s per week, corporals and drummers 10d and privates 8d.

As just seen, the Hospital took ten years to build, and as it was still far from completion when King James II succeeded to the throne in 1685, he resolved to introduce interim measures for the relief of the disabled and infirm soldiers who would be eligible for admission to the Hospital when it opened. In December 1685 he issued a Warrant directing that such soldiers should receive pensions out of the monies allotted for the Hospital. Whatever failings King James exhibited as a ruler, he must be credited with the initiation of the first systematic pension scheme in the British Army. Entitled *Establishment and Regulations of Rewards and other Provisions to be made for his Majesties Land Forces*, the Royal Warrant laid down the following daily rates:

Private soldier	5d
Drummer	7d
Sergeant	11d
Corporal	7d
One of the troops of Guard	18d
One of the Light Horse	12d
Corporal of Light Horse	18d
Dragoon	6d
Corporal of Dragoons	9d
Master gunner	14d
Other gunners	7d

In addition the Warrant provided for wound gratuities to be paid out of Army funds and not from those of the Hospital. These lump sums ranged from £2 for the loss of an eye to £8 for loss of two limbs.(17)

The scale of pensions for Out-Pensioners was adopted by William and Mary in 1689 and continued in force, with some minor modification by the Duke of Marlborough after Blenheim, until drastic cuts ordered by the Government following the Peace of Utrecht in 1713. Although the reward for twenty years' service to King and Country, and possibly disablement, may seem niggardly enough, we must remember the relative values of money between then and now. Whether or not the soldier considered his reward adequate, at least he could now look forward to some official remuneration for those years of service.

To end this chapter we can reflect on an extract from a letter of advice written in 1678 by an anonymous ex-officer to a friend just commissioned. Whether the writer was a typical seventeenth-century officer is conjectural, but the hints give some insight into the attitudes and practices of the time.

Despise all base ways of enriching yourself, either by cheating the King with false musters, or defrauding or abridging your men any part of their due: such practices have been the undoing of many a good cause, and are so far more worthy a gallows than common robberies.... Consider your men are equal sharers in danger, though not in the profit or honour of war, and that as you are the head, they are the body, containing, besides the trunk the usefullest members, hands, arms, legs, feet, without whose executive power, all your contriving facilities will prove insignificant; so that you must not think you discharge the duty of a good or prudent commander when you only shew yourself bold, and bring them on bravely to battle: your care must be, both before and afterwards, to see that they have as wholesome food (and physick when it needs) and as good quarters as the place will afford; and since English constitutions cannot easily endure famine as the people born and bred in less plentiful countries, you must make it a principal part of your endeavours, to have them sufficiently provided, and when upon any action, your under-officers or others have deserved well, you ought to use your interest to get them encouraged and promoted.

A good commander will use his soldiers, just as a good father uses his children.... But though I would have you love your men well, because you can do nothing without them, I would not have you spoil them with overmuch kindness. It is the wise dispensing of rewards and punishments which keeps the world in good order. They never had their business well done, who through an excess of goodness reward mean services too highly, or punish great miscarriages too lightly. Therefore, as you must take care of the back and the belly, the pay and provisions of your soldiers, so you ought to be very severe in your discipline; the two former will gain you the love of your men, the latter their fear, and all mixed together, produce complete obedience: or to express it better in the martial phrase, 'Pay well, and hang well, makes a good soldier.'(18)

2

MARLBOROUGH'S MEN

The oft-quoted maxim about no bad regiments, only bad officers, was undoubtedly as true in Marlborough's time as it is today. So far little mention has been made of the officer corps of the early Standing Army, for this book deals primarily with rank-and-file, but to understand fully the working of the military machine we should give a modicum of attention to its governing mechanism.

Although social status and class background are no longer of prime importance, traditionally those who held the King's or Queen's commission were expected to be 'officers and gentlemen'. And the latter term implied not only good breeding, but the possession of some wealth. Until the purchasing of commissions was abolished in 1871, a young man had small hope of becoming an officer in the Army unless he enjoyed adequate private means. Not only was he obliged to pay for his first commission as Cornet of Horse or Ensign of Foot, plus the cost of his uniform and equipment, but proportionately larger sums were payable for every step up the promotion ladder to the rank of Colonel. There was nothing peculiarly military, or even British, about this system, for the buying and selling of civil offices was common practice, while the purchase system flourished in the French Army. There were spasmodic attempts to stamp it out in Britain, but after an unsuccessful effort by George I in 1719, he was driven merely to regularise the official prices.

In the 1680s an Ensign paid between £400 and £600 for his commission; a Major of Foot seeking to purchase his promotion to Lieutenant-Colonel would have to put down about £3,400.(1) In a Royal Warrant signed by George I in February 1719 prices were laid down 'not to be exceeded', as listed overleaf.(2)

Despite these regulations however, it was tacitly accepted that an officer wishing to sell his commission could bargain for higher figures, and 'over-regulation' trafficking continued down to the Victorian era,

	Regiments of Horse	Dragoons	Foot Guards	Infantry
	£	£	£	£
Colonel	9000	7000	—	6000
Lieut-Colonel	4000	3200	6000	2400
Major	3300	2600	3600	1800
Captain	2500	1800	2400	1000
Lieutenant	1200	800	900	300
Cornet or Ensign	1000	600	450	200

when peers such as Lord Cardigan happily paid out some £20,000 above regulation for command of fashionable light cavalry regiments.

As far as the Government was concerned the purchase system made economic sense, for there was no need to apportion large sums for retired officers' pensions: when they finally sold out (at a profit, of course) the cash realised formed a sort of life insurance sum. Moreover, since the day of Charles II Government had claimed ten per cent of the sale proceeds, ostensibly for the Chelsea Hospital funds. An officer's pay of rank barely covered his expenses: in 1713 a Cornet of Horse received 5s per day; a Major, 19s 6d and a Lieutenant-Colonel £1 2s. Regardless of inflation, these rates remained unchanged for nearly fifty years. It must be added that promotion was sometimes attainable without purchase. If a serving officer died or was killed in action, the next senior in the regiment could step up without paying, but obviously this was a case of waiting for dead men's shoes. Occasionally an officer might be promoted free as reward for some distinguished conduct in the field.

As for the rank-and-file, a commission by purchase was of course beyond imagination: the only path by which a soldier might become an officer lay through perhaps twenty years' service and successive ranks up to Sergeant-Major, when he might be promoted Quartermaster or Riding Master with Lieutenant's rank. However, on very rare occasions an NCO, or even a private soldier, might be granted an Ensign's commission as reward for some particularly gallant conduct in action. Fortescue cites the instance of a Sergeant Littler of the 1st Guards being so promoted for his valour at the siege of Lille in 1708. But while the purchase system prevailed, a newly-commissioned 'ranker-officer' was unlikely to be able to afford further promotion.

Once an officer achieved general rank he ceased to be paid in peacetime, unless he held a staff appointment or other office. Since most General officers were Colonels of regiments, they naturally ensured that their income from that source was as much as could be contrived.

With the officer corps drawn exclusively from the upper strata of society, the gulf between regimental officers and their men was wide and unbridgeable. Even if there had been any organised leisure activities in the Army, it would have been unthinkable for an officer to join in with the other ranks. To the soldier, his officers were creatures apart, representing only authority and discipline, and normally seen only on parade, or behind the Orderly Room table when punishment was to be meted out.

A letter of July 1701 from a newly-joined private of Schomberg's Horse (later 7th Dragoon Guards) to his parents, probably typifies current attitudes:

> … Our Sarjent has served 12 yeares and is a good man tho strict. The Corprals I say not much of. Captain Coursey [Courcy] is Troop Captain and we have another Cornet. We being in Billetts we scarce see them but on Drill and Stabels, and the Coronel I have not set eyes on. Sarjent says the officers serve us good if we serve them good, which I mean to do. I have not yet spoke with the Capt or Cornet. We only speak when they speak to us. I pray you are both well as I am.
>
> Your dutifull and loving son
James Wilcocks(3)

Before a more democratic spirit pervaded the Army in more recent times, it was neither unnatural nor unusual for the regimental officers to be firmly entrenched behind caste and rank barriers, and to leave the men very much to their own devices in off-parade hours — provided they got up to no mischief. Doubtless there were exceptional officers, such as the sage veteran whose letter was quoted in the previous chapter (p. 18), and who counselled his young friend: 'You should not be absent from your men oftener, or longer, than you need, although you have nothing for them to do; for vulgar minds are generally busy, and depraved, and will rather be contriving ill, than doing nothing. It will therefore be an act worthy of your prudence, to exercise them at convenient times (above what is usual) in matches at leaping, running, wrestling, shooting at marks, or any other manly and innocent sports, which may render them healthy, and hardy, and give them no leisure to study mutinies, or other mischief.'

Evidently, if the soldier was expected to trust his officers, the reverse did not always hold true.... the devil finds work for idle hands. However, one characteristic of the British officer shines out constantly through the ages, and that is his bravery in action, coupled with utter disregard of personal safety. Whatever his other failings, his men would follow where he led.

It was King William III who led the British Army on its first full-scale campaigns, in Ireland and Flanders, but it was under Marlborough that the Army was forged into the superb fighting machine that had no equal among the professional troops of Europe; it was under him that the British redcoats gained the reputation for valour, discipline and endurance that was inherited by successive generations. The secret of Marlborough's pre-eminence as a commander was not merely his brilliant generalship, but his genuine concern for the welfare of his troops. 'He secured the affections of his soldiers by his good nature, care for their provisions, and vigilance not to expose them to unnecessary danger, and gained those of his officers by his affability; both one and the other followed him to action with such a cheerfulness, resolution and unanimity as were sure presages of success.'(4) It is significant that Marlborough was known throughout the Army as 'Corporal John' or 'the Old Corporal'. The British soldier could never have applied any such compliment (for so it was) to Wellington, nor to Kitchener, still less to Haig.

There is no denying that the great Captain-General was a strict disciplinarian; but the soldier respects firmness provided he knows that it is tempered with justice and due regard for his rights. In December 1703 Marlborough wrote thus to his newly-appointed Quartermaster-General, Colonel William Cadogan:[1]

> You do well apprehend that good order and military discipline are the chief essentials in an army. But you must be ever aware that an army cannot preserve good order unless its soldiers have meat in their bellies, coats on their backs, and shoes on their feet. All these are as necessary as arms and munitions. I pray you will never fail to look to these things as you may do to other matters....(5)

What happened when 'these things', or in modern parlance, logistics,

1. Later General 1st Earl Cadogan; Colonel, 5th Dragoon Guards, Grenadier Guards, Coldstream Guards.

were not looked to, had been disgracefully exposed during the early phase of King William's campaign of 1689 in Ireland, when through the abject failure of the Commissariat, the men were starved and uncared for. In just over three months 6,300 soldiers out of a total of 14,000 succumbed to malnutrition, exposure and disease.

Marlborough's genius for organisation and administration was never better displayed than in his celebrated march to the Danube in 1704, when he moved his entire force of some 40,000 horse, foot and guns 250 miles from the Netherlands to the banks of the Danube, thereby deceiving both his obstinate Dutch masters and the enemy, and culminating in his first great victory of Blenheim. Constantly on the march for six weeks, and fighting one major action at the Schellenberg en route, the 'scarlet caterpillar' arrived at the scene of Blenheim not only fighting fit but without having lost one man through sickness or privation. And moreover, no soldier, or horse, went short of rations or forage. In collaboration with his splendid Quartermaster-General, Marlborough had meticulously organised every logistical detail in advance, arranging for adequate supplies of bread, meat and forage at each night's halt, even ordering 12,000 pairs of new boots for the infantry at the half-way halt, besides constant supplies of 'fitt iron' for horseshoes. March discipline was such that the local populace along the whole route could not find a single complaint to make about the conduct of the soldiers.

There are two well-known diaries of soldiers who marched with Marlborough to the Danube, and both are complimentary. Sergeant Millner of the Royal Irish Regiment (18th) wrote: 'I must say he [Marlborough] perform'd that march with very good conduct, by beginning every day's March by Break of Day, or Sun-rising, so that every day, before it was extreme hot, or noon, we were fully encamped in our new Camp; so that the remaining part of the day's Rest was nigh as good as a day's halt.'(6)

Captain Robert Parker of the same Regiment:

As we marched through the countries of our allies, Commissaries were appointed to furnish us with all manner of necessaries for men and horse; these were brought to the ground before we arrived, and the soldiers had nothing to do, but to pitch their tents, boil their kettles, and lie down to rest. Surely never was such a march carried on with more order and regularity and with less fatigue, both to man and horse.(7)

That redoubtable female trooper in the Scots Greys, 'Mother Ross' (see over, p. 26) says little of the March itself, but singles out the following incident:

> I cannot help taking notice in this place, though it breaks in upon my narrative, of the duke of Marlborough's great humanity, who seeing some of our Foot drop, through weariness, took them into his own coach.

As Fortescue observes, the magic of Marlborough's personality was the more remarkable when one reflects that the soldiers whom he led to victory were, like those of Wellington's army, mostly 'the scum of the earth'. There was of course a good leavening of long-serving men, especially among the NCOs, but as was always the case, on the outbreak of the Spanish Succession War in 1701 the Army, pruned by Parliament after the Peace of Ryswick in 1697, found itself woefully short of manpower, and questionable recruiting methods were resorted to. Among these was an Act of 1703 authorising certain classes of convicts to be released from gaol if they agreed to enlist. In the following year another Act legalised conscription within certain limits. Magistrates were empowered to raise and levy any able-bodied man who was unemployed and could show no visible means of supporting himself. The result of all this was that Commanding Officers found themselves burdened with recruits who did little for the morale or discipline of their regiments. 'Criminals were drafted in wholesale, and the debtors' prisons were emptied into the Army.... The Recruiting Acts were seized on as a chance to rid the countryside of poachers and suspected persons and to pay off personal or political scores.'(8) Captain Richard Pope of Schomberg's Horse was scathing of some of the recruits willed on him by Government decree: 'Such a set of ruffians and imbeciles you never beheld,' he wrote to his cousin, 'you may call them canon fodder, but never soldiers. None of them have sat a horse, and when they get their swords I fear they will cut their horses' heads off rather than the enemy's.'(9) The contemporary chronicler Narcissus Luttrell records in March 1705 that 'about 350 pickpockets, housebreakers etc..... got to be soldiers in the guards, the better to hide their roguery.'(10)

In 1705 Lieut-Colonel Robert Killigrew of the 8th Dragoons wrote (in singularly illiterate terms) to his Colonel concerning some recruits sent out to his regiment in Barcelona: 'As to my like or dislike the recrouts, Mr. Jasen may afarm what he please, I have only this to say, I returned sevverell, wich ware either lame, or to old, or Blind, and I sent them for England, and thare wos amongest them severell Boyes wich I made to be taken for Dromes [Drummers] or sarvants…'(11)

Of course, in theory all recruits were supposed to undergo a medical examination before being accepted, but this formality was often glossed over, while the civilian doctors were not above taking bribes to pass an unfit man so that the recruiters could pocket the fee. As we have just seen, the halt and 'blind' found their way into the ranks, and incredibly enough, so did women masquerading as men. The best-known example of the latter is the celebrated 'Mother Ross', or Christian Davies, who joined a Foot regiment as a private in 1693. After being wounded at the Battle of Landen she transferred, as trooper, to the Scots Greys and fought throughout the early part of Marlborough's campaigns. It was only after again being wounded at Ramillies that her sex was discovered by the surgeons tending her. On her subsequent discharge she was granted a pension of one shilling a day for life by Queen Anne. The remarkable aspect of her career is not so much that she managed to enlist, but that she succeeded in concealing her sex from her comrades throughout thirteen years' service, most of it in the field. She was born Christian Cavenaugh in Dublin and was thrice married to soldiers, the first two being killed with Marlborough, the third admitted to the Chelsea Hospital as a pensioner. After his death in 1739 she too succumbed and was buried in the Hospital cemetery.(12)

Such was the make-up — in part, at any rate — of the army which gained Marlborough's 'glorious quartet' of victories and set the prestige of the British redcoat on a pinnacle not surmounted again until Waterloo. What motivated these uncouth, ignorant youths to stoical endurance of hardship, mutilation and violent death? In later times the British soldier's morale was fed not only by patriotism ('Your Country needs you!') but by the unique regimental spirit that has been the envy of other armies down to the present day: one cannot let the Regiment down. But in Queen Anne's time such a spirit must have been almost non-existent. When the Battle of Blenheim was fought in 1704 no regiment could look back on more than forty-odd years' service, while some had only just come into existence. Pride of regiment and its traditions takes longer than that to be nurtured. The local origins shared by the soldiers of a regiment were not a significant factor until much later, towards the end of the eighteenth century. At this period the private soldier was little more than an automaton, functioning by reflexive obedience to orders.

Obedience implies discipline, and discipline, training. Until well into the twentieth century parade-ground drill was the basis of all training. In the eighteenth and nineteenth centuries the accepted tactics of professional armies demanded the manoeuvring of regiments in rigid close-order lines, and thus close-order drill to perfect the complex evolutions was an essential.

The object of parade-ground drill was two-fold: first to enable a commander to manoeuvre his regiment, or battalion, or company, into any desired formation, and second, to inculcate in all ranks, instant, unhesitating obedience to words of command. Until the advent of more fluid methods of warfare, troops were formed and fought in the field in exactly the same manner as practised on the parade ground. Even though today such methods have been obsolete for a century or more, the value of close-order drill is still recognised as an aid to discipline, and the modern recruit still endures many hours of 'square-bashing' as part of his basic training. But today's soldier, and his officer, are spared the chores of learning and practising the 120-odd separate 'motions' and words of command considered necessary to manoeuvre a battalion in the eighteenth century.

Weapon training, or the 'handling of arms', occupied as much time as foot drill. When Queen Anne succeeded to the throne infantrymen were armed with the pike and the clumsy matchlock musket, but by 1704 the pike had been abolished and the infantry soldier carried the improved flintlock weapon, with bayonet. By 1730 the flintlock had developed into the famous 'Brown Bess' or Tower Musket, a formidable weapon which with various modifications was to remain the British infantry's principal firearm for nearly a century.

In order to prime, load and fire, the soldier had to obey twenty-one words of command, and when fully trained he could achieve a rate of fire of two rounds a minute — double the rate of the old matchlock. Of course, there was only one 'posture' for firing, and that was bravely standing erect to face the enemy. No thought was given to the use of cover until Colonel Coote Manningham demonstrated the revolutionary tactics of his Experimental Corps of Riflemen (The Rifle Brigade) in 1800.

In addition to practising the stereotyped 'six cuts' with his sword, the cavalryman was supposed to master the drill of 'giving fire' with his pistol and carbine, on horseback. But such a hazardous exercise was seldom resorted to in action. There are authenticated instances of excited troopers blowing off their horses' heads, and the drill (with blanks) seems to have been designed more to impress inspecting Generals rather than the enemy. In the artillery, gun detachments ('crews' to the ignorant layman) were constantly practised in the complicated drill of laying and firing their pieces. The loader placed a bagged charge in the bore, the spongeman rammed it home, while the ventsman primed the vent with loose powder. When the piece had been layed by the 'Number one', the firer ignited his portfire from the continuously burning slow-match, or linstock, the loader rammed home the projectile, and the gun was reported 'ready to fire'. The firer applied his portfire to the vent and the discharge sent the gun recoiling back on its wheels. When it was run up again by three of the detachment, the spongeman thrust his wet sponge down the bore to extinguish any smouldering remains of powder, and after the dense white clouds of smoke had cleared, the gun was relayed. The extreme range of a 9-pounder field gun was about 1,000 yards, but battle ranges were usually much shorter, often no more than 200 yards. All laying was done by lining the piece by eye, or what we should term 'open sights'. Indirect fire was of course impossible; the target had to be visible, which meant that the gun position was also visible to the target, so that the gunners often got as good as they gave. Thus, in the face of shot and shell, and musketry, it was essential that the detachments carried out their drill with instinctive, automatic precision.

The eighteenth century saw little change in the general conditions of the soldier but there was one novel feature which was to sully the name of military discipline for more than a hundred years and to call forth periodic public outcry. As we have seen, corporal punishment inflicted with a cane or 'rod' had been common practice ever since the raising of the Standing Army (and earlier), but now the barbaric, flesh-searing cat-o'-nine-tails, or lash, was substituted. Exactly when 'the reign of the lash' commenced it is difficult to say, but Grose, writing in 1786, asserts that the cat-o'-nine-tails had been in use 'these thirty years at least'.(13) Whoever devised such an instrument of punishment (or torture) must have borne a grudge against the human body. There was never any 'sealed pattern' for the cat, but it generally comprised nine lengths of whipcord, about two feet long, attached to a wooden handle. To ensure the maximum laceration of the victim, each lash had from three to nine knots spaced along it.

At first there seems to have been no limit to the number of strokes inflicted: neither the Mutiny Acts nor the Articles of War laid down any maximum, merely specifying 'corporal punishment', with the proviso that it was not to extend 'to life or limb'. Apparently twenty-five strokes was the absolute minimum, for minor offences, but for serious crimes such as theft, 'disgraceful conduct' and striking a superior officer, the sentence was left entirely to the caprice of the commanding officer, and rose to the horrifying proportions which not only endangered life but brought the whole question of flogging into open dispute in Parliament. The extreme case is surely that of a Guardsman in 1712 who, convicted of slaughtering his Colonel's horse and selling the hide, was awarded seven separate floggings of 1,800 lashes each, or an incredible total of 12,600. Since the man had nearly succumbed after the first 1,800 strokes the Queen remitted the remainder of the sentence.(14) Until 1807, when King George III was 'graciously pleased' to approve an Army order recommending a limit of one thousand lashes, sentences of 1,500, 1,800 and even 2,000 were quite common.

In order to create the maximum impression on potential wrong-doers, all floggings were performed at a parade of the whole of the victim's unit, which was formed up in a hollow square. In the centre stood the 'triangles', originally sergeants' halberds, but later a timber tripod to which the prisoner was lashed, stripped to the waist. The Commanding Officer, Adjutant, Drum-Major and Medical Officer stood by. The lashes were delivered by the drummers under the eye of the Drum-Major who was charged to ensure that they did not spare their effort. The Adjutant called out the number of strokes, and in order that the drummers did not tire, they were relieved after every twenty-five strokes. Blood was always drawn after the first few, and after about fifty the man's back would become raw flesh. If he showed signs of collapse he would be examined by the surgeon and 'restored' with cold water thrown in his face. The punishment might then be resumed, or postponed, depending on the surgeon's opinion. If he advised postponement the victim would be admitted to hospital until his back had healed, all the while his suffering aggravated by the knowledge that the ordeal was to be repeated.

In 1787 Dr Robert Hamilton, a regimental surgeon, wrote:

Hall was sentenced to receive five hundred lashes for house-breaking; he got four hundred of them before he was taken down; and in the space of six weeks was judged able to sustain the remainder of his punishment, as his back was entirely skinned over. The first twenty-five lashes of the second punishment tore the young flesh more than the first four hundred, the blood pouring at the same time in streams. By the time he got seventy-five his back was ten times more cut by the 'cats' than with the former four hundred — so that it was thought prudent to remit the remaining twenty-five.... Hall declared that his first punishment was trifling to what he suffered by the second. Other examples might be added, but to multiply cases of this kind is disagreeable.(15)

One of the rare personal accounts from victims of the 'cat' is that of Alexander Somerville who enlisted as private in the Scots Greys in 1831 and was sentenced to 150 lashes for writing a seditious letter to the Press. Although chronologically this case belongs to a future chapter, it is appropriate to quote it here:

The regimental Sergeant-Major, who stood behind with a book and pencil to count each lash and write its number, gave the command 'Farrier Simpson, you will do your duty'.... Simpson took the cat as ordered; at least I believe so; I did not see him, but I felt an astounding sensation between the shoulders, under my neck, which went to my toe nails in one direction, my finger nails in another, and stung me to the heart, as if a knife had gone through my body.... He came on a second time and then I thought the former stroke was sweet and agreeable compared with that one.... [After twenty-five strokes] Simpson stood back and a young trumpeter who had not flogged before, took his cat and began. He gave me some dreadful cuts about the ribs, first on one side and then on the other.... [After fifty strokes Farrier Simpson takes over again.] The strokes were not so sharp as at first; they were like blows of heavy weights, but more painful than the fresh ones.... He travelled downwards, and came on heavier than before, but, as I thought, slower. It seemed a weary slowness for the sergeant-major, to be only counting the fifteenth and sixteenth of the third twenty-five. I then uttered the only words which I spoke during the whole time, namely, 'Come on quicker, Simpson, and let it be done; you are very slow.' The poor fellow was slow from aversion to the task; I do not know if he gave the strokes more quickly; they all seemed to last too long.

When the other youngster had reached, or nearly, his second twenty, I felt as if I could yield, and beg forgiveness; but the next moment the coward thought was rebuked within me, and banished, but I prayed to God to put it into their minds to stop, and pardon me the remainder. When this twenty-five was completed, which made a hundred, the commanding officer said 'Stop, take him down, he is a young soldier.'(16)

Somerville was just twenty-one. After eight days in hospital he was back at duty.

Our present-day society which disputes the morality of caning naughty schoolchildren can only regard the bloody flagellation of naked backs as inhuman torture. And torture it undeniably was. But contemporary views during the whole period were surprisingly divided, even among the sufferers themselves. Somerville himself later declared that 'nothing but the most severe punishment could have any influence on some of the ruffians that had enlisted solely for cheap spirits and were born mischief-makers.' He was writing in Victorian times, but the same view probably applied with greater force in the previous century. In 1840 Dr Henry Marshall, Deputy Inspector of Army Hospitals, had this to say: 'It is a notorious fact that when flogging was at its height it was counted no great disgrace, indeed it was sometimes made a boast of, and instances have occurred where to have suffered under the lash was reckoned qualification necessary for becoming a good comrade.'(17)

But just as there were hardened cases, there were others who were sickened and revolted by the savagery of the more severe sentences. An ex-drummer wrote:

At the lowest calculation, it was my disgusting duty to flog men at least three times a week. From this painful task there was no possibility of shrinking, without the certainty of a rattan over my own shoulders from the Drum-Major, or of my being sent to the black hole.... After a poor fellow had received about one hundred lashes, the blood would pour down his back in streams.... so that by the time he had received three hundred, I have found my clothes all over blood from the knees to the crown of the head. Horrified by my disgusting appearance, I have, immediately after the parade, run into the barrack-room, to escape from the observations of the soldiers, and to rid my clothes and person of my comrade's blood.(18)

The soldier continued to suffer under the 'cat', for even petty malpractices, until 1881, and subsequent chapters will notice the continuing controversies it aroused and the spasmodic attempts to abolish it.

Meanwhile, we must constantly remind ourselves that before such terms as 'human rights' and 'corrective training' came into currency, society expected that malefactors should suffer for their crimes, and should be seen to suffer, the better to deter others. Murderers, thugs and robbers, were public enemies and should be treated as such. Perhaps a soldier whose back was flayed for 'unseemly language' to his platoon sergeant had not offended against society, but he had struck at the very fundamental of his calling, military discipline. And we must again recollect that it was not only the soldier who suffered under the lash: flogging was still a common penalty under civil law, although oddly enough its practice did not seem to arouse the same passions from the abolitionists. Men, and women, could be flayed half-naked 'at the cart's tail' through the streets for some petty larceny, or the crime of vagrancy.

Like his civilian counterpart, the soldier could suffer the ultimate penalty for murder and other lesser crimes, though in these cases he was granted the privilege of being 'shot to death' by his comrades instead of the not always swift end on the hangman's rope. As noted in Chapter 1, the seventeenth-century Articles of War specified no fewer than twenty-five offences which carried the death penalty. By 1781 the Mutiny Act was listing only eight military crimes punishable with death. These included mutiny or incitement thereto; desertion; fraudulent enlistment; sleeping at post; abandoning post; correspondence or treating with an enemy; striking or offering violence to a superior officer, and disobeying a lawful command. As previously, however, the death sentence might be commuted to 'such other punishment as by a Court-Martial shall be inflicted' — the lash.

Public executions remained common practice until late Victorian times and the Army was no exception — the object, as with flogging, being to create the maximum impression on the witnesses. This it certainly did, for a military execution was performed with awesome ceremony. Among the many soldiers who have left us first-hand descriptions is Rifleman Harris, who in 1802 at Portsmouth had the unwelcome duty of acting as one of the firing party for the execution of a deserter:

> The place of execution was Portsdown Hill, near Hilsea Barracks, and the different regiments assembled must have composed a force of about 15,000 men.... The sight was very imposing and appeared to make a deep impression on all there.... When all was ready we [the sixteen-strong firing party] moved to the front, and the culprit was

brought out. He made a short speech to the parade, acknowledging the justice of his sentence, and that drinking and evil company had brought the punishment upon him.

He behaved himself firmly and well, and did not seem to flinch. After being blind-folded, he was desired to kneel down behind a coffin, which was placed on the ground, and the drum-major of the Hilsea depot, giving us an expressive glance, we immediately commenced loading.

This was done in the deepest silence, and the next moment we were primed and ready. There was then a dreadful pause for a few moments, and the drum-major, again looking towards us, gave the signal before agreed upon [a flourish of his cane], and we levelled and fired. We had been previously strictly enjoined to be steady, and take good aim, and the poor fellow, pierced by several balls, fell heavily upon his back; and as he lay, with his arms pinioned to his sides, I observed that his hands waved for a few moments, like the fins of a fish when in the agonies of death. The drum-major also observed the movement, and, making another signal, four of our party immediately stepped up to the prostrate body, and placing the muzzles of their pieces to the head, fired, and put him out of his misery. The different regiments then fell back by companies, and the word being given to march past in slow time, when each company came in line with the body, the word was given to 'Mark Time', and then 'Eyes Left', in order that we might all observe the terrible example.(19)

Although Harris omits mention, the Chaplain was always in attendance on the prisoner, and usually offered up a prayer for his soul just before the firing party did their duty.

Meanwhile officers whose behaviour incurred punishment — if their conduct was deemed 'unbecoming an officer and gentleman' — might be cashiered, or suffer a loss of seniority, or merely be reprimanded. And while the offending soldier could be punished with severity, he could expect little reward for good conduct and loyal service; even acts of bravery in the field normally went unrecognised, for gallantry awards and decorations did not appear until the mid-nineteenth century. Contemporary thinking was simple: it was deemed no more than a soldier's duty to display courage on the battlefield, fortitude in adversity. There could be no circumstances 'beyond the call of duty'. The most the good private soldier could hope for was normal promotion through the ranks, though as we have seen, on very rare occasions a signal act of bravery might earn him an Ensign's commission.

The latter part of the eighteenth century brought an innovation which was to have a profound effect on the living conditions of the soldier. Hitherto, as already related, there were few permanent barracks and it was the practice to billet scattered detachments of troops in taverns and ale-houses, although in Ireland there had been barracks — of a sort — almost since the creation of the Standing Army. In 1792 William Pitt, Prime Minister, established the office of Barrackmaster-General, with responsibility for constructing permanent barracks throughout the Kingdom.[2] By 1797 there were 81 Government-owned buildings in existence, besides 49 rented or 'temporary' barracks. Apart from London, where the Knightsbridge and Kensington barracks appeared, most of the building was concentrated in strategic areas, such as the south coast to combat any French invasion, and in large towns like Chelmsford and Colchester. Eventually by 1805 the building programme had extended to the completion of 203 barracks with accommodation for 17,000 cavalry and 146,000 infantry.(20) All this was not without opposition from the anti-military lobby in Parliament and among the public, who feared that the concentration of large numbers of troops presaged 'bayonet-dictatorship'. The shades of Cromwell and his Major-Generals still haunted dark corners. As early as 1740 General George Wade, former C-in-C Scotland, had averred that 'the people of this Kingdom have been taught to associate the idea of barracks and slavery so closely together that, like darkness and the devil, tho' there be no connection between them, yet they cannot separate them, nor think of the one without thinking at the same time of the other.'(21)

The barracks programme coincided with the spread of brick as a building material, and nearly all the new quarters were so constructed. While as regards weather-tightness and durability they were a vast improvement on the early hovels of Irish 'barracks', they offered little

2. The first holder of the office was Colonel Oliver Delancey (late of the 17th Light Dragoons), who does not seem to have been a particularly happy choice. Fortescue records that he not only misappropriated large sums of the £9M public funds allotted, but appointed hordes of subordinate 'barrack-masters' in locations where there were no barracks and none planned.

comfort or amenities to the inmates other than stout walls and roof. It was still considered necessary to disperse troops piecemeal throughout the country, for policing duties, and most of the new barracks were small, housing no more than one squadron or company. Apart from the large garrison towns such as Colchester, Maidstone, Chester and Edinburgh, nowhere was there accommodation for a complete regiment. The Barrackmaster-General evidently deemed his duty done if he provided merely a weatherproof building: little or no thought was given to basic facilities. It is recorded that of 146 barracks in England and Scotland, 89 lacked any proper washing facilities for the men, while 77 had no means for washing dirty linen. In Ireland, conditions were even worse: 130 of the 139 barracks surveyed were devoid of men's ablution arrangements.(22) Even in the larger barracks where facilities were available, this did not always imply running water from a tap. Very often the soldier's only means of washing his person or his underclothes was by drawing water from a well in the barrack square.(23) Especially in winter, there was little to encourage personal hygiene. The cramped barrack rooms were foetid with the stench of unwashed bodies, compounded with the odour of the dual-purpose tub which served as a urinal at night and a washtub by day.

> In winter the men would block up all the ventillation with old sacking, etc., and when I had to visit the rooms in the morning as Duty Officer, the atmosphere was so nauseating that I felt disinclined to touch my breakfast afterwards. Of course the soldiers had only an outside tap to wash from, which was often froze up, and even when it was not, you may imagine that few of them were bold enough to strip and swill themselves in the cold and darkness of a January morning.... You can smell some soldiers' feet before you enter their rooms.(24)

In the smaller barracks one room was allotted to every eight men, in which they ate, slept, cleaned their arms and kit, and stowed such worldly goods as they possessed. The barrack regulations specified that each soldier should have a minimum space of 450 cubic feet: a convict in prison was allowed 1,000. Until the 1790s no beds were provided: instead, the men slept on straw-filled 'bolsters' or palliasses, which were refilled with fresh straw every two months. The only form of lighting after dark was by candle. When the luxury of bedsteads — wooden cots — was permitted, it was on the niggardly scale of one for every two men, so that the term 'bedfellow' acquired a literal meaning. Whether such sharing of beds contributed to the crime known as 'unnatural conduct' is conjectural.

The larger permanent barracks could accommodate a whole cavalry regiment with its horses, or an infantry battalion, and many of these structures built between about 1790 and 1810 continued in use until well into the twentieth century. For instance, the cavalry barracks at Piershill, Edinburgh, were erected in 1793, and although condemned in 1909 were not demolished until the 1930s. Nearly all barracks were of the standard layout which is still familiar to many old soldiers of today: two-or three-storey brick blocks arranged in a hollow square, the central space reserved as the parade ground. The men's barrack rooms, or 'dormitories', were usually on the first floor, reached by exterior iron staircases and each accommodating a Troop or Platoon of about thirty men. In cavalry barracks the horses were stabled on the ground floor, so that at night the troopers slumbered to the accompaniment of rattling head-chains and stamping of hooves, while the odours of their four-footed comrades rose to mingle with their own. Barrack furniture was sparse: apart from cots, there was usually one wooden trestle-table and a couple of benches in each room, and later each man was given a wooden box in which to keep his few private possessions. Sanitary arrangements were still primitive, confined to one urinal tub in each room, though this would be placed on the exterior balcony where one was provided. Separate latrines and ablution rooms did not appear until the latter half of the nineteenth century. Nor were there any separate cooking or dining facilities: the men cooked and ate in their own rooms. 'Cooking' is perhaps a rhetorical term, for only two copper boilers were issued, one for meat and one for vegetables. Consequently, boiled beef, broth or stew was the unchanging diet, eked out with bread and occasionally cheese. The scale of rations constantly varied slightly, but the average for nearly a century was 1½ lb bread and ¾ lb meat per man per day — the meat being weighed with bone and gristle. The only beverage provided was beer, but on active service rum was issued.

The rations may have been issued, but they were not free, for as already noted, the private soldier was docked sixpence a day out of his pay of eightpence to pay for them. If all soldiers complained of hunger this was because they existed on only two meals a day: breakfast between 7.30 and 8 a.m. and dinner at 12.30 p.m. The pangs of that hiatus from dinner until the next morning could only be assuaged by what a man could afford from the few pence remaining of his weekly pay. William Cobbett who enlisted in 1784 recalled that he had seen young soldiers 'lay in their berths... actually crying on account of hunger. The whole week's food was not a bit too much for one day.'(25)

Since the Army was bedevilled by the deplorable prevalence of drunkenness almost down to the twentieth century, it might be thought that authority would frown on alcohol, but on the contrary it was made officially available. Until 1802 beer was issued to the amount of five pints per day per man. In that year Government imposed a heavy tax on malt, so that beer became expensive, its issue was discontinued, and in lieu each soldier was granted one penny per day as 'beer money'. Now he could spend it (and often the rest of his pittance) on the more potent neat spirits which were available in officially authorised canteens or 'grog-shops' which were opened in each barracks by civilian contractors.

Commanding officers were enjoined to exercise proper control over these establishments, but it proved impossible for them to do much more than limit the hours of opening, with the result that the grog-shop became the prime source of drunkenness and indiscipline.

> The spirits in particular were rank fiery poison, more deadly and potent than were sold in public houses, and this was a fertile source of crime. Insubordination in barracks, and particularly the striking of non-commissioned officers, was very common and was almost invariably the result of a visit to the canteen.... The soldier had two meals a day, breakfast at 7.30 and dinner at 12.30, so that he was left for nineteen hours without food. Since he lost appetite for the eternal beef-broth and boiled beef, he was naturally hungry and weak in the evening, and took refuge in drink.... To be brief, the State offered every inducement in the way of monotonous diet, monotonous occupation, climatic discomfort, bad housing and abundant alcohol that could lure men to drink; and then deplored the drunkenness of the Army.(26)

In fairness to the soldier, however, we should remember that addiction to alcohol was just as rife in civilian life as in the Service; the sleazy taverns and grog-shops of the towns, even the village ale-houses, were more infamous than the barrack canteen for debauchery and riotous behaviour. But to the civilian drunkenness was merely a vice; to the military it was a crime, punishable with the lash.

The Army always frowned upon marriage, as a hindrance to absolute loyalty and obedience, though tacitly accepting that a soldier had the basic right to wed and propagate his species. The official attitude is reflected by the restrictions on the number of wives permitted in a unit. Until the nineteenth century only six soldiers in every hundred were allowed to marry 'on the strength', and then only with the approval of the commanding officer. Their wives lived in barracks and enjoyed free rations, in return for which they were expected to perform menial chores, such as washing and mending clothes, cooking, and cleaning the barrack rooms. In official returns officers' wives were listed as 'ladies', soldiers' as 'women', for of course the latter came from the same lowly caste as their husbands whose living conditions they shared. This even extended to sharing the same barrack room with the unmarried men, their only privacy being a couple of blankets slung across one end. In such conditions a bridal couple would spend their wedding night to ribald commentary from twenty or thirty room-mates.

There were no regulations to prohibit a soldier marrying 'off the strength', but there was little to recommend such a union, for it was anything but that. 'Off-the-strength' wives were not allowed in barracks, nor were the husbands permitted to sleep out with them; they received no rations or allowances, and as few soldiers could afford to maintain a spouse out of their own pay, most of the latter were forced to take some humble employment or even to live off the parishes as paupers. All in all, Mr Punch's later advice to those about to marry could be applied specifically to generations of British soldiers.

The daily routine in barracks kept the men fully occupied from 'Reveille' to 'Lights Out', their comings and goings being regulated by trumpet in the mounted units and bugle or drums in the Foot[3] In summer months 'Reveille' roused the soldier at 6 a.m., in winter at 7. Before breakfast the cavalryman mucked out his horse's standing, brushed it down, watered and fed it, while the infantryman might endure an early-morning session of 'smartening-up' footdrill. The rest of the morning would be taken up with mounted or dismounted drill by troops or companies, arms drill, and the Commanding Officer's 'Orderly Room', when punishment would be meted out to offenders, or men with requests or complaints could be interviewed. A daily ceremony in mounted units was 'Stables', usually

---

3. The official trumpet and bugle calls, or 'sounds' were first codified and issued in 1798, and with slight modifications remained in use until 20th-century technology banished the trumpet and bugle as means of communication. But the venerable 'Last Post' and 'Reveille' are still to be heard at military funerals and other occasions.

held at 11 a.m. and compulsory for all ranks. Here the horses were thoroughly groomed and inspected by the Squadron officers, while the farriers attended to any necessary shoeing. Further parades might be held in the afternoon, especially for recruits, but this was the period for the chores aptly termed in the Army as 'fatigues', which could be anything from peeling potatoes for the Officers' Mess, sweeping the barrack square, or such other tasks devised to keep the soldier busy. Since he had no further meal to look forward to until next morning's breakfast, severe physical exertion must have been unwelcome. The trumpets or bugles sounded 'Tattoo' (later First and Last Post) between 9.30 and 10 p.m., at which hour every soldier had to be in his barrack-room, and at 10.15 came 'Lights Out' when the order was, into cots and no noise.

From about 4 p.m. in winter and 6 in summer, the soldier's time was theoretically his own, though the cavalryman still had to water, feed and bed down his mount. But spare time did not necessarily spell leisure. The latter half of the eighteenth century saw the Army afflicted with sartorial vexations which were as much a source of unnecessary expense as of barrack-room blasphemy. Under the influence of the Hanoverian George II with his fetish for Prussian fashions, the soldier was obliged to attire himself in extravagant uniform which may have been impressive on a Review Order parade, but was hardly practical in the field, and involved much time and toil in off-duty hours. 'Each garment became more close-fitting; belts and straps grew tighter; pipeclayed breeches and long white-buttoned gaiters came into wear; strange head-dresses were invented.'(27) Apart from the multitude of metal buttons to be polished, breeches, gaiters, belts and strappings needed to be pipe-clayed every day, and the pipe-clay itself had to be made up from fine white powdered clay and water. The pristine whiteness of newly pipe-clayed attire and accoutrements made a splendid foil to the scarlet coats on parade; but a heavy shower of rain could undo hours of labour.

The most absurd and time-consuming feature of the Georgian soldier's toilet was the ritual of hair-dressing — a form of military *frisure* almost as involved as that of a lady of fashion. The hair was to be tightly drawn back and finished at the nape of the neck with a club or queue and then the whole head was powdered. John Shipp describes the procedure:

I went into the town to purchase a few things that I needed such as a powder-bag, puff, soap, candles, grease and so on. As soon as I got back I had to undergo the operation of having my hair tied for the first time, to the no small amusement of the other boys. A large piece of candle-grease was applied first to the sides of my head, and then to the long hair behind. After this, the same operation was gone through with nasty, stinking soap, the man who was dressing me applying his knuckles as often as the soap... that part was bad enough, but the next was worse. A large pad, or bag, filled with sand, was poked into the back of my neck, the hair twisted tightly round it, and the whole tied with a leather thong. When thus dressed for parade, the skin of my face was pulled so tight by the bag stuck at the back of my head, that it was impossible so much as to wink an eyelid. Add to this an enormous high stock which was pushed under my chin, and I felt as stiff as if I had swallowed a ramrod or the Sergeant's halberd.(28)

In 1795 the Regimental Standing Orders for the 106th Regiment of Foot laid down that, 'The whole Regiment must be absolutely uniform to the size of the club, and the shape of it, from the Officer to the Private, so they must all have their hair clubbed with the regimental clubbing iron. It must be tied close to the head, the top and bottom must both be nearly equal in size, the bottom a little less than the top, and the whole must wear the regimental strap, and Officers the rosette.... the hair must be powdered before the strap or rosette is put on, so that it may always appear black and clean, and the hair must be quite white, but not clotted together.'(29)

The bane of the military coiffure continued to afflict the soldier until the early years of the nineteenth century. By 1804 the queue had grown into a pigtail of fifteen inches, but in that year seven inches was fixed as the maximum length. Then in 1808 the queue itself, and the whole absurd business of greasing and powdering were finally abolished — after nearly half-a-century.

But the soldier still had plenty to occupy his spare time. For instance, his cleaning materials, such as pipe-clay and boot polish, were not to be bought ready-made as in later times, but had to be laboriously made up in the barrack room. Here is a contemporary recipe 'to make Black-Balls for Boots':

Take six ounces of bees-wax, two ounces of virgins-wax, one ounce of hard tallow, and one barrel of lamp black, well mixed and boiled together in an earthen pot glazed; when you take it of [*sic*] the fire, take one ounce of plum gum beaten very small, which pour in gradually, stirring it continually till it is quite cold and incorporated; then preserve it for use.(30)

Arms cleaning was naturally of prime importance, and there were numerous recipes for rust-proofing, polishing brightwork and staining of stocks. These activities, wrote a military mentor in 1768, 'habituating soldiers to such remarkable neatness about every part of their appointments, not only gives employment for many of those idle hours they otherwise must have (a circumstance in itself alone quite worthy of consideration) but beyond all doubt, encourages in them a kind of liking for those arms, etc., which they are taught to take such care of.'(31)

Leaving the men to while away their 'idle hours', we must glance at two important changes which can round off this chapter. In 1751 the age-old practice of designating regiments by their Colonels' names was abolished by Royal Warrant (32) and there came into use the numerical titles which in some cases are still familiar today. Furthermore, the Warrant expressly forbade the display of Colonels' arms, crests or livery on regimental Colours or appointments. Then in 1782 came the allotment of 'territorial' or County sub-titles to most of the infantry regiments, the idea being that the association of a regiment with a particular county would stimulate recruiting and encourage local interest in a regiment. Thus originated, for example, the 22nd (Cheshire) Regiment, which is still proud to bear that title.

Predictably, many of the Colonels resented what they regarded as deprivation of their personal influence (and so it was intended), but there is no doubt that these reforms helped to foster regimental pride among both officers and men. Before 1751 a man might say he served in Colonel Brown's Regiment of Foot. When he had joined, it had been Colonel Smith's Foot; and before very long it might well become Colonel Robinson's Foot. These ephemeral titles meant little to the young soldier, who rarely set eyes on the titular head; to other units they meant nothing. Now there was a durable thread of continuity and identification, the basis of the splendid regimental spirit that has characterised the British Army down to the present day (despite the welter of amalgamations). While officers and men might come and go, the regiment lived on, an abiding family with its cherished, unique traditions and idiosyncrasies. It was fast becoming '*The* Regiment'.

When in 1799 an act was passed whereby recruits could not enlist for a specific regiment, but for 'General Service', this proved so unpopular that it was rescinded in 1816 and a man could once more opt for the unit of his choice. As Lord Palmerston declared in the House, 'I believe there is a great disinclination on the part of the lower orders to enlist for General Service; they like to know that they are to be in a certain Regiment, connected perhaps with their own County and their own friends.'(33)

3

THE AGE OF WELLINGTON

The advent of the nineteenth century saw the British Army matured as a formidable fighting force. It had been blooded in Continental wars, in the Americas, and in India, and the redcoat had laid the firm foundation of those traditions of valour and stoicism that were to be built on with even greater effect by succeeding generations.

But although the public had conceded some ephemeral acclaim to the soldier after such great victories as Blenheim, Dettingen, Minden, Quebec and the rest, the general mistrust of the Army was still prevalent. The squirearchy and the wealthy merchant classes had little love for it because they were obliged to pay heavy taxes in order to keep it in being, while the lower orders actively disliked the soldier who, in the absence of any organised constabulary force, acted as policeman and symbolised oppressive authority. The Navy, whom many still regarded as the real defenders of our shores, escaped such anathema, for the sailor was hidden away on board his ship at sea and had little or no contact with the populace, whereas the armed soldier was everywhere to be seen — especially when he was required to quell disturbances of the peace, which could be anything from pub brawls to riots of factory labourers.

> Our God and soldiers we alike adore
> Ev'n at the brink of danger, not before:
> After deliverance, both alike requited,
> Our God's forgotten, the soldier slighted.[1]

In 1796 one of the leading barristers of the time, Lord Erskine, publicly denounced at the Old Bailey what he termed the 'uncontrollable licentiousness of a brutal and insolent soldiery'. Such attitudes were to linger on until Kipling's day.

1. There are numerous variants of this well-known aphorism. The above version is preferred by the *Oxford Dictionary of Quotations*, and attributed to Francis Quarles (1592–1644).

One man dominated the Army and British military thinking for practically the first fifty years of the nineteenth century. Arthur Wellesley, Duke of Wellington, first emerged as a leader during the Mahratta War of 1803–04, after which he was scathingly dubbed by his home-based contemporaries as 'only a sepoy general'. But his real genius was displayed when he drove the French out of Spain, and on his final triumph at Waterloo his name became the household word that it remains today. There was no more fighting for him after Waterloo, but as successively Master-General of the Ordnance, Commander-in-Chief, Prime Minister, Constable of the Tower, his influence on all aspects of the Army, and of British politics, was immense.

Although an avowed admirer of Marlborough, Wellington was in many respects the very antithesis of 'Corporal John'. To the end of his life he was doggedly conservative (with a capital C as well, one could add) and was opposed to any degree of reform or modernisation. He stubbornly resisted the abolition of the contentious purchase system, and was adamant that nothing but flogging with the 'cat' could preserve proper discipline among soldiers. He disputed a proposed increase of pay because '. . . these men will only spend it on drink.' The Duke's reference to the soldiers who won his victories as 'the very scum of the earth' was to dog his memory ever after, but his realistic attitude is better revealed by a passage in one of his letters:

People talk of their enlisting for their fine military feeling — all stuff — no such thing. Some of our men enlist for having got bastard children — some for minor offences — many more for drink; but you can hardly conceive such a set brought together, and it really is wonderful that we should have made them the fine fellows they are. (1)

There is a certain characteristic conceit here, for of course it was the writer who had made them the 'fine fellows'.[2] Marlborough too, transformed his 'scum' into a magnificent fighting machine, but he would never have insulted them with that epithet. Conversely, the troops had no endearing nickname for Wellington: he was known simply as 'The Duke', or more familiarly as 'Old Nosey', referring to his prominent facial feature. In later life Wellington once complained that he had been 'much exposed to authors'; throughout his reign in the Army and in politics, the troops were much exposed to his foibles.

2. Having described his army as a 'rabble' in his despatch of May 31st, 1809, Wellington added 'I am endeavouring to tame them.'

Nevertheless, with all his ambivalence of character, the Duke exerted an extraordinary sense of loyalty among both officers and men. 'If ever England should require the service of her army again, and I should be in it, let me have "Old Nosey" to command. Our interest would be sure to be looked into, we should never have occasion to fear an enemy.' So wrote a sergeant of the 51st Foot after Waterloo.(2) And yet those soldiers who gained Wellington and the British Army the crowning repute throughout Europe endured sufferings and hardship which make dreadful reading in the many journals and diaries which emanated from the campaigns. The Duke may have 'looked into the interests' of his troops, in that he always led them to victory, but he was no Marlborough, and his Commissariat department was usually a shambles. Again and again we read of the men having to live as best they could off the country because rations were not forthcoming, while the cavalry horses starved for want of forage. The shoes supplied to the infantry were so inferior that they quickly wore out and many units were reduced to marching barefoot. During the withdrawal from Burgos to Ciudad Rodrigo in 1812 Wellington lost nearly 5,000 men from sickness and privation, while four of his cavalry regiments were so depleted in men and horseflesh that they had to be dismounted and sent home. The Duke's only reaction after the miseries of the retreat (in appalling weather) was to issue a scathing circular castigating the regimental officers for not preserving better discipline and denouncing the soldiers who had 'suffered no privations . . . nor any hardship excepting . . . the inclemency of the weather.'

Bearing in mind the types of men in the ranks — the Duke's 'scum' — and the exertions and hardships they were subject to, it is not surprising to learn that a distressingly large number resorted to alcohol, of which they seemingly never went short. Drunkenness had always been the bane of Authority, but in the Peninsula it smote the regiments with unparalleled excess and disgraceful instances of looting, rape and carnage, which even the Iron Duke's heavy hand and the lash were powerless to repress. A sergeant of the 43rd Light Infantry wrote:

The conduct of some men would have disgraced savages, drunkenness prevailed to such a frightful extent . . . . It was no infrequent thing to see a long string of mules carrying drunken soldiers to prevent them falling into the hands of the enemy. The new wine was in tanks particularly about Valladolid and the men ran mad. I remember seeing a soldier lying fully accoutred with his knapsack on in a large

tank, he had either fallen in or been pushed in by his comrades I
saw a dragoon fire his pistol into a large vat containing thousands of
gallons; in a few minutes we were up to our knees in wine, fighting like
tigers for it. (3)

Wellington himself complained that a vast number of men enlisted solely
for drink, and this was probably true. But it is a curious anomaly that the
discipline and morale that enabled Marlborough's men to march the
length and breadth of Europe without any such excesses should
apparently break down under the most eminent general in British history,
among men who gained him his supreme triumphs.

By the time Wellington had soared in the military firmament, the
Army had been moulded into the pattern it was to retain almost to the end
of the century. A recruit could be posted to any one of thirty-one
regiments of cavalry, three regiments of Foot Guards or 104 of line
infantry. The supporting arms comprised only the Royal Regiment of
Artillery, raised in 1716 (and since 1793 including the Royal Horse
Artillery), and the Corps of Royal Engineers, which was formed as an
officer-only branch in 1717, with a separate other-ranks corps of Royal
Military Artificers. The latter of course demanded men of higher
intelligence and education than the line regiments, while both artil-
lerymen and engineers were really a separate force of their own, being
controlled and administered by their civilian masters of the Board of
Ordnance, not by the War Office, (or Horse Guards as it was then
termed).

The new century saw the emergence of a new type of infantry. In 1800
an 'Experimental Corps of Riflemen' was raised at Shorncliffe, soon to be
joined by battalions of light infantry. This was the nucleus of the elite
Rifle Brigade and Wellington's equally elite Light Division in the
Peninsula. The novel corps raised eyebrows among the martinets of the
old Prussian school, for as skirmishers and reconnaissance troops the
men were trained to fight not in the conventional rigid, close-order ranks,
but in dispersed order and taking all advantage of cover. In other words,
they practised field-craft. More startling was the concept of the 'Light'
soldier as a 'thinking fighting man', the emphasis being on the initiative
and self-reliance of the individual. The formation of the Rifle Brigade,
with its provisions for regimental schools, and examinations, rewards for
good conduct and bravery, even the encouragement of sport, was the
basis of the modern military system, and as Fortescue observes, 'marks a

new era in the history of the British infantry.' But more than a century was to pass before these revolutionary ideas became generally assimilated throughout the Army.

Britain still prided herself on having volunteer defence forces and, with the demand for more recruits during the early part of the Napoleonic Wars, various means were devised to tempt them. In 1805 the enlistment bounty was raised from £7 12s 6d to twelve guineas, but as usual, few would-be recruits learned until too late that nearly a third of that sum would be deducted for their 'necessaries' on joining. In the following year a 'Limited Service' was introduced. Instead of enlisting for 'life', a recruit could opt for a limited number of years, after which he could take his discharge, or re-engage for a further period, with increased pay. He could then take his discharge with a pension equivalent to half pay, or sign on for a third period, after which he would be discharged with a pension nearly equal to his pay. The three periods varied slightly according to arms: in the infantry they were each of seven years; in the cavalry ten, seven and seven, and in the artillery, twelve, five and five.

There was mixed reaction to this innovation. Many senior officers (including, predictably, Wellington) were opposed to it, maintaining that a man choosing the profession of arms should be committed enough to devote the whole of his active life to his career, and the scheme would open the ranks to 'uncommitted opportunists who have no intention of becoming real soldiers'.(4) Surprisingly enough, however, the men themselves evidently chose to become 'real soldiers', and limited service seemed to have little appeal. Statistics for 1814 show that of 3,143 recruits a vast majority of 2,371 signed on 'for life'.(5) Since the scheme proved so unpopular with the men it was abandoned in 1829 and 'life' service was reintroduced, which in effect was about twenty-one years, or approximating to the total of the previous three 'short service' engagements. But the reforming lobby remained active, and in 1847 limited service was once more introduced, this time to stay (although with modifications). A soldier could now enlist initially for ten years in the infantry and then re-engage for another eleven years. In the cavalry, artillery and engineers the periods were twelve and twelve. There was a catch in this scheme, not always explained to the recruit before enlistment: a soldier was not entitled to any pension unless he re-engaged for the second period.

Another source of recruits was the Militia, a part-time volunteer force administered not by Horse Guards but by the Lord Lieutenants of Counties, and liable only for home service. Until 1805 Militiamen were exempt from regular service, but in that year they were permitted to transfer to regular regiments of their choice, and a remarkable total of 13,580 did so. The Army profited not only by numbers, but by the fact that the Militia recruit had already received some training and was generally a steadier type of man than the usual run.

In the 1790s the basic pay of a private in the infantry was raised from 8d per day to 1s, and at that sum it remained, not only throughout the age of Wellington but until the end of the century. A cavalry trooper was a little better off with 1s 3d, a Foot Guardsman minimally so with 1s 1d; the elite Life Guardsman enjoyed 1s 11¾d.

But as hitherto, the soldier did not see the whole of the above sums. He was stopped 6d per day for his rations, about 2d for laundry and 'maintenance of necessaries' and other sums for hair-cutting and 'barrack damages', which could cover anything from a broken window-pane to replacement of a leaking urinal-tub. He would be fortunate if his spending money amounted to more than one penny a day. Yet again we must compare these pittances with the average earnings of one of his class in civilian life. In the 1840s a farm labourer's wages varied from 7s per week to 9s — hardly more than the private soldier's, and although the labourer might enjoy a few perks, this was all he had to house, clothe and feed himself.(6) There is in fact surprisingly little evidence to show that the average soldier considered himself underpaid: it was a case of what he never had he never missed. And there were even some who considered the pay over-generous: in the debate on the Army Estimates in the House of Commons, in March 1834, William Cobbett, himself an ex-soldier and radical reformer, objected that '7s 7d per week was too much for the common soldier'.(7)

It was possible for the soldier to supplement his regimental pay. A much sought-after (if strictly limited) opportunity was employment as officer's servant, one being allowed for each junior officer and two for field officers and above. Many smart and intelligent men did very nicely out of such jobs, for in addition to gratuities from their officers they often received perks in the way of extra rations from the Mess — which also employed soldiers as waiters and orderlies. In the cavalry a trooper could earn a few extra pence by acting as groom to officers and troop sergeants. Finally, in 1836 a munificent Whig Government passed a Bill granting good conduct pay for soldiers of 'unblemished conduct'. This amounted to one penny a day for every five years' service, which scarcely compensated for all stoppages still in force. It is hardly necessary to add that good conduct pay was disapproved of by Wellington, who was averse to 'bribing men to become good soldiers'. Incidentally, the Duke did not discountenance the practice of promoting rankers to a commission for distinguished conduct in the field, and during the Peninsular Campaign he personally directed the Commanding Officers of the Light Division regiments to recommend deserving sergeants for such promotion. But this was very exceptional, and he once declared of the ranker-officers 'their origins would come out and you could never perfectly trust them.'(8) Writing of the Peninsula period, Sir Charles Oman remarked, 'In command they were not as a rule successful, and I have only come on a single case of one [ex-sergeant] who reached the rank of full Colonel, and of two who were fortunate enough to obtain a majority.'(9) Conceivably the ranker-officer was ill-considered by the traditional officer-class, while failing to gain the full respect of the common soldier from whose social class he originated — however, in the absence of solid evidence, this has to remain a matter for speculation.

Marriage was still discouraged, in the Army, but as some commanding officers were inevitably lax about the numbers of men permitted to have wives in barracks, in 1829 the Commander-in-Chief (Viscount Hill) was obliged to issue a General Order reminding them of the regulations. Stressing that in no circumstances was the authorised number of six women per hundred men to be exceeded, his Lordship added:

> It must be explained to the men, that their comforts as soldiers are in a very small degree increased by their marriage, while the inconvenience and distress, naturally accruing to them from such connexion are serious and unavoidable, particularly when regiments are ordered to embark for foreign service, when only *six women to one hundred men* are allowed to proceed with their husbands:- on these occasions commanding officers are placed under considerable embarrassment, in making selection of the women who are to be permitted to accompany their husbands abroad, and of those who are to be compelled to return to their friends, or to their parishes.(10)

In the *United Service Journal* for November 1833 the Editor expressed his own views: 'It must be recollected, that Barracks are properly the abode of a *male* community . . . the admission of females is an indulgence, contingent on their own conduct and usefulness and the due accommodation and recreations of the men. The wives of soldiers are to be held strictly to this understanding.' Wives of soldiers, however, unless they could support themselves, were to remain an exception until the pay structure made provision for them, so the question may have remained somewhat academic. One assumes that the Oldest Profession found gainful employment in garrison towns.

Although the Army had to wait until almost the end of the century for any radical reforms, there were earlier, niggardly attempts to improve the soldier's lot and encourage recruiting. In 1829 George IV issued a Royal Warrant laying down regulations for pension settlements. Briefly, pensions were divided into three categories, based on length of service, wounds in action, and disabilities suffered while serving. To be eligible for the long-service pension a private soldier had to put in at least twenty-one years' service (twenty-four in the cavalry), when he would be entitled to one shilling a day after discharge. NCOs received slight increases according to rank: thus a sergeant-major got an extra 2½d per day, a corporal one halfpenny. If a soldier was so severely wounded as to be incapable of supporting himself (e.g. by the loss of two limbs or both eyes), the Royal Warrant rewarded him with from 1s 6d to 2s per day according to the circumstances.

The rules for disability pensions were extremely complex, but were basically dependent on whether the disabled man had less or more than fourteen years' service. To summarise, a disabled soldier with less than fourteen years received an extra 6d a day depending on his injury or illness; over fourteen years he was entitled to a maximum of 9d — which was all he could claim if he had become totally blind (not as a result of wounds). Apparently the one-eyed man was still capable of further service: the Warrant emphasised that 'No soldier shall be discharged for the loss of one eye only, whether it be the right or left.' But in such cases ' . . . the loss may be considered by the Commissioners (of Chelsea Hospital) at their discretion, in apportioning the rate of any pension.'(11)

Both the Royal Hospitals at Chelsea and Kilmainham had been functioning for nearly 150 years by the time of Waterloo, and in theory an eligible discharged soldier could apply for admission to one or other as an in-pensioner. But accommodation was limited: Chelsea could take 500 men, Kilmainham only 200 and as some 8,000 soldiers became eligible for pensions every year during the 1830s, the vast majority had to fend for themselves as out-pensioners.

If a serving soldier decided to take his discharge before his time was up, the regulations allowed him to do so by purchase — a system still in force today. The rates varied according to length of service: under seven years a cavalryman had to pay £30, an infantryman £20. After fifteen years the figures were reduced to £6 and £5. Since those who resolved to 'soldier no more' were usually the younger types, few of them could find the £20 or £30, roughly twice the yearly pay, and thus they would resort to desertion. The longer-serving man had little to gain by throwing up his secure job and chances of promotion, for if he purchased his discharge he renounced all claims to a pension, while should he subsequently decide that the Army was a better life after all and sign on again, he was not allowed to reckon his former service.

In the first half of the nineteenth century we detect a stirring of conscience regarding the education of the soldier (and his officer). Besides instituting the first training establishment for cavalry and infantry officer-cadets at High Wycombe in 1802 — later to become the Royal Military College, Sandhurst and the Staff College — the Duke of York persuaded King George III to grant a Royal Charter for the founding of a boarding school at Chelsea for the children of the rank-and-file, preference being given to those whose fathers had been killed in action or who had died in service. Opened in 1803 as the Royal Military Asylum, this school offered free board, clothing and tuition, at first to children of both sexes, but from 1850 only boys were admitted. In 1815 a similar establishment was opened in Dublin and known as the Royal Hibernian Military School. The latter closed down in 1922 but the Royal Military Asylum is still flourishing as the Duke of York's Royal Military School at Dover (where it has been since 1909). There was of course an ulterior motive behind the benevolence of these establishments, for, run on military lines, both became sources of a superior class of recruit for the Army. Although there was no compulsion for a boy to join up after attending either school, there was inducement to do so, for if he declined, none of his family's children would be eligible for admission. Between 1803 and 1830 the Chelsea Asylum provided 1500 recruits, regarded as potential NCOs. In this respect the scheme could be seen as a forerunner of the modern Junior Leaders Regiments.

Perhaps spurred on by the above, certain individual regiments began to open their own schools, but as before, the emphasis was on the soldiers' children rather than the men themselves. If he wished to better himself, a soldier could attend with the infants, who were probably no less literate than himself. In 1832 the Commanding Officer of the 15th (King's) Hussars directed that 'Every Private should aspire to promotion, nor need anyone despair of attaining it, as he has the power fully to qualify himself by attendance at the Regimental School . . .'(12)

By 1844 Regimental Schools had become obligatory throughout the Army, and Queen's Regulations and Orders for that year enjoined all commanding officers to give 'their personal care and attention'. They were reminded that the object of the schools was the care and instruction of the children of non-commissioned officers and soldiers and 'to give them that portion of learning which may qualify them for Non-Commissioned Officers and to enable them to become useful members of the community.' Boys were taught by a sergeant-schoolmaster, girls by a civilian schoolmistress. In addition to the normal 'three R's', the boys were taught the rudiments of the trades of armourers, tailors, saddlers and shoemakers — obviously useful in the Army — while girls were taught 'plain needlework and knitting'. The 1844 Regulations devoted thirteen clauses to Regimental Schools and their child pupils; almost as an afterthought, the penultimate clause added;'Officers Commanding Regiments are to encourage, by every means in their power, the attendance of the young Non-Commissioned Officers and Soldiers at the Regimental Schools for two hours in each day: this instruction is to be afforded free of expense.'

Although doubtless many COs 'encouraged' their men to improve themselves, book-learning was not a favoured pursuit among the general run of soldiers, unless they were ambitious for promotion; and even then not much was demanded from the NCO other than ability to read and write orders and do simple arithmetic. The proliferation of rank-and-file diaries, memoirs and other literary effusions during the Wellington period might seem to imply a burgeoning literacy in the ranks; but these are exceptions, and many of them were compiled and polished in the writer's later years. The well-known *Recollections of Rifleman Harris* (1848) were actually edited and set down by a retired officer named Curling. The equally familiar *Letters of Private Wheeler* were carefully polished up and prepared for printing when Wheeler had become a schoolmaster-sergeant, aged forty.

A step in the regularisation of education came in 1846 with the formation of a Corps of Army Schoolmasters, but there was still no compulsion for a soldier to better himself — nor was there for a civilian until the Education Act of 1870. Even with official encouragement, illiteracy remained as high in the Army as it was in civilian life among the equivalent classes. As late as 1857 the total percentage of soldiers unable to read or write was recorded as 20.5, while 18.8 per cent could read but not write, and were barely able to sign their names.(13)

In any spare time he might have after parades the soldier gravitated to the canteen, later familiar as the 'Wet Canteen', which had been established in most barracks during the early nineteenth century. There was nowhere else for him to relax, other than the spartan barrack rooms, and the atmosphere of neither was conducive to any form of study. But in 1830 the enlightened Colonel of the Black Watch founded a Regimental 'Library', or reading room, where soldiers so inclined could indulge in recreations more improving than swilling ale or spirits. This example was followed by several other regiments. In 1841 the scheme was given official blessing with Horse Guards' approval of the setting up of regimental libraries throughout the Army, although the Commander-in-Chief, Viscount Hill, expressed concern about 'the men collecting in societies of that sort'.(14)

Whether such amenities had any effect on general standards of education is doubtful: only the handful of literates sought the intellectual ambience of the reading room, the vast majority preferring the robust environment of the canteen where they could fill bellies rather than minds.

Despite a few military voices crying in the wilderness, the attitude of Authority towards the education of the rank-and-file remained basic: not only was it totally unnecessary to teach a soldier anything but the duties and skills of his trade, but it would surely prejudice good order and military discipline to develop his thought processes. The C-in-C's view, noted above, reflected such suspicions. Earlier, when Colonel Le Marchant had put forward his plans for the Royal Military College, he had included provisions for a similar school for NCOs, but this was firmly rejected by Horse Guards who considered it 'inconsistent with the habits of this country to raise private soldiers to so close an equality with their officers'.(15)Until his death the Duke of Wellington stubbornly opposed the schooling of soldiers, although he advocated 'a superior education' for officers, as gentlemen. The slow progress towards the 'thinking bayonets' gathered momentum during the latter part of the nineteenth century, and we shall revert to it in the next chapter.

Meanwhile we must glance at medical matters. It would seem an elementary maxim that if a soldier is to be kept fit for service his body must be kept fit and healthy. Yet, as we have seen, such arrangements as existed for the care and treatment of the sick or wounded left much to be desired. There was no organised medical department in the Army, and the regimental surgeons were not always professionally qualified. Dr James McGrigor, Principal Medical Officer to Wellington in the Peninsula, and subsequently prime mover in military medical reform, described many of the so-called Medical Officers with the regiments as little more than apothecaries and even 'druggists' apprentices'. On the outbreak of the Napoleonic War it was the practice to advertise for these men, 'offering commissions to such as could pass some kind of examination . . . and it was the occasion of many uneducated and unqualified persons being introduced to the service, not a few of whom . . . found means to pass through the different grades to regimental and staff surgeon.'(16)

Of course it is dangerous to generalise, and there were many conscientious, hard-working doctors who did their best within the limits of the contemporary state of their art. There were no analgesics or sedatives to ease a badly-wounded man's sufferings, and no anaesthetics. If a limb had to be amputated, the only easement for the patient was a stiff dram and the proverbial bite on the bullet while the surgeon's assistants held him down. The stoicism of soldiers undergoing such ordeals is well illustrated in a description by a sergeant in the Coldstream Guards of the amputation of his gangrenous leg at Bergen-op-Zoom in 1813:

They had got me fixed upon the end of a long barrack-room table, sitting upright, with my legs hanging down: a basin was brought for me to drink out of. I said, 'Sir, let me have a good draught.' He poured out nearly a pint [of rum] which I eagerly drank off. In an instant it raised up my spirits to an invincible courage . . . The serjeant was preparing to blindfold me. 'Oh no,' I said, 'I shall sit still and see as well as the rest.' One of the surgeons sat on a stool, to hold the leg steady; the second ripped up my trousers and took down the stocking low enough, then he waited on the head surgeon . . . the tourniquet being placed painfully tight above the knee, he put his hand under the calf of the leg and setting the edge of the knife on the shin bone, at one heavy, quick stroke, drew it round till it met the shin bone again . . . The blood, quickly following the knife, spread around and formed like a beautiful red fan, downwards . . . Next the surgeon with his hand, forced up the flesh towards the knee, to make way for the saw. When the saw was applied, I found it extremely painful; it was worn out . . . it stuck as a bad saw would when sawing a green stick. I said 'Oh sir, have you not a better saw?' He said he was sorry he had not, as they were all worn out. The bone got through, the next thing to be done was still more painful — that of tying up the ligatures; then followed the drawing down of the flesh to cover the end of the bone, and tightly strapped there with strips of sticking plaster; after this, strongly bandaged: and thus ended the operation, which lasted about half an hour.(17)

The worthy sergeant was invalided home, discharged on a pension of a shilling a day, and fitted with a wooden leg 'free, a gratuitous national gift'.

Diseases, and particularly tropical diseases, carried off more soldiers (and their officers) than did the enemy. The West Indies were described as the graveyard of the British Army in the late 1790s. Between 1794 and 1796 the 23rd Foot lost twelve officers and 600 soldiers from yellow fever while serving in St Domingo; during the same period the 13th Light Dragoons, with an establishment of 452 all ranks, lost nineteen officers and 296 other ranks from the same cause. The appalling total losses of the Army in that period are given by Fortescue as 25,000.(18)

Even the higher echelons of the medical profession were largely ignorant of the causes and therapy of such tropical diseases as cholera, dysentery, malaria, and in India these ravaged the ranks with melancholy regularity. Cholera was the dreaded scourge, for it struck with terrifying suddenness, and when it did there were few survivors among the smitten. A unit might parade up to strength in the morning and by nightfall a dozen or more men would be dying in agony. The mortality from cholera may be gauged from records of an epidemic at Karachi in June 1845. In the 86th Foot 410 men were afflicted and 238 died; the 104th Foot lost 83, and within four days the garrison of eight regiments buried a total of 753 officers and men.(19) On their three-month march from Calcutta to Cawnpore in 1843 the 9th Lancers, 450 strong, lost one officer and eighty soldiers, together with fourteen wives and eight children.(20) Similar depressing statistics can be found in the records of most regiments which served in India during the nineteenth century. In his autobiography, *Forty-One Years in India*, (1878) Field-Marshal Lord Roberts wrote: 'In the fifty-seven years preceding the Mutiny the annual rate of mortality amongst the European troops in India was sixty-nine per thousand, and in some stations it was even more appalling.'

There was no known prophylactic for cholera, nor any cure. Native troops were no more inured to these epidemics than were European troops — none bred the appropriate antibodies. In 1853 an anonymous contribution to *The Lancet* confessed 'All is darkness and confusion, vague theory and speculation. What is cholera? Is it a fungus, an insect, a miasm, an electrical disturbance . . .? We know nothing; we are at sea in a whirlpool of conjecture.' Ex-Private Frank Richards of the Royal Welch Fusiliers later recalled (21) that as late as 1902 it was generally believed that an invisible germ-laden 'cholera cloud' swept through a barrack-room at a level of two or three feet from the ground, and he cites the instance of a single survivor who had fallen in a drunken stupor on the floor, the rest of his mates in their beds being stricken down. 'Every unit serving in India had the same story,' adds Richards, and the present writer can confirm that the myth was still remembered among the lower ranks in India in the 1930s.

The virulent cholera bacillus breeds in conditions of filth such as cesspits and fouled water sources, and is transmitted through the mouth by drinking such water or consuming food contaminated by flies. Not until the twentieth century was it fully appreciated that the root causes of cholera epidemics were the low standard of hygiene and the insanitary conditions prevailing in India. Before the Mutiny most of the British troops' barracks 'up country' were of the primitive native-style construction, with walls of mud and cow-dung, thatched roofs, and floors of plain rammed earth, which was often 'finished' with a washing of cow-dung. Such conditions were hardly conducive to hygiene. But the sanitary arrangements were even worse. The latrines (or 'bogs' as they were commonly termed by the soldiers) consisted of wooden boxes fixed over a cesspit in an outbuilding between two barrack-rooms, drainage being non-existent. Periodically the ordure would be carried away by the low-caste *mehtars*, or sweepers, and dumped in a main cesspit, where it would drain into the subsoil — to pollute the nearby wells which supplied the drinking water. Although improved barrack blocks — brick-built with tiled roofs, stone or brick floors and deep verandahs — had made their appearance by the 1850s, the sanitary arrangements remained primitive. In place of the cesspit, each latrine had a metal pan under each seat, and this was removed by the sweepers through trap doors at the rear of the building, whence the contents were emptied into tubs for disposal as before. A member of the Royal Commission to investigate the sanitary arrangements of the Army in India commented on the stench from the latrines. 'As you ride through the barracks you go through those places in going to the general parade ground — and it is invariably most offensive. There is never any time of the day or night that you do not smell them.'(22) As at home, urinal tubs were placed either within the barrack-rooms or on the verandahs, these too being emptied daily by the sweepers, who would often spill the contents when staggering with a full tub slung on a bamboo pole.

When it is recalled that before separate messing blocks were introduced, all meals were cooked and eaten in the barrack-rooms, infested with myriads of flies during the hot weather, it is scarcely surprising that the soldier was smitten with cholera, typhoid, dysentery and other enteric ailments.

The only 'preventive' measure on the outbreak of cholera was for the whole regiment or battalion to move itself into a 'clean' area and go into temporary camp away from the barracks, in the fond belief that the infected atmosphere would thus be left behind to spend itself. It was not realised that this 'cholera-dodging' as it was termed, was of little avail, for more often than not the deadly virus was carried with the men.

The importance of personal hygiene was recognised, but it was no simple matter to persuade soldiers to wash or bath when adequate facilities were not available, or to wear clean underclothes. The Standing Orders of the 15th Hussars in 1832 directed that 'As personal cleanliness conduces greatly to the preservation of health, the men are therefore ordered to wash their feet every Sunday morning before parade, and in summer their bodies also' (in winter, presumably, they were excused the latter ordeal). They were also enjoined to put on clean drawers every second Sunday, and clean shirts and socks on Sundays and Wednesdays. Similar orders by the Commanding Officer of the 7th Dragoon Guards in 1823 advised 'every Dragoon to thoroughly wash his private parts at least once a week, since irritation in this portion of the body can greatly inconvenience a cavalry soldier in the saddle.'(23)

Both at home and overseas, regiments had their own hospitals, although that term was hardly justified, for the 'hospital' was merely a separate barrack block, with the same conditions of overcrowding, lack of proper sanitary arrangements and bad ventilation. It was staffed by the regimental surgeon and a squad of untrained orderlies who could do no more than dress wounds and apply bandages. In India, if a man could not be cured by the regimental doctor he died, for there were no central hospitals with better qualified staff. In the United Kingdom a soldier suffering from a serious disease or injuries needing long-term care might, if lucky, be sent to one of the general hospitals located at Chatham, Dublin and Cork, where superior facilities were available. But none of these could accommodate more than 300 patients. Unless he were seriously ill, the soldier did not altogether welcome a spell in hospital, regimental or otherwise, for in addition to the other stoppages from his pay, he was docked tenpence a day towards his diet and drugs.

Throughout the Wellington era Army discipline was founded on the bedrock of flogging. It is true that by 1832 some humanitarian influence had prevailed, and instead of the barbaric sentences of one thousand and more lashes, the Mutiny Act restricted the maximum number to three hundred, on the sentence of a General or District Court Martial. A regimental court could award no more than two hundred. There was constant agitation, at Westminster and among the Press, for total abolition, but this came to nothing. In 1834 a motion in the House for such reform was soundly defeated by a majority of 133, the voting being 227 against and 94 for.(24) Although Wellington was no longer Commander-in-Chief, he was a member of the Cabinet and his influence was still dominant on all military matters. His views on abolition were entirely in character: having declared that 'British soldiers are taken entirely from the lowest order of society,' he went on: 'I do not see how you can have an Army at all unless you preserve it in a state of discipline, nor how you can have a state of discipline, unless you have some punishment . . . There is no punishment which makes an impression upon any body except corporal punishment.' The prime object of punishment, he continued, was to deter others by making examples, and not merely to improve the conduct of an erring individual. 'I have no idea of any great effect being produced by anything but the fear of immediate corporal punishment. I must say, that in hundreds of instances, the very threat of the lash has prevented very serious crimes . . . '(25)

Some medical and political luminaries who might have been expected to hold opposite views to the Iron Duke were surprisingly in accord. The distinguished physician, Sir Gilbert Blane, wrote a counterblast to the abolitionists in *The United Service Journal* of March 1830 in which he likened the flogging of soldiers to the caning of schoolboys. 'Members of the House might have been asked whether they felt themselves degraded, or their spirits broken, by having been whipped at school . . . Neither school-boy nor soldier will bear any ill-will to his master or Officer, provided the punishment has been justly inflicted.' Quite the contrary, added Sir Gilbert, 'a little reflection on the part of the culprit brings perfect acquiescence . . . and even gratitude.'

It is clear that, from the Duke of Wellington downwards, the proponents of flogging were not motivated by any spirit of vindictiveness, but sincerely believed that proper discipline could not be maintained without it. And the Duke and others were convinced that the substitution of prison sentences, as proposed by the abolitionists, would not prove such an effective deterrent, for the offender must be *seen* to be punished — 'a striking and prompt example'. If a man were sent to prison, his punishment was not visible to his comrades, and furthermore a prison sentence would deprive his unit of his services, and this 'would be quite impractical on actual service' (Blane).

However, such was the pressure from the anti-flogging lobby that in March 1834 a Royal Commission was appointed 'for inquiring into the system of military punishments in the Army'. After deliberating for nearly twelve months and interrogating 71 witnesses, the Commissioners, headed by Lord Wharncliffe (Lord Privy Seal) produced their report, which came down firmly in favour of flogging. Their summary was 'that the opinion of almost every witness whom we have examined, is that the substitution of other punishments for corporal punishment in Your Majesty's Army, upon actual service, and in the field, is impracticable, and if practicable, would be insufficient for the maintenance of proper discipline.' Nevertheless, they conceded that every effort should be made 'to make its infliction less frequent', and there should be clearer guidance as to the types of offences warranting corporal punishment.

As a result of this Commission there was some mild concession to public conscience: the maximum number of lashes to be awarded by a General Court Martial was reduced from 300 to 200; a district court martial could award 150 and a regimental 100. The next issue of Queen's Regulations clearly specified the offences for which punishment could be inflicted: (1) Mutiny, insubordination, using or offering violence to superior officers; (2) Drunkenness on duty; (3) Sale of, or making away with arms, ammunition, accoutrement or necessaries, and stealing from comrades 'or other disgraceful conduct'.

The terms 'insubordination' and 'disgraceful conduct' were of course subject to different interpretations by different commanding officers: a man might be awarded one hundred lashes for swearing at his platoon sergeant in a moment of provocation, while a dirty turn-out on parade could be classed as 'disgraceful', with consequent penalty.

Although prison sentences were not regarded as a satisfactory alternative to flogging, a soldier could be so punished for certain offences, and hitherto the sentence was to be served in a civilian gaol, the most notorious being those at Millbank and Pentonville, London. The Commissioners felt that men so imprisoned would be subject to 'moral contamination' in the company of felons and other undesirable characters, and accordingly they recommended that special detention barracks should be provided for military offenders. This was put into effect in 1844, and by 1856 there were ten military prisons or detention barracks in the United Kingdom, and ten overseas. One of the largest was that erected at the new garrison town of Aldershot in 1855, and its later nickname came to be dreaded by generations of erring soldiers, besides being commonly applied to all similar establishments. When reconstructed in 1870 its main roof over the three-storey block of cells was entirely of glass, so that it became known throughout the Army as 'the Glasshouse'.

For minor offences several lesser punishments than flogging or prison sentences were specified in Queen's Regulations. Commanding Officers could award confinement to the 'Black Hole' (the detention cell in the Guardroom); confinement to barracks (for not longer than one month), extra drill in full marching order (not exceeding fourteen days) or ordinary defaulters drill, without packs, up to a period of one month. Confinement to barracks, or 'CB', remained one of the commonest punishments meted out by Commanding Officers and/or Squadron/Company commanders down to post World-War II days; and so did extra drills, which involved being marched around the parade ground with full pack and arms, in quick and double time. Hence the once-familiar term 'pack-drill'. Men undergoing these regimental punishments were known as defaulters, and in addition to the above penalties they were required to report to the Guardroom every hour during the evenings, at the summons of 'Defaulters Call' on the bugle or trumpet, there to answer their names and be inspected by the Guard Commander. There was little respite for the defaulter.

Offending NCOs received some discrimination commensurate with their rank. Queen's Regulations (1844) directed that they were never to be confined in the Guardroom with private soldiers, but merely to be placed under arrest (which meant confinement to barracks), while an officer should not reprove a NCO within the hearing of privates ' . . . indeed, admonition conveyed in mild terms, and without exposure of the individual, whatever may be his Rank, will in general be found to have a much better effect than that which tends to humiliate him in the eyes of his inferiors or his comrades, or to lower him in his own estimation.'

The reductions in the maximum flogging sentences motivated by the Royal Commission of 1834–35 did little to appease the abolition lobby, and just eleven years later another storm of protest raged over the tragic case of Private Frederick White of the 7th Hussars. While stationed at Hounslow in June 1846 this 27-year-old soldier had been found guilty of insubordination and received 150 lashes with the 'cat'. After treatment in hospital he was discharged fit for duty, but later complaining of pains in the chest and legs, he was readmitted to hospital, where he died on July 11th. A regimental autopsy attended by a medical officer appointed by Dr James McGrigor reported that death had been caused by inflammation of the pleura and the lining membrane of the heart, and 'was in no way connected with the corporal punishment received on 15 June.' However, at a public inquest on August 4th the Coroner's jury were unanimously of the opinion that the man had died from the effects of a 'severe and cruel flogging', adding the rider that the Government should once more be urged to abolish 'the disgraceful practice of flogging'. Amid renewed outbursts in the radical press, the House debated the question yet again, with predictable result: the motion for abolition was defeated by 90 votes to 37. But public feeling was now so strong that Government was forced to make another concession, this time more generous, and on August 11th it was announced that the maximum punishment by any court martial would be limited to 50 lashes. Another thirty-five years were to pass before the 'cat' disappeared altogether in the Army. (26)

SOLDIERS OF THE QUEEN

By 1850 the British Army had been in existence for nearly two hundred years. During these centuries neither officer nor soldier saw very much in the way of radical change either in tactics, training, or in living conditions. It is true that barracks had appeared, pay was minimally increased, there were a few military hospitals, the soldier was encouraged to acquire a degree of literacy. Nevertheless, if a private of Charles II's army could have been reincarnated in that of Queen Victoria shortly before the Crimean War, he would not have been unduly perplexed by what he found.

Yet well within the lifetime of a soldier of the thirty-year-old Queen, the Army would see sweeping reforms that transformed it into something nearly resembling that which crossed the Channel in 1914.

> You must not look upon the soldier as a responsible agent, for he is not able to take care of himself, he must be fed, clothed, looked after like a child and given only just enough to make him efficient as part of the great machine for War. Give him one farthing more than he really wants, and he gives way to his brutal propensities and immediately gets drunk.(1)

Such an attitude, expressed by a Captain of the Rifle Brigade at the time of the Crimea, was probably typical of that of many Victorian officers, especially the more senior ranks, but this too was to be modified within the next fifty years or so.

The seeds of reform were sown in the Crimea, where the appalling inadequacies of the medical and commissariat services were publicly exposed to shock the readers of *The Times, Illustrated London News* and other journals. The sufferings of the soldiers through shortage — even absence — of rations, warm clothing and shelter, and the bungling efforts to evacuate casualties have been so fully chronicled in the numerous writings by the sufferers themselves that it is not necessary to detail them here.

Anaesthetics had been used in surgery as early as 1847 and in 1853 Queen Victoria herself was given chloroform during the birth of her seventh child. But there was ethical and clinical opposition to its use, and when Dr (later Sir) John Hall arrived in the Crimea as Principal Medical Officer and Inspector-General of Hospitals, he issued a memorandum to all medical officers cautioning them against the indiscriminate use of chloroform when operating on badly wounded men: 'for, however barbarous it may appear, the smart of a knife is a powerful stimulant; and it is much better to hear a man ball lustily than to see him sink silently into the grave.'(2) We may note that Dr Hall had been the surgeon who denied the allegation that Private White of the 7th Hussars had died from the effects of flogging, as recounted in the previous chapter.

The strictures about gross mismanagement published by William Russell, *The Times* correspondent, were amply confirmed by regimental writers. 'Certainly the Army Staff could not be worse. We might as well have an old woman to command us as Lord Raglan. Then our commissariat is nearly useless. Our ambulance totally useless, and our medical department very bad . . . '(3)

On the declaration of War the Horse Guards had made a gesture of medical organisation by despatching with the Expeditionary Force a Hospital Conveyance Corps, or ambulance corps. This consisted of some 300 decrepit old pensioners who succumbed either to their privations or to the bottle. Since even Lord Raglan admitted that the ambulance corps was 'a complete failure', Whitehall conceived another plan, initiated by Sidney Herbert, Secretary-at-War. This was for a formed body of selected NCOs 'of good character and able to read and write', who would be trained to act as medical orderlies and hospital assistants. The proposal was approved in December 1854, but it was not until February 1856 that the Corps was recruited and officially established. It was almost too late to be of service in the Crimea, but later that year it was embodied in the Regular Army, with the title Medical Staff Corps, and as such was the origin of the non-commissioned ranks of the later Royal Army Medical Corps.(4)

Of course it is Florence Nightingale's name that is indissolubly linked with the improvements in the sick and wounded soldiers' lot in the Crimea and the establishment of the properly run hospital at Scutari. But her efforts were fully backed by Sidney Herbert, who had instigated her posting to the Crimea, and the influence of both these personalities was to exert a profound effect on later reforms.

The British public were aghast to learn of the administrative incompetence and the casualty toll in the Crimea. In the seven months from October 1854 to the following April, thirty-five per cent of the total strength of the Expeditionary Force died, not through enemy action but from sickness, malnutrition and exposure. It seemed that the heroes of the Alma, Balaclava and Inkerman were left uncared for and the British Army was being destroyed by the bunglings of its masters. But such scandals were by no means unprecedented: in the calamitous Walcheren expedition of 1809 practically an entire army had perished from sickness; in the Peninsula Wellington lost thousands of men from the same cause, and the dreadful mortality rate in the West Indies has already been mentioned (p. 55). Harrowing details of soldiers' sufferings in these and many other theatres are to be found in journals and diaries. But these were not read by the general public: the Crimean Campaign was unique in that for the first time an accredited war correspondent accompanied the army and, to the discomfiture of Authority, fearlessly reported everything he saw.

William Russell's despatches created a furore of indignation: these as much as the efforts of Sidney Herbert and Florence Nightingale sowed the seeds of army reform.

> Its sacrifices and heroism at the Alma, Balaclava, at Inkerman and in the first bitter winter of the war had not only hastened the long-needed overhaul of an outdated military system, but awakened the realisation in the minds of the British public, at least for a time, that the despised, often hated redcoat was a human being of surprising, often noble qualities, whose valiant steadfastness deserved better of his countrymen. Sadly the best of them had to perish before this was grasped.(5)

One immediate result of the Crimean War — actually while it was in progress — was the institution of awards for acts of gallantry and distinguished conduct in the field, which had hitherto gone unrecognised. The first of these was what ultimately became known as the Distinguished Conduct Medal, authorised by Royal Warrant of December 1854, and restricted only to non-commissioned ranks. Then in August 1855 came the Warrant instituting Britain's supreme award for gallantry, the Victoria Cross, open to all ranks. Both awards entitled non-commissioned holders to annuities or gratuities, the annuity for the VC being £10, irrespective of rank.[1] The gratuities for the DCM varied with rank, a sergeant receiving £15, a corporal £10 and a private £5. In 1862 the gratuities were abolished, the emphasis being solely on the honour of the award.

Of more direct concern to the soldier and his welfare were several Royal Commissions of Inquiry which the Crimean scandal inspired. The most important of these was the Royal Sanitary Commission appointed in 1857 to inquire into the conditions of army barracks, the administration of hospitals and the care of sick and wounded soldiers.[2] This was entirely due to the efforts of Florence Nightingale who had been campaigning ('bothering' as some politicians termed it) for such an inquiry ever since she left Scutari. She herself drew up the brief, which was approved by the Queen. The Chairman was of course her friend and co-reformer, Sidney Herbert.

After inspecting barracks and hospitals throughout the Kingdom and taking voluminous files of evidence, the Commission produced their Report a year later. The findings were almost as shocking as the circumstances which had initiated the inquiry. First, they revealed an alarming mortality rate in the home-based army, which was nearly double that of the civilian population. It was recorded that in the infantry 18 men per thousand died every year from disease, while the Foot Guards figure was even worse, at 20.5. In addition, during 1854 the infantry as a whole lost 20.8 per cent of its strength through men invalided from the service. The root causes of this casualty rate were ascribed to three main reasons: insanitary conditions in barracks and hospitals, inadequate diet, and 'enervating mental and bodily effects produced by ennui', in other words, lack of any facilities for recreation in off-duty hours.

Nearly all the barracks inspected were deficient in sanitary arrangements and ventilation, the result being that the soldier 'lives by day and sleeps by night in a fetid and unwholesome atmosphere, the habitual breathing of which, though producing, for the most part, no direct

1. In 1898 the annuity was increased to £50, and in 1959 to £100, at which it remains today. In view of subsequent inflation this does not seem over-generous.
2. The full title of the Commission was *Royal Commission appointed to inquire into the Regulations affecting the Sanitary Condition of the Army, the organisation of Military Hospitals and the Treatment of the Sick and Wounded*.

perceptible effects, probably lays the seeds of that pulmonary disease which is so fatal to the British Army.' Overcrowding was still one of the main shortcomings: 600 cubic feet per man was considered the minimum acceptable space, yet although the existing minimum was supposed to be 450, the average was found to be less than two-thirds of this figure, and in many cases only one half, with scarcely room to walk between men's cots. One imagines that the conditions of overcrowding and poor diet endured on board the British man o' war at this time were scarcely more salubrious.

The siting of barracks also came in for criticism: nearly all of them were located in cities and large industrial towns, situations not conducive to a healthy atmosphere, while, reported the Commission, 'residence in towns offers great facilities for sexual debauchery, and the diseases which are thereby generated.' Statistics showed that venereal disease was one of the most serious causes of unfitness for service, 206 men per 1000 in the cavalry and 250 per 1000 in the infantry being permanently affected. It was asserted that more than five per cent of the whole army were in hospital or off duty from this cause, and of these one half would never be fit for duty again.(6)

The question of diet received much attention, it being urged that greater variety, both of foodstuffs and of preparation, was necessary to improve health standards. 'The soldier is provided with neither change in kind nor in cookery, he is often condemned to live on boiled beef for twenty-one years. The constant repetition of the meal of sodden meat becomes so disgusting that the soldier, in fact, throws his food to the dogs; out of $\frac{3}{4}$ lb allowed, not more than half is consumed, and of course, the soldier falls off in strength.' Vegetables were essential, but generally these were monotonously limited to boiled potatoes and sodden cabbage.(7)

A sequel to the Royal Sanitary Commission was the setting up (at Sidney Herbert's urging) of four sub-commissions with specific tasks: (1) the supervision of sanitary improvements in barracks; (2) founding of a statistical branch of the Army Medical Department; (3) establishment of an Army Medical School; (4) reorganisation of the Army Medical Department, revision of Hospital Regulations and the preparation of a new Warrant for the promotion of Medical Officers.

It was inevitable that all the adverse publicity given to the Army administration by the Commission should evoke indignation from the Horse Guards hierarchy. In a debate in the House of Lords on March 26th, 1858 the Duke of Cambridge, Commander-in-Chief, assured their

Lordships that it was not the case that the soldier had been neglected in the past; it was merely that he was more appreciated at the present day. The Earl of Cardigan, Inspector-General of Cavalry (and still basking in his Balaclava glory), dismissed the criticisms of the soldiers' welfare as 'grossly exaggerated'.

Despite initial inertia and antipathy, the Commission, aided and abetted by Florence Nightingale, pressed on, and the fruits of their labours became apparent during the next decade. In 1858 the first Army Medical School was opened at Chatham to provide specialised training for medical officers. By 1860 this had moved to Netley, near Southampton, where it became the military hospital familiar to generations of officers and soldiers. Three years later a new general hospital was built at Woolwich, and this too, as the Royal Herbert Hospital (commemorating its initiator) continued to treat military patients down to the twentieth century. Between them, these two could accommodate 1600 patients, with facilities for the treatment of bacteriological and tropical diseases, together with remedial care and physiotherapy for disabled soldiers. But they remained the only military hospitals of this stature until the opening of a similar establishment at the garrison town of Aldershot in 1879 and named after the Commander-in-Chief, the Duke of Cambridge. There were reforms in the Army Medical Department (to which the Regimental Medical Officers belonged), all Army doctors being given an increase in pay, for which they had to pass professional examinations. But their assistants were still the inadequately trained men of the Army Hospital Corps, which remained an entirely separate body, its detachments being under command, not of the medical officer, but of the senior combatant officer. Thus there was frequent friction between the commander of a garrison and his medical staff. This anomaly persisted until 1873 when the Army Medical Department was granted full responsibility for the training and discipline of the Hospital Corps. But unification of medical officers and other ranks in a single corps only came about in 1884 with the resurrected title of Medical Staff Corps. Another fourteen years were to pass before this in turn became the Royal Army Medical Corps.

By 1861 statistics compiled by the Commission on Barracks and Hospitals showed that some reforms had been put into effect. Proper ventilation was provided in 2,996 barrack rooms, 67 schoolrooms, reading rooms and workshops and 500 hospital wards. Piped water had been supplied to one-third of the barracks and one-fifth of the hospitals, and proper latrines had replaced the old cesspits and privies in 45 barracks. However, this was only a very modest beginning, for thirty per cent of the barracks and ten per cent of the hospitals were still without adequate ventilation, and more than half the barracks lacked sanitary latrines. In the vast majority of barracks the only form of lighting was still the primitive candle and oil lamp. Although in 1861 gas lighting was common throughout the major cities and towns of Britain, the Commission reported that only nine barracks and five hospitals enjoyed this amenity.(8)

In 1863 the practice of allowing regimental canteens to be entirely run by civilian contractors was modified. Queen's regulations ordered the setting up of a Canteen Committee in each regiment, comprising an officer not below Captain as President and two others as members. The barmen and stewards were also to be drawn from the regiment, and the stock was to be purchased by the Committee at the most favourable rates obtainable. All retail profits went to regimental funds. This was a step in the right direction, for the canteens were now in the hands of the regiments themselves and not of profiteering civilians.

Overcrowding was still endemic, particularly in the regimental hospitals, where the basic problem was simply lack of space. It was only in the 1870s that individual regiments' hospitals began to be replaced by larger, purpose-built garrison hospitals, such as that at Aldershot.

As we have seen, the actual nursing of soldiers in the regimental hospitals was entirely in the not very skilled hands of soldier-orderlies of the Army Hospital Corps. Until Florence Nightingale took her volunteer band of female nurses to the Crimea it had been unthinkable that a lady (in any sense of the word) should be exposed to the rude ambience (and language) of the common soldiers' hospital ward. In civilian life nursing had come to be regarded as a suitable occupation for 'respectable young females'. Nevertheless, Miss Nightingale was successful in introducing female nurses in the large military hospitals at Woolwich and Netley, and in 1866 the Queen approved the employment of trained civilian nurses in all garrison hospitals. This was the modest origin of the justly renowned Queen Alexandra's Royal Army Nursing Corps, whose development will be outlined in the next chapter. The fact that the new nurses were civilians and therefore not subject to military discipline, caused misgivings among both medical officers and the authorities. 'If, as surely must happen on occasions, friction arises between any of these young women and the Surgeon nominally in charge of them, the latter will be placed in a very difficult situation, since he has no powers of compelling them to follow his orders. Furthermore, it is debatable whether a private soldier should be subjected to the dangers of familiarity with these same young women, whose background and attitudes are so different from those of the military profession.'(9) Nevertheless, the young women were there to stay, and no doubt the sick soldier welcomed their ministrations. There is no evidence that these proved dangerous to his morals.

Although the Crimean legacy of furore over the soldier's living conditions did not extend to the betterment of his mental state, some tentative steps were taken to facilitate Army education. In 1860 the Council of Military Education, first formed in 1857, assumed control over all army schools and libraries and became responsible for the appointment and promotion of army schoolmasters. In the same year the first Army Certificates of Education were introduced, although there was no compulsion for a man to obtain any of them, unless he were bent on promotion. There were three Certificates. The lowest or Third Class merely demanded the ability to read aloud and write from a short passage of dictation and to do simple arithmetic. A man achieving this standard was deemed educationally qualified for promotion up to the rank of corporal. If he aimed at sergeant, a more ambitious Second Class Certificate was necessary. Corporal John Acland of the 4th The King's Own Regiment, sat for his Second Class in 1874 and describes it thus:

> The examination consisted of two pieces of writing from dictation, including a lot of orders with officers' names, etc., reading prose and poetry, difficult examples of the elementary rules in arithmetic up to vulgar fractions, balancing a Dr. and Cr. account, keeping an imaginary savings bank account for a year, and making up the accounts of a mess for one day — i.e. all about groceries, vegetables, etc. etc.(10)

The First Class Certificate, necessary for promotion to Warrant Officer and for commissions from the ranks, was much more demanding. Besides dictation and reading from the classics of English literature, a candidate had to be familiar with more complex mathematics, including algebra, and to offer an additional optional subject, such as geography or English history, or a foreign language.

Despite the obvious potential advantages, few soldiers bothered to improve their education. In 1874 the Director-General of Military Education boasted that 32 per cent of the rank-and-file had achieved a 'superior degree of education', by which was meant only the Third Class Certificate. By 1877 some 51 per cent still possessed no Certificate at all.(11)

Predictably, many senior officers and not a few regimental commanders were averse to cramming soldiers' minds with learning that they had no aptitude for and would benefit little therefrom: their time would be better spent on drill and weapon training. However, in 1870 Parliament passed the Elementary Education Act which was the first step towards compulsory education throughout the country, and thus prompted, the military authorities decreed that all recruits should attend their schools for a minimum of five hours per week. A year later a Fourth Class Certificate of Education was introduced as the basic goal to be achieved by all soldiers. Even more elementary than the Third Class, its standard has been described as being about equal to that obtainable by a child of eight. Once a soldier had achieved that standard, there was no compulsion for him to struggle further.

Despite all official encouragement, the average soldier remained obstinately unenthusiastic about improving his mind, and tended to regard the schoolroom merely as a restful alternative to physical exertions on the parade ground. As late as 1882 Private Grenville Murray recalled that there were still some ten per cent of his comrades who were totally unable to read or write, and some of these had enjoyed up to 2,000 hours in the schoolroom during their service.(12) The same writer describes a typical garrison schoolroom of the period — about a hundred soldiers divided into classes:

Here were the forms for beginners who could neither read nor write — fearful dolts some of them, who bleated through their spelling most ruefully; further on, some recruits were tracing pothooks and hangers with clumsy fingers. Then came a class which contained several middle-aged corporals who had got their third-class certificates but were trying to qualify for sergeantships by getting second classes . . . some of these unfortunates, who were splendid soldiers, fairly sweated over the difficulties of compound interest and rule of three . . . and there was a dazed frown between their eyes as they tried to comprehend the patient demonstrations of their teacher expounding to them that 1/2 and 6/12 meant the same thing.

The patient teachers were qualified instructors attached from the Corps of Army Schoolmasters, which had been in existence since 1846. All male teachers underwent quite a comprehensive two-year course of training[3] at the Royal Military Asylum, Chelsea, and when qualified ranked as non-combatant sergeants. Generally, the schoolmasters were not popular, either with officers or rank-and-file. Although they wore three stripes, they were not proper soldiers, yet by virtue of their superior education they tended to regard themselves as a class apart from the common herd, and there was often friction between them and the officers and warrant officers, who looked upon the garrison or regimental schoolmaster as nothing more than a clerk in uniform.

The children of 'on-the-strength' married personnel were obliged to attend school until they reached the age of fourteen.

By the 1860s regimental, and in the larger stations, garrison libraries and reading rooms had become well established. They were encouraged for two reasons: first, it was accepted that soldiers should be provided with facilities for utilising their 'superior education' (i.e., their ability to read), or, as Queen's Regulations put it, 'to employ their leisure hours in a manner that shall combine amusement with the attainment of useful knowledge, and teach them the value of sober, regular and moral habits.' The latter lofty aim reveals the second reason for official approval. Drunkenness was still the besetting crime in the Army, and it was fondly believed that the amenities of the reading room would lure men away from the temptations of the Wet Canteen and the local pubs. Although these amenities were well patronised, it might have been foreseen that they attracted only those who were naturally quiet and sober and averse to the rowdyism of the canteen. The patrons of the latter remained unconverted: 'there are and always will be some characters who will not be satisfied with the quiet employment of the library and recreation room.'(13) In 1868 Commanding Officers were empowered to inflict fines for drunkenness, and statistics showed that far from decreasing, drunkenness actually increased over the next decade or so. In 1869, 16 per cent of the whole of the Army were so punished; this rose to a dramatic peak of 28 per cent in 1876, and then began to decline.(14) The

3. The curriculum covered mathematics, including algebra, geometry and trigonometry, mechanics, British history, English grammar and literature, geography, penmanship, chemistry, physics, fortification, drawing, mapping, religious knowledge, and even singing.

proliferation of libraries and reading rooms did not seem to have encouraged 'sober, regular and moral habits'.

The moralists of the Army, and successive governments, always professed to be deeply shocked by the soldier's addiction to alcohol. But, as we have already observed, drunkenness among the equivalent civilian classes was just as rife. The well-known Victorian diarist, the Rev. Francis Kilvert, is constantly inveighing against the 'disgraceful' brawls and rowdyism disturbing his evenings from the inn opposite his lodgings in the Welsh border village of Clyro.(15) Far worse went on in the 'gin palaces' and taverns of the manufacturing towns. Writing of the Victorian period, Trevelyan declared 'Drunkenness and excessive expenditure on drink constituted one of the major evils of city life, one of the chief causes of crime and the ruin in families, especially since spirits had largely taken the place of beer.'(16)

The fact is, drunkenness as such was not regarded as a crime in civil law: a man could be dragged insensible from a pub and dumped in the street until he came round sufficiently to stagger homewards, and provided he caused no damage or hurt, he was innocent of any offence. But if a soldier were guilty of such conduct he would be clapped in the guard room, to be brought before his commanding officer next morning and punished accordingly. And so another digit would be added to the statistics.

At least the soldier-drunk was not now automatically subjected to the torture of the 'cat'. As a result of constant campaigning by the abolition lobby, the maximum number of strokes awarded by *any* court-martial, was limited to fifty by the Mutiny Act of March, 1860, and while flogging was still a permissible punishment for drunkenness, it was seldom resorted to. Fines of a penny a day up to a maximum of 168 days, and/or confinement to barracks and extra drills, were the norm. But as a result of further heated debate in the House, in March 1868 a Bill was passed whereby flogging was restricted solely for offences committed on active service,(17) although it remained a permissible punishment in military prisons. The final victory for the humanitarians came with the revised Army Act of 1881 which expressly forbade any form of corporal punishment, whether on active service or no. Thus the barbaric 'Reign of the Lash' which had aroused so much passion and seen so much mutilation during nearly three hundred years, was at last ended.[4] In its place was

4. Officially, that is. There are recorded cases of illegal infliction of corporal punishment down to quite recent times. In 1946 a Major was court-martialled

introduced Field Punishment No. 1 which, as the term implies, was limited to active service. The offender was lashed to a gun- or carriage-wheel for up to four hours a day, in all weathers, while during his periods of release he was subjected to pack-drill and extra fatigues. With some modification, such as the substitution of handcuffs for the wheel, Field Punishment remained in force until the Second World War.

The humanitarians had always maintained that flogging was degrading for a man's self-esteem. Oddly enough, the practice of branding deserters and 'bad characters' never seemed to have aroused similar criticism, though it was surely just as degrading — if not more so, for its effect was permanent. The term itself was something of a misnomer, for the hot iron had been abolished in the previous century and the marking was now done by a form of tattooing. Convicted deserters were marked with the letter D 'Two Inches below and One Inch in rear of the Nipple of the Left Breast', and the needle punctures were to be impregnated 'with some Ink or Gunpowder, or other preparation, so as to be clearly seen, and not liable to be obliterated.'(19) Bad characters, i.e. those discharged with ignominy for habitual drunkenness, insubordination or both, were to be marked with the letters BC on the upper part of the right forearm. The Army authorities justified branding as an assurance against the fraudulent re-enlistment of undesirable characters; but as part of the general reforms to popularise the service it was finally abolished in 1871.

Capital punishment remained the ultimate penalty for offences so punishable under criminal law, such as murder, and for certain military offences committed on active service, which included desertion, mutiny, treacherous conduct, offering violence to a superior officer. As previously, the usual method of execution was by firing-party, the unhappy members being selected at random from the victim's own unit. Usually from eight to twelve men were so detailed, under command of an officer armed with a revolver. The rifles were previously loaded by the officer and it was the practice for one to be loaded with a blank round, the idea being that right up to the moment of taking aim each member of the firing party could continue to hope that he alone might be absolved from

---

for having ordered two of his men to be caned for sleeping on sentry duty during a Chindit operation in Burma. In his defence it was stated that General Wingate had recommended flogging for offences endangering comrades' lives, and the men themselves had signed a paper agreeing to be caned rather than take the alternative punishment of 28 days field punishment (which was impracticable in the circumstances). The Major was acquitted.(18)

playing a part in the killing of a comrade. Once having fired, however, that hope would vanish for all except one, for no trained soldier could fail to distinguish between the 'kick' of a live round and a blank. The blindfolded prisoner was strapped either to a stake or in a chair (he was often in a state of collapse), and should he show any sign of life after the volley it was the officer's duty to approach him and give the *coup de grâce* with his revolver.

When specifying the death penalty the Mutiny Act and the later Army Discipline and Regulation Act (1879) always added the proviso 'or such other Punishment as by a Court-Martial shall be awarded', which usually meant penal servitude, or until the 1850s, transportation. And the nineteenth century saw a marked decrease in the number of death penalties actually carried out. Between 1826 and 1835 there were 76 death sentences in the Army, out of which 33 were commuted to transportation. In the period 1865–1898, 44 men were so sentenced, and 33 were executed.(20)

In December 1868 a new Secretary of State for War was appointed by Gladstone after the sweeping Liberal victory in that autumn's election. His name was Edward Cardwell, and it is familiar to this day by the term 'Cardwell reforms', reforms which were to mould the Army into a near resemblance of the modern force.

Of immediate concern to the soldier was Cardwell's Army Enlistment Act of 1870, under which, instead of enlisting for twelve years with the Colours as hitherto, men now signed on for six years, after which they could be discharged but were automatically placed on the Reserve for a further six years. This was the first time that a properly-trained reserve force had been formed, to be available in the event of general mobilisation, and although there have been variations in the periods with the Colours and on Reserve, the system survives today. If he so desired, and was of good character and medically fit, a soldier could extend his Colour service to the full twelve years, and could then, with the same proviso, re-engage for twenty-one years. However, the short-service man was not eligible for a pension: instead he received what was termed 'deferred pay' on transfer to the Reserve. This amounted to 4d per day. Cardwell retained the right of a man to purchase his discharge, if he could afford to do so. A recruit of three months' service had to find £10; after that £18 was the price — more than the total annual pay of a private soldier.

Turning to organisational matters, Cardwell initiated what became the 'linked battalion' system in the infantry, which survived until the welter of amalgamations following the Second World War. In 1870 there were 141 regular battalions of infantry, all but 50 more or less independent regiments, known by their numbers (or ranking) in the Line; none had any permanent static depots or recruiting centres, and when a battalion was posted overseas it left one or two companies at home to act as temporary depot for the supply of drafts. Since 1857, however, certain of the regiments had been given two battalions, the object being that they would take turns for foreign service, the home-based battalion forming the depot and replacement pool for its overseas partner. Cardwell proposed to extend this well-proven system to the whole of the infantry, but instead of creating new battalions, he advocated the linking of pairs of existing single battalions, each pair becoming to all intents and purposes a new two-battalion regiment. In addition all the infantry regiments were to be 'localised', each one allotted a specific county or other territorial area in which it would set up a permanent depot and seek its recruits. This idea was not entirely new, for as already noted, an attempt at 'territorialising' was made in 1782 when some infantry regiments were given County sub-titles. But the proposal of fusing two different entities, each with its own jealously preserved traditions and customs, into a single new regiment naturally aroused opposition, if not passion. Officers, and indeed some long-serving soldiers, were outraged that their Regiment, which had served the Crown since King William III's days, should be merged with one that had not even formed part of the British Army until 1861 and could display only one solitary Battle Honour.[5]

There was also some criticism and discontent about the proposal that all infantry regiments should lose their numerical titles and adopt the names of the counties to which they were to be allotted. Thus, there seemed little logic in renaming the 24th (2nd Warwickshire) Regiment 'The South Wales Borderers' just because its depot happened to be Brecon, while neither the 40th (2nd Somersetshire) nor the 82nd (Prince of Wales's Volunteers) were overjoyed to merge as 'The South Lancashire Regiment'.

In the face of opposition, not only from the senior officers, but from certain members of Parliament who feared that the marriage of diverse

5. An example is the case of the 27th (Inniskilling) Regiment of Foot, raised in 1690, and merged with the 108th (Madras Infantry) Regiment which had been raised for the Hon. East India Company in 1854.

regiments and the loss of time-honoured numerals would 'gravely reduce the morale of the Army', Cardwell had to defer this plan, and it was left to his successor, Hugh Childers, to implement it.

Cardwell managed to carry through the actual localisation scheme, the regiments being allotted 66 'Brigade Areas' (later 'Regimental Districts') each made up of two Regular battalions with two Militia battalions attached. Apart from rationalising the somewhat chaotic infantry organisation, the scheme had the objects of 'attracting the agricultural population to the Colours and encouraging the Militia to volunteer into their own Line regiments'.(21)

Although not directly concerning the rank-and-file, mention must be made of Cardwell's revolutionary reform, the abolition of the purchase system whereby a young gentleman bought his commission and subsequent promotion steps up to Colonel. When Cardwell introduced his Army Regulation Bill in the House in February 1871 it let loose a storm of almost paranoiac protest and criticism, both in the House and in the Press. The diehards predictably vociferated that what had been good enough for Britain's greatest leaders, Marlborough and Wellington among them, should not be tampered with by a politician who had never led so much as a platoon. Nevertheless, by dint of persuading the Queen to issue a Royal Warrant, thus nullifying further dispute in both Houses, the Army Regulation Act came into force in July 1871, and from November of that year the age-old system of purchase ceased to exist. As *Punch* remarked in a 'Notice to Gallant but Stupid Young Gentlemen', they could purchase their commissions in the Army 'up to the 31st day of October. After that you will be driven to the cruel necessity of deserving them.' In the House of Commons the initiator put it less acidly: 'For the first time', said Cardwell, 'the Regular Army will become in reality as well as in name, the Queen's Army, instead of belonging to those who have paid for their commissions.' Not unnaturally there was apprehension among existing officers, particularly those in the more fashionable regiments, that the discarding of the key to commissions and promotion — personal means — would result in their having to admit to 'the club' types who would previously never have survived the obligatory interview with the Colonel or Commanding Officer. In fact there proved to be little cause for concern. Until well after the First World War the officers continued to be largely drawn from the Public School class who enjoyed some private means. Without the latter, few even in the least expensive infantry regiments, could hope to pay their way and keep up appearances. One of the few to rise from the ranks was Field-Marshal Sir William Robertson who tells us that when he was serving as a corporal in the 1870s the chief obstacle in the way of a commission from the ranks was lack of private means: 'without some £300 a year in addition to Army pay it was impossible to live as an officer in a cavalry regiment at home.' The infantry was less expensive of course, but the chances were that any young officer without private means would 'be miserable in himself and a nuisance to his brother officers'.(22)

Evidence that the make-up of the officer corps changed little after the abolition of purchase is to be found in some statistics as late as 1891 from the Royal Military College Sandhurst. Out of a total of 373 cadets, no fewer than 237 had entered from the leading Public Schools, Wellington topping the list with 37 entries, followed by Eton with 29 and Harrow and Marlborough with 16 each. Thirty-four cadets came from universities, the remainder from 'Private Schools and Tutors'.(23) At that time these embryonic officers ranked as 'Gentlemen Cadets', and it is unlikely that any of them did not warrant that classification in every sense of the term. They or their parents would have been able to purchase commissions had not the system been abolished — just as they could now afford the boarding and tuition fees and other expenses at Sandhurst.

Turning to 'ranker-officers', these were still rare, principally because of the financial obstacle quoted above. During the year 1877–78 no more than 2.2 per cent of cavalry and infantry officers emanated from the ranks, and most of these had been long-serving senior NCOs promoted Quartermasters or Riding Masters with Lieutenant's commissions.(24) To be considered for a commission a man had to possess a First Class Certificate of Education, to be of exemplary character and to have reached the rank of at least sergeant. It goes without saying that he also had to be recommended by his commanding officer. Unlike the civilian candidate, however, he did not have to undergo the cadet course at Sandhurst (or Woolwich). Since 1845 an initial outfit allowance of £150 was granted on first commission, but this scarcely covered the cost of full dress uniform, let alone the cavalry officer's two chargers he was required to buy. On being commissioned many senior NCOs found themselves considerably worse off financially than before. In the 1870s a sergeant-major's basic rate of pay amounted to roughly 4s a day, besides which he received free clothing and rations, and if married on the strength, free education for any children. On promotion to Ensign, or 2nd Lieutenant (after 1871) he got 7s 6d per day, but by the time he had paid his mess bills, band subscriptions and other expenses (including any necessary replacements to his kit and accoutrements) there was little left. Age was another factor that militated against the ranker-officer. As a senior NCO, he would probably be in his late twenties or early thirties on becoming a subaltern, and, unless on active service, he could hardly hope to achieve his captaincy for at least another ten years, when he would be regarded as somewhat aged for a junior officer.

In fact statistics show that before 1876 very few 'rankers' rose higher than Captain.(25) But there were of course notable exceptions, probably the best known being 'Wullie' Robertson, already quoted, who was unique in being the only man to rise from the lowest rank in the Army to the highest.[6] Scarcely less remarkable was his contemporary, Major-General Sir Hector MacDonald who at eighteen joined the 92nd (Gordon Highlanders) as a private in 1870. For gallantry during the Second Afghan War Colour-Sergeant MacDonald was awarded an immediate commission in the field, and after serving in successive ranks in numerous 'small wars', during which he earned the sobriquet 'Fighting Mac', he became a Major-General in 1899, his KCB following in 1900. His brilliant career was tragically terminated in 1903 when, accused of a homosexual act, he pre-empted a court-martial by shooting himself.

Both Robertson and MacDonald were true rankers, coming from humble backgrounds, proud of it, and never making any effort to modify their homespun manner of speech. Of very different origin was the lesser-known Major-General Sir Gerald Farrell Boyd, who could have been a prototype for one of Kipling's 'Gentlemen rankers'. Born in London in 1877, of a wealthy well-connected family, he failed the entrance examination for the Royal Military Academy, Woolwich, but determined on the Army, enlisted as a private in the Devonshire Regiment in 1895. For conspicuous bravery as a sergeant at Colenso he was awarded the Distinguished Conduct Medal, and in 1900 was commissioned in the East Yorkshire Regiment. In the same year he earned the DSO, and became the only officer to wear both ribbons. In the Boer War he fought as a Captain of Mounted Infantry. There followed several staff appointments until in 1918 he was promoted Major-General and given command of the 46th North Midland Division

6. Enlisted as Private (aged 17) in the 16th Lancers, in 1877. Became Troop Sergeant-Major 1885; 2nd Lieutenant 1888; Lieutenant-Colonel 1900; Major-General 1910; General 1916; Field-Marshal 1920.

which distinguished itself, and him, by smashing the Hindenburg Line at Bellenglise in September 1918 — one of the most decisive victories of the war. His active service now ended, he had added CB, CMG and Croix de Guerre to his DSO and DCM, and at forty was one of the youngest Major-Generals in the Army. After commanding the Dublin District during 'the Troubles', he was successively Commandant of the Quetta Staff College, Colonel of the Leinster Regiment, and Military Secretary to the Army Council. Had Boyd lived, it is probable that he would have rivalled 'Wullie' Robertson with a Field-Marshal's baton, but in 1930 he was striken with cerebro-spinal meningitis and died in Millbank Military Hospital, aged 53. Unlike Roberston and other ranker officers, Boyd was never hampered with money problems, while he came of course from the 'officer class' so that he was the equal of any member of the Mess. But even if he had not enjoyed these advantages, he would surely have reached the heights, for he was a brilliant, dedicated soldier, much loved by his men. Characteristically, he was supremely proud of the fact that he was the only General Officer to wear the DCM.

5

HIGH NOON

When the Indian Mutiny erupted in 1857 units of the British Army had been serving in the subcontinent for just over a century.[1] But British soldiers had fought and bled in 'the East Indies' from much earlier times, for until after the Mutiny the Honourable East India Company's three armies of Bengal, Madras and Bombay maintained a leavening of 'European' (*ergo* British) units of cavalry, artillery and infantry in their preponderantly Indian establishments. The Company's armies were entirely separate from the British Army; they were not part of the forces of the Crown but were virtually private armies of a chartered commercial company. They were administered, armed and paid by the Company, and obeyed their own Commander-in-Chief.

The British officers, both of European and Indian (or 'Native') regiments held their commissions from the Company, not from the Crown, while the purchase system was never countenanced, and promotion was exclusively by seniority. This being so, the H.E.I.C. forces attracted the less wealthy officers who could not afford a commission in a 'Royal' or British Army unit, with the consequence that the 'Royal' officers tended to look down on the 'Sepoy officers', even if the latter happened to command European troops. There was also animosity over the seniority ruling whereby a Royal officer was automatically senior to a Company officer of the same rank, no matter what their respective lengths of service. Thus a Company subaltern with ten years in that rank could find himself under command of a raw youth just out from England.

The rank-and-file were mostly enlisted at home (at a depot near Brentwood, Essex) and posted to units on arrival in India. Some, however, were sons of soldiers already serving in the Company's forces

1. The first British regiment to land in India was the 39th Foot, who did so at Madras in 1754. Their present-day descendants, The Devonshire and Dorset Regiment, still bear the Motto *Primus in Indis*.

and these were allowed to join their fathers' regiments. Every recruit was well aware that he was taking a bold step in volunteering for 'John Company'. If he survived the hazards of the climate, disease, and almost constant active service, he would not see England again perhaps for twenty-one years. The Company's forces existed primarily for Indian service though they could and did fight in Afghanistan, Burma, Java and Ceylon. Joining the Company was almost tantamount to joining a Foreign Legion.

Just as the officers owed their commissions and allegiance solely to the Company, not the Queen, so the soldiers' terms of enlistment specified service exclusively in that Company's forces, not in those of the British Army. It was this factor that sparked off the most serious revolt of British soldiers since 1743 when The Black Watch had broken into open mutiny, with very similar motivation.

After the final suppression of the Indian Mutiny it was clear that the Honourable East India Company had become an anachronistic body: it had long since ceased to have any trading or commercial functions. Thus in November 1858 a Royal Proclamation announced the abolition of the Company and the transfer of the government of India direct to the Crown. This of course meant that the British ranks of the defunct Company would also transfer their allegiance to the Queen, becoming in fact, part of the British Army. Neither Lord Canning, now the first Viceroy of India, nor the Government, were prepared for the troops' reaction, which has become known as 'the White Mutiny'. A fortnight after the Proclamation, all the men of the Madras Fusiliers staged a 'sit-in' in their bungalows, protesting that they had enlisted solely for the Company's service and strongly objecting to being peremptorily transferred to the Queen's 'like so many cattle'. Shortly afterwards all the soldiers of the 1st Bengal European Cavalry at Allahabad followed suit, uttering such seditious slogans as 'We are not Queen's men' and 'We won't soldier for the Queen.' Their example was followed by other units of the Bengal European Cavalry: at Meerut the 4th Regiment refused to parade, while all manner of subversive graffiti appeared on the barrack walls. 'Unity is strength.... Stick up for discharge or bounty... John Company is dead: We will not serve the Queen.' At Behrampur the 5th Regiment paraded 'under their own arrangements and gave three cheers for the Company and three groans for the Queen.'

All the mutinous soldiers were unanimous in their demands: if the Government intended to break the terms of their enlistment, then they should be granted a free discharge and passage home, while any man willing to transfer to the British service should be allowed to re-enlist voluntarily — with a bounty.

The disaffection reached a climax in June 1859 when the 5th Bengal European Cavalry barricaded themselves in their barracks and shouted abuse at their officers. This at last prompted a show of force by the authorities, who despatched a 'Queen's' battalion and two Horse Artillery guns to overawe the mutineers. No shots were fired, and after a week's blockade of the barracks the men were starved into submission.

Perhaps because Lord Canning, and the home authorities, felt some guilt about the unjust and arbitrary nature of the proposed transfer, surprising leniency prevailed. No arrests were made, but Courts of Inquiry were set up in all the affected stations, at which the soldiers were allowed to state their case. It seemed that the mutiny had petered out and in June 1859 the Government retracted and granted all the men's demands — free discharge, with the option of re-enlistment with bounty for the Queen's service. As a result, 10,116 men were shipped home and discharged free, but of these only 2,809 proved willing to re-enlist.

But this was not quite the end of 'the White Mutiny'. Although their case had been won, the militants among the 5th Bengal European Cavalry seemed determined to demonstrate contempt for their new masters, and again broke into open mutiny, with a private as self-elected 'commandant' and others appointed 'officers'. Law and order was not restored until September, when the men were again cowed into submission by a show of force, the ringleaders arrested and all but one sentenced by court martial to ignominious discharge and penal servitude. The exception was the 'Commandant', Private William Johnson, who received the death penalty, and was executed by firing party in November 1860.(1)

In fairness to the generality of British soldiers of the defunct Company, it must be stressed that the mutineers were almost exclusively men of the five regiments of Bengal European Cavalry. It is true that there was initial unrest among the 1st Madras Fusiliers (a regiment raised in 1839), but the men allowed themselves to be mollified by their officers — whether or not the latter shared their grievances. Four of the cavalry regiments had been hastily raised in England in 1858 as reinforcements for India; the men were a motley sweeping of layabouts, ex-sailors, vagrants, who were pushed out to India and active service with a minimal three weeks' 'training'. Discipline and morale were virtually non-existent, and these qualities were not conspicuous among the officers, who were mostly seconded from Bengal Native Infantry regiments who had mutinied and been disbanded. The fifth regiment (actually numbered 2nd) was raised in India, chiefly from volunteers from 'Queen's' infantry regiments already in the country, and there was little or no trouble with them, or with the rest of the Company's European troops.

The old adage about 'no bad regiments, only bad officers' had some relevance. Colonel Douglas Mackenzie, who forced the capitulation of the 5th Regiment, reported that the officers were 'demoralised, incompetent and slack, and afraid to do their duty', while Shadwell described all of them as 'alike unacquainted with their men and inexperienced in dealing with European troops'.(2)

It was 'the White Mutiny' that influenced the garrisoning of India by British troops after the demise of the East India Company. There were proposals for a 'local force' of soldiers enlisted solely for Indian service, as in the Company's days, but General Peel, Secretary of State for War, was convinced that it was 'an absurd anomaly for British soldiers to form part of an army that was essentially native', while it was known that the Queen herself was strongly in favour of all the European troops being transferred to the British Army, as at first envisaged. Thus in April 1861 General Order No. 332 directed the transfer of nine battalions of European infantry, and three of the Bengal European Cavalry (the other two, the 4th and 5th, had been disbanded).[2]

Although the anomaly of maintaining the three original Presidency Armies (now exclusively Indian) persisted until the amalgamation of all three as Britain's Indian Army in 1895, henceforth no British soldiers could serve in a force that was essentially 'native'.

Whether the divorce of British regiments from their Indian counterparts had any effect on the soldier's attitude to his Indian brother-in-arms, and to the native populace in general is debatable. For generations the British soldier in India had regarded himself as a 'sahib' (as, indeed, he was addressed by the Indian servants and menials); he represented the master race, and although he might be generous enough to acknowledge

2. The three cavalry regiments became the 19th and 20th Hussars and the 21st Lancers. The nine infantry regiments eventually emerged as battalions of The Royal Inniskilling Fusiliers, Royal Sussex Regiment, King's Own Yorkshire L.I., Durham L.I., Prince of Wales's Leinster Regiment, Royal Munster Fusiliers and Royal Dublin Fusiliers. The latter three were disbanded on the establishment of the Irish Free State in 1922.

the fighting qualities of native troops, he never accepted them as equals. The sole exceptions were the Gurkhas, with whom he felt much in common, and would happily fraternise given the chance.[3] Normally the only indigenous classes that he had daily contact with were the low-caste sweepers, *bhisties* (water-carriers), *syces* (in the cavalry) and the non-martial races who provided the barrack servants and the shop-keeping fraternity in the bazaars. It is a sad fact, but true, that his attitude to these generally remained one of arrogance, if not contempt. He might refer to Indian soldiers as sepoys, but the rest were simply 'wogs' or even 'black soors' (pigs). It is also a fact that the authorities, far from encouraging a better understanding between British and Indian, actually seemed to discourage it. In all Indian stations the white population both military and civil, was strictly segregated from the native, being quartered in the Cantonment which consisted of the British troops' barracks, officers' and civil officials' residences and offices, places of worship, together with its own shopping centre or Saddar Bazaar. The Indian troops' barracks were usually remote from the Cantonment, and the majority of the Indian populace dwelt and had their business in the City, which was the ancient Indian township, separated from the Cantonment. The City was strictly out of bounds to British soldiers: the only occasions on which they glimpsed its teeming bazaars and narrow *gallis* were when called to put down the periodic sectarian riots. Conversely, the British barracks and the Cantonment were forbidden areas for the majority of the Indian inhabitants: only those with legitimate business were allowed in.

British soldiers were not allowed to enter the Indian troops' lines, so that any fraternisation between the two races was impossible. This was in no way regretted by the British soldier, for it was simply not done to strike up any degree of friendship with a 'native'. A few officers with a genuine interest in Indian culture and religions might do so, but they would risk disapproval by their brother-officers who might accuse them of 'going native'.

Thus the soldier could spend eleven or more years in the subcontinent, from Madras to Peshawar, and return home almost completely ignorant of its peoples. He did however bring back a legacy of his service in the smattering of Hindustani words and phrases he had picked up to employ with the barrack menials and bazaar shopkeepers, and which, handed

3. The Gurkhas never regarded themselves as 'Indian', being subjects of the independent State of Nepal.

down through generations, became an established element of the British Army vocabulary. Since 1947 when the last British troops left India, much of this Anglo-Indian argot has been forgotten, but a vestige has survived, even if today's soldiers are unaware of its origin. The following are some of the terms which were once familiar throughout the Service (original Hindustani, or Urdu, versions in brackets where known).

Acha (*Achchha*)	All right, good, O.K.
Bat (*Bat*)	Speech, language, matter
Beesti (*Bahishti*)	Water-carrier
Bibbi (*Bibi*)	Woman, girl, 'bit of skirt'
Bolo (*Bolo*)	Speak, talk (e.g. to 'bolo the bat' — speak the language)
Buckshee (*Bakhshi*)	Free, gratis
Bundook (*Banduk*)	Gun, rifle
Bundobust (*Bandobast*)	Arrangement, matter, affair
Burgoo	Porridge
Burra (*Bara*)	Big, great, important
Butti (*Batti*)	Lamp
Char (*Chae*)	Tea
Charpoy (*Charpai*)	Bed, cot
Cheez (*Chiz*)	Thing, matter, affair
Chikko	Small boy, child
Chokra	Boy
Chit, chitti, (*Chitthi*)	Written note, message, letter
Chubbarow! (*Chhabarao!*)	Be quiet! shut up!
Dekko (*Dekho*)	Look, see
Dobi (*Dhobi*)	Laundryman
Duftur (*Daftar*)	Office
Durzi (*Darzi*)	Tailor
Gurrum (*Garm*)	Hot
Gooli (*Goli*)	Bullet, ball (hence, testicle)
Idderow! (*Idharao!*)	Come here!
Jow! (*Jao*)	Go away! Get out!
Jeldi, or Jildi (*Jaldi*)	Hurry up, get a move on
Karna, or Konna (*Khana*)	Food, meal, grub
Kooshi (*Khushi*)	Pleasant, enjoyable, easy
Krab (*Khrab*)	Bad, wrong, evil (e.g. 'Krab Bat' — bad language)

Kud (*Khad*)	Hill, mountain
Loose-wallah (from *Lut* — theft)	Thief
Myla (*Maila*)	Dirty
Nappi (*Nai*)	Barber
Pawni (*Pani*)	Water
Pi-dog (from *paraiyah*)	Mongrel, cur
Pukka (*Pakka*)	Good, well-made, proper (e.g. 'Pukka sahib' — a real gent)
Puggle(d) (*Pagal*)	Mad, crazy
Punkah (*Pankha*)	Fan
Rooti (*Roti*)	Bread
Rooti Gong	Long Service and Good Conduct Medal (comes up with the rations!)
Sarf (*Saf*)	Clean
Soor (*Sur*)	Pig
Soosti (*Susti*)	Lazy, idle
Teek (*Thik*)	Correct, right, very good, O.K.
Tiffin (*Tiffin*)	Lunch, Light midday meal
Topi (*Topi*)	Helmet, hat
Usti (*Ahista*)	Slow(ly), gently
Wallah (*Walla*)	Person, man, thing, agent, doer

Oddly enough, although British soldiers were stationed for lengthy periods in Aden, Egypt and later Palestine and Iraq, they never seemed to acquire a similar degree of Arabic phraseology. Such expressions as *Bint* (girl), *Shufti* (look, see) and *Imshi* (go) were among the very few that became established slang.

Just as the latter half of Queen Victoria's reign saw significant reforms in the Army at home, so it did in India. After the Mutiny, living conditions were greatly improved. The squalid *matti* (mud-built) and thatched bungalows were replaced by quite elegant brickbuilt and tiled barrack blocks (still called 'bungalows') with deep, colonnaded verandahs to keep out the searing hot-weather sun. Inside they were spacious and airy, at least 1,000 cubic feet per man being provided, while there was adequate ventilation from clerestory windows and wide doorways opening on to the verandah. In the hot-weather months ('summer' was too mild a term) the doorways were hung with reed mats known as *khas-khas tattis*. Periodically dowsed with water by the *chokra* (boy) squatting on the verandah, these provided wafts of cool air redolent with the aromatic scent of the wet reed. Most of the bungalows conformed to that term by being single-storeyed, but in some of the larger garrisons, such as Delhi and Lahore, two-storey blocks were erected towards the end of the century. The bungalows were well spaced out and often shaded by pipal and nim trees, while the Battalion or Regimental headquarters area and officers' mess usually contrived some attempt at graciousness with lawns and flowerbeds, tended by the hosts of *malis* (gardeners) and *bhistis* (beestis).

Each bungalow had its ablution room with running water (if only cold) and tin baths, while married families were no longer huddled into one corner of a barrack room, but enjoyed the privacy of separate accommodation in the purpose-built married quarters bungalows. Originally these were known as the 'patchery', but the soldier soon came to refer to them as the 'married patch'. They were out-of-bounds to non-married personnel.

Other amenities included the provision of separate dining halls, so that the men no longer had to eat in their barrack rooms, while meals were prepared in properly-equipped cookhouses by Indian cooks, known to the troops as 'bobberjees' (from Hindustani *bawarchi*), under the supervision of the Messing Officer and his deputy, a sergeant. In India, beef (or mutton) and bread were still the staple official ration of the British soldier, but since such extras as chicken, eggs, bacon and vegetables could be bought cheaply in the bazaars, these formed welcome additions to the diet. Every unit now employed a native contractor to run its own 'coffee shop' or Regimental institute, where those who preferred tea or coffee to the Wet Canteen beer could indulge their taste, and where commodities such as tobacco, cigarettes,[4] toilet necessities and cleaning materials could be purchased at rates controlled by the Regiment.

Compared with soldiering at home, service in 'the Shiny' had numerous attractions, so much so that many soldiers preferred to transfer to another unit relieving their own when the latter was posted back to the U.K. Down to the demise of the British Raj after the Second World War, it was generally agreed that, apart from the periodic 'trouble' on the

4. Cigarettes were introduced to Britain following the Crimean War, and by the 1880s had rivalled the traditional pipe in the Army, both at home and overseas. Oddly enough, the chewing of tobacco, so common in the Navy, never caught on in the Army.

Frontier, and the hazards of the climate, life in India was 'cushy'. When the young soldier joined his unit from home he found that, humble private or no, he had become a 'sahib' and as such was exempt from many of the menial chores that were his lot in England. All such fatigues as sweeping and cleaning barrack rooms and environs were carried out by the native sweepers; the native cooks performed all the cookhouse chores; all his clothes-washing was done by the *dhobi* (washerman), while by clubbing together with his mates he could employ a 'bearer' who, for a few annas a week, would relieve him of all the burden of kit-cleaning which had occupied so much of his leisure hours at home. Only his arms remained for his personal attention: no weapon could be touched by the servants. In a mounted unit the horse lines were mucked out by the *syces* and their 'dung boys' who also humped all the fodder and bedding. Every morning at Reveille the *nappi* (barber) came round the bungalow and any soldier could enjoy the luxury of a shave while lying half-awake on his cot, for one anna or so.

In the hot weather, from April to October, all parades were completed by noon (though that meant Reveille at the ungodly hour of 5 a.m.) and the rest of the day was free until the cool of the evening. Well into the present century it was considered hazardous for the British soldier to be exposed to the fierce sun and soaring temperatures of the Indian hot-weather season, and thus he usually indulged in a post-tiffin siesta with a book (if he could read) or a game of 'pontoon' (from *vingt-et-un*) with his mates. On all the hot-weather parades and duties between Reveille and sunset it was obligatory for all ranks to wear a 'spine-pad', a lint pad secured next to the skin by tapes round the shoulders and waist. The idea was that this would prevent the deadly rays of the sun penetrating to the spine and thus causing heat-stroke. In fact, its only effect was to promote excessive perspiration down the back, and the encouragement of that hot-weather scourge, prickly heat. Not until the early 1900s did the medical profession concede that spine-pads were not only useless but harmful, and they were abolished. However, it was still mandatory for a soldier to wear his sun-helmet at all times when outdoors during daylight hours, even if he were simply stepping across from his bungalow to the latrines. He was liable to be put on a charge if caught without it. This regulation remained in force down to the Second World War.

*

In 1876 Queen Victoria assumed the title Empress of India, and in celebration of this all British troops in India were granted an extra day's holiday per week. From then until the end of the Raj, Thursdays were sacrosanct as rest-days, the soldier was exempt from all military duty apart from the essential ones of quarter guards and, in mounted units, watering and feeding the horses. Officially, Sundays too had always been 'free' days, but since all British soldiers were assumed to be Christians (practising or not), they were required to attend Divine Service every Sunday morning. This was not only a religious, but a military ritual, for Church Parade was very much the ceremonial occasion of the week for all but the few who might claim exemption. Full Dress was the order — white cotton drill in the hot weather, serge in winter — and turnout had to be as immaculate as for any General's inspection. Most of the English infantry and cavalry soldiers were nominally Church of England, so that virtually the whole unit paraded at about 10 a.m., first for inspection by the eagle-eyed Adjutant and RSM, followed by the Commanding Officer. Woe betide any churchgoer whose tunic or trousers were not freshly-creased or whose rifle butt-plate was not highly polished. This ordeal over, the battalion marched off to the garrison church, led by the Band and Drums. Since the Mutiny, every man was armed with rifle and bayonet, and five rounds of live ammunition: the British Army never forgot that Sunday of 1857 at Meerut. 'I always thought this was a good idea,' wrote Private Frank Richards in *Old Soldier Sahib*, 'but I don't know what the One Above thought of it: I expect He did many a grin when He looked down over Northern India on his armed worshippers.' Depending on the loquacity of the Chaplain, the service itself lasted at least an hour, so that by the time the battalion had reformed, marched back to barracks and been dismissed, half of the 'free day' had been divinely expended. And next morning there would be the usual crop of 'dirty on parade' offenders outside the Orderly Room, for whom worship of the Almighty spelt extra drills and/or confinement to barracks. It is hardly surprising that this form of compulsory worship was never popular. As Richards averred, 'Ninety-five per cent of the Battalion heartily detested Church Parade and would do anything in reason to get out of it.'

Cunning recruits, who had perhaps been warned by old soldiers, would claim on joining that they were Primitive Methodists, Baptists, Plymouth Brethren, or subscribed to some other 'fancy religion' as the term had it. Since few garrisons (and none in India) enjoyed facilities for such nonconformist worship, there was no Church Parade for them. Roman Catholics, however, did not escape, for RC Chaplains had been accepted in the Army since 1836 and as most Irish regiments were preponderantly Catholic there was usually a Catholic service in every garrison or cantonment. Similarly, Scottish regiments had their Presbyterian services.

Even in the overtly pious atmosphere of late Victorian days there were some radical minds that questioned the wisdom of compulsory religion in the Army:

Having served for more than twenty-five years, in this country and in the East, I am of the opinion that it is no more than counter-productive to thrust religion upon a soldier as though it were a military duty, rather than a matter for his own conscience. We do not compel our civilian populace to attend Divine Service every Sunday: they are free to do so as and when they wish, or not at all. The past quarter of a century has seen great and worthy endeavours to improve the soldier's mind by education and everything that contributes to his mental and moral make-up. Surely as regards worship he should be given the same freedom of choice as he would enjoy in civilian life. In my opinion you do not make a soldier into a God-fearing Christian by subjecting him to the ordeals of Church Parade on his one day of rest, and forcing him to sing hymns and listen to a discourse which means little or nothing to him. The compulsory Church Parade is not an act of Worship; it is simply another irksome duty, and I can categorically affirm that it is resented by most soldiers, whether they have religious inclinations or no.(3)

These sentiments were echoed by Field-Marshal Sir William Robertson who wrote: 'Of all days of the week, Sunday was the most hated — a sad confession to make, but none the less true. After morning stables there was a general rush, often with little or no time for breakfast, to turn out in Full Dress for Divine Service — attendance at which was compulsory…. It was only natural that the men should resent being hustled about on the one day of the week observed by everybody else in the country as a day of rest.'(4)

Nevertheless, compulsory worship remained part of the soldier's duties, wherever he was stationed, until after the Second World War. Queen's Regulations for 1899 dictated that 'All officers in command are to take care that divine service is regularly performed for the troops under their orders.... soldiers of the various denominations are to be regularly marched to and from their own places of worship.... Every soldier, when not prevented by military duty, is to attend the worship of Almighty God according to the forms prescribed by his own religion.' However, a man was not to be compelled to attend the services of any religious body not of his own denomination, and as we have seen, this often provided an escape for those of 'fancy religions'. The military authorities seemed to harbour surprising doubts about the politics of the civilian clergy:

> Whenever seditious or inflammatory language is made use of during the service in any place of worship not under military control, the Senior Officer present will use his discretion in withdrawing the troops with as little interruption as possible and marching them back to their quarters.... Officers commanding will prevent their men from attending divine service if such language is likely to be used in sermons.

> (Queen's Regulations)

Perhaps this was a legacy from the days of King James II and the seven Bishops. But, slightly modified, the paragraph continued to appear until the 1940s. Despite the efforts of regimental padres[5] who periodically lectured the men on their obligations as Christians, the evils of vice and so forth, the British soldier has never been markedly devout, at least not since the era of Cromwell's psalm-singing troopers. Few were avowedly atheistic, while equally few were genuinely religious-minded, but the general attitude to 'God-bothering' was one of amused tolerance. There was something slightly unmanly about a soldier who was overtly pious, and anyone who had been accustomed to kneeling in prayer at his bedside every night at home, might do so in the barrack room only at the risk of ribaldry from his comrades. Acland who was sincerely devout, relates that he was resigned to saying his nightly prayers unseen in some quiet corner of the barracks.(5)

A feature of the Victorian Army was the establishment of institutions known as Soldiers' Homes. Concerned at the 'godlessness' of the average soldier, and his addiction to the demon drink, certain evangelistic philanthropists founded social centres in the larger garrisons which were

5. Chaplains had been granted officer-status in 1816 and were uniformed in 1860. At first only Church of England chaplains were accepted, but in 1827 Presbyterians were admitted, followed by Roman Catholics in 1836, Wesleyans in 1881 and Jews in 1892.

intended to lure men away from the canteens and liquor bars by ostensibly offering home comforts, recreational facilities and a complete contrast to the military atmosphere. The first such Home was opened at Chatham in 1861 by the Wesleyan preacher Charles Henry Kelly. It consisted of a small basement club-house with reading-room, chapel and tiny dormitory. The following year Mrs Louisa Daniell, an officer's widow, established her Soldiers' Home and Institute at Aldershot, which soon expanded into a large complex of 500-seating lecture hall, tea and coffee bars, smoking and games rooms, baths, laundry facilities, sleeping quarters, and even an annex for soldiers' wives and children. The Daniell Homes later became familiar features of other garrisons.

Another well-known institution was the Sandes Soldiers' Home, founded in Ireland in 1877 by Elise Sandes. In 1895 Miss Sandes established the first Soldiers' Home in India, at Rawalpindi, and by 1905 Sandes Homes were flourishing in many other Cantonments, including Quetta, Meerut, Lucknow and Ambala. Yet another evangelist was Miss Sarah Robinson who opened her Soldiers' Institute at Plymouth in 1874, which enjoyed the accolade of a visit by the Duke of Cambridge (Commander-in-Chief) and the Prince of Wales two years later. Miss Robinson soon extended her ministrations to sailors, with similar institutions at Portsea and Landport, and finally set up her Sailors' and Soldiers' Institute at Alexandria in Egypt — the first overseas 'Home'.

The real motive behind the efforts of these godly ladies was not so much the provision of comforts for the troops, but the saving of their souls. Those who frequented the Homes might find themselves obliged to attend Bible lessons, temperance lectures, and on occasions to bawl out hymns accompanied by a harmonium. They had to be satisfied with tea or coffee instead of beer, to divert themselves with 'innocent pastimes' such as chess or draughts or spelling games. Moreover, in the company of worthy females they had to keep a tight rein on their language. Not surprisingly, most of the regulars patronising the Homes were the rarities among the ranks who preferred 'Bibles and buns' to what was available in the Canteen, so that the proselytising was really a case of preaching to the converted. Although the homes certainly provided comfortable 'homely' surroundings and amenities generally lacking in barracks, there is little evidence that they exerted any effect on the spiritual or moral character of the general run of soldiers. Drunkenness remained the most common crime in the Army, while that other more serious problem of venereal disease continued to be rampant. And down to modern times barrack-room language has remained as unprintable as ever.

Of more practical benefit to the soldier, serving and discharged, and to his dependents, were the several welfare organisations which came into being during the late Victorian era. One of the earliest of these was the Army and Navy Pensioners Employment Society, founded in 1855 primarily to provide suitable civilian jobs for wounded and discharged servicemen invalided home from the Crimea. Another result of public concern for Crimean soldiers was the founding of a Home for Daughters, whether orphans or not, 'of those brave men who have served or are serving in the Present War'. Housed in premises in Hampstead, this charity was patronised by the Queen, the Prince Consort and the Duke of Cambridge and £11,000 was raised for its support. The 'Soldiers' Infant Home' as it was first called, took girls 'from the tenderest years until the age of thirteen', keeping them until sixteen. In 1887 the age limits for admission were from six years to eleven. On discharge from the Home, the girls were found suitable employment, mostly in domestic service. The Royal Soldiers Daughters' School, as it became known, still flourishes in Hampstead.

In 1859 Captain Edward Walter, retired from the 8th Hussars, set up his Corps of Commissionaires to help wounded ex-soldiers, who were found posts as hotel door-keepers, night watchmen and bank messengers. The corps was run on military lines, members being uniformed, and they were paid out of a central fund, based on a small joining fee. From modest origins the Corps expanded rapidly, and its smart and disciplined members became much sought after. By 1907, when it was inspected by King Edward VII at Buckingham Palace, there were more than 3,000 men on its books, including ex-sailors who were now accepted in addition to soldiers. For his services (at first single-handed) Captain Walter was knighted in 1885. Today the Corps of Commissionaires is not only inter-service, providing for soldiers, sailors and airmen, but also accepts ex-policemen, fire service and Merchant Navy men, with nation-wide branches or 'outquarters'.

One of the most familiar services welfare societies of today is The Soldiers', Sailors' and Airmens' Families Association, or SSAFA. It was founded in 1885 as the Soldiers' and Sailors' Families Association, by Major (later Colonel Sir) James Gildea of The Royal Warwickshire Regiment. This energetic philanthropist had already raised donations of some £12,000 for widows and orphans of soldiers killed in the Zulu War, and a similar sum after the Second Afghan War. Patronised by Princess (later Queen) Alexandra, his Soldiers' and Sailors' Family Association went from strength to strength, with voluntary helpers and branches throughout the Kingdom. During the South African War, 1899–1902, it administered funds totalling £1¼m. Then as now, its objects were to provide practical and financial help to Services families and to perform health and social work, together with 'counsel and friendship'.

The growing awareness of the plight of ex-servicemen when trying to find civilian employment led to the formation in 1884 of the National Association for Employment of Reserve and Discharged Soldiers, resulting from the initiative of Major-General (later General Sir) Edward Chapman, Royal Artillery. The scheme was supported by HRH The Duke of Connaught and in 1885 the Queen was pleased to become a patron and contributor to the funds. With headquarters in London, provincial branches were set up in Berkshire and Cambridgeshire, while three Regimental agencies were affiliated — those of the Royal Engineers, Royal Warwickshire Regiment and the Devonshire Regiment. Three years later this number had risen to eighty-five, including batteries of the Royal Artillery. The primary object of the Association was not so much the direct provision of employment, but the establishment of liaison between prospective employers and the Army. It was envisaged that the scheme would also benefit 'employers of labour by enabling them, at any time, to lay their hands upon men of good character and varied qualifications'. Funding was principally by voluntary donations and subscriptions, the War Office making an annual grant. In 1920 the Association absorbed the Army and Navy Pensioners Employment Society, and two years later the Admiralty and Air Ministry agreed to cooperate in the registering of sailors and airmen on the Association's books. Thus in 1922 the present title was adopted: National Association for Employment of Regular Sailors, Soldiers and Airmen. This is usually abbreviated to Regular Forces Employment Association.

The last year of the century saw the emergence of yet another charitable body in the Soldiers and Sailors Help Society, founded in 1899 under the patronage of King Edward VII and HRH Princess Christian. Later assuming its present title, The Forces Help Society and Lord Roberts Workshops, this voluntarily-supported body assisted ex-servicemen to find jobs, and provided convalescent homes for the sick and wounded. The Lord Roberts Workshops were set up to offer special training for disabled soldiers and sailors and to secure suitable employment for them. Today the activities have been extended to helping serving personnel with personal and domestic problems, such as obtaining compassionate leave and grants for meeting civilian commitments. Since the Second World War members and ex-members of the women's services have been included.

One of the best-known and most popular events in London is the Royal Tournament, held annually at Earls Court. Apart from being a splendid public relations exercise, the *raison d'être* of the Tournament is to raise funds for Service charities, who benefit by shares in all the profits — as they have done for more than a century. In 1880 a group of Army officers and civilian promoters resolved to mount a 'Military Tournament and Assault-at-Arms' in the Islington Agricultural Hall. At first there was no thought of contributing to any charity, but when the Duke of Cambridge, Commander-in-Chief, was approached for patronage and permission for Regular soldiers to take part, he agreed only on the condition that the promoters would guarantee him the sum of £500 for his own charity, the Royal Cambridge Asylum for Soldiers' Widows.[6]

The first Tournament was held in June 1880, and proved a financial disaster. The Duke did not get his £500, for the promoters suffered a heavy loss. Nevertheless, the event was staged again the following year, with further loss, but in 1882 the public were attracted by the first Musical Ride to be seen — more to their taste than the rather dull skill-at-arms competition — and £3,000 was handed over to the Cambridge charity. This prompted the Duke, in a committee meeting, to 'hope that every Regiment in the Army will soon have a widow in the Asylum'.

Thenceforward the event never failed to contribute handsomely to the deserving widows: by 1891 it had handed over a total of £26,000. In 1905 the Admiralty became involved, and the title was changed to 'The Royal Naval and Military Tournament'. Profits were now shared between the two Services, and by 1914 had amounted to £132,000. The Royal Air Force participated in 1919, which meant the adoption of the cumbersome title 'Royal Naval, Military and Air Force Tournament'. This was too much of a mouthful, and in 1920 it became simply 'The Royal Tournament', which it remains today. In 1950 the venue was moved from Olympia (where it had been since 1906) to the present location at Earls Court.

6. This had been founded in 1851 in memory of the 1st Duke of Cambridge who had died in 1850. It still flourishes as The Royal Cambridge Home for Soldiers' Widows, and still benefits from the Royal Tournament.

From 1919 the Tournament has been a truly inter-Services endeavour, both in presentation and in profit sharing. Each year's total is handed to the Secretary of State for Defence who divides it between the Services, to be apportioned out among their own individual charities and welfare organisations.(6)

In a different category to these charitable organisations, but one contributing greatly to the 'comforts' of Servicemen is that whose common abbreviation has long been familiar to all who have served in the Forces, and to the general public — the NAAFI. This organisation had humble origins. As previously remarked, regimental canteens had been firmly established in the 1860s, but the management of these, and particularly the purchase of stock, was not always competent, and often subject to abuses.

Being dissatisfied with the existing arrangements, Major Harry Crauford, Canteen-President of the Guards Depot at Caterham, joined with his friends Captain Lionel Fortescue,[7] 17th Lancers, and Surgeon-Captain Herbert Ramsay, Scots Guards, and in 1894 the three founded a co-operative society with capital of £400 collected from friends. Registered under the Industrial and Provident Societies Act, this was called the Canteen and Mess Co-operative Society. Although it flourished during the Boer War, it foundered shortly afterwards — but not without having pointed the way to a more efficient canteen service. In 1916 an Army Canteen Committee resurrected the original aims of Captain Fortescue that all canteens should be conducted by a central organisation under the ownership and control of the Army itself. By 1917 more than 2,000 canteens were so organised, serving the troops at home and in France. In the same year the Admiralty joined in, and the organisation became the Navy and Army Canteen Board. Finally in 1921 the Air Ministry asked to be included, and so in January of that year the Navy, Army and Air Force Institute came into being. Since then the NAAFI has expanded into big business, running thousands of shops and canteens in the U.K., in Germany and on board ship. The NAAFI can supply, at competitive prices, anything from bootlaces and razor-blades to motor cars and boats, besides groceries and household goods, and a percentage of profits is paid into the welfare funds of individual units. Although the Board of Management and staffs of canteens and shops are

7. Fortescue was a brother of the Hon. J. W. (later Sir John) Fortescue, historian of the British Army. He was killed in the Boer War.

civilian, control of its affairs is in the hands of a council of senior officers. The NAAFI is truly the 'Forces Co-op', run by the Services for the Services, a policy originally conceived by the three founders of the Canteen and Mess Co-operative Society.

The proliferation of welfare organisations during the late nineteenth century marked the growing awareness of the common soldier as a member of society and not an outcast whose subsequent fate after years of service was of no concern. Oddly enough, the individual who did most to popularise the rank-and-file among the general public was not himself a soldier and had no personal experience of military life. Yet his name has always been linked with the British Army as the troubadour of its soldiers. With his *Soldiers Three* (1888) and *Barrack-Room Ballads* (1892) Rudyard Kipling achieved remarkable success as the first writer to deal extensively with the serving private soldier and to depict him as a lovable human being, with his foibles perhaps, but basically decent and honest. The public had never before been offered such literature, and they took to 'Mulvaney', 'Ortheris' and 'Learoyd' and the Ballads with astonishing avidity, accepting the stories of barrack-room life and soldiering as faithful portraits. Kipling was writing for the civilian market, and whether his portraits were faithful is debatable, although he tells us in his autobiography, *Something of Myself* (1937), that he based his characters on real-life soldiers with whom he had chatted in Lahore. Many who have known the British soldier better than Kipling have criticised his characters as being stagey and unreal, their dialogue artificial and their behaviour contrived. 'Old Soldier Sahib' Frank Richards said 'his knowledge of barrack-room life seemed to us a bit hazy' and although he confesses to having read the stories, he much preferred *Kim*, which was 'in my opinion the best thing he wrote' — a verdict confirmed by much of the public. In his percipient biography of Kipling Lord Birkenhead wrote: 'His characterization was weak because it was difficult for him to escape from his own subjectivity, so that his characters were apt to melt rapidly in the mind.' Birkenhead goes on to criticise Kipling's chief failing in his barrack-room stories — his abuse of dialect which alienated many military readers:

It is a curious fact that when Kipling wrote dialect his ear was far from perfect. He often uses it when it would be more effective not to do so. It is carried to ridiculous lengths in the Mulvaney stories, and the effect of the stylized cockney and preposterous Irishisms is, in the end, one of fundamental falseness which falls on the ear like an untuned piano ...

Of course the Victorian public could never have stomached genuine barrack-room language with its repetitive four-letter words, even if Kipling had dared to reproduce it, and civilian readers who knew no better accepted the watered-down dialogue in good faith, as they did all the rest. Field-Marshal Earl Roberts, who knew Kipling well in India and must at least have glanced at his soldier tales and ballads, makes not a single reference to him in his autobiography *Forty-One Years in India.* Similarly, Major-General Lionel Dunsterville, the 'Stalky' of *Stalky & Co.*, ignores the writings in his own autobiography *Stalky's Reminiscences.*

The fact is, *Soldiers Three* and much of the *Ballads* were too contrived to ring true to the average soldier, and the few who perused them regarded the characters as rather comic caricatures. When the present writer was serving in India in the 1930s, Kipling was totally unread in the barrack room, and hardly at all in the Mess.

Nevertheless, the Army owes him gratitude for the massive public-relations effect that the stories and verses achieved. Some achieved more. During the Boer War his *Absent-Minded Beggar* verses were set to music by Sir Arthur Sullivan, and selling in millions of copies raised more than £250,000 for the soldiers in South Africa.

We tend to speak of 'the Victorian Army' as though it were something that came into being when the young Queen ascended the throne in 1837 and was transformed into something else when she died in 1901. But as we have seen, the Army had constantly changed during that long reign. A soldier who had fought in the Sikh Wars that added the Punjab to the Raj would have been dumbfounded at the transformation could he have been projected into the Army that confronted the Boers in South Africa. Happily, most of the changes were to his benefit. When the twentieth century dawned the soldier was better educated, better fed, adequately housed, the barbarous 'Cat' was just a shocking memory, and although the RSM might still terrify the recruit, discipline was no longer based on Draconian punishment. His medical care was properly organised by the new Royal Army Medical Corps (1898); the Army Service Corps (1889) supplied and fed him, the various welfare organisations looked after his interests while serving and when discharged. In his off-duty hours he could (but was not compelled to) take part in such organised sports as football, cricket, hockey, boxing and swimming, all of which were non-existent when Victoria came to the throne.[8]

> The soldier was no longer treated, as he used to be, as a being without intelligence and without the remotest chance of ever developing any, down whose throat it was the business of the non-commissioned officers to force as much parrot-like drill as possible, but never to attempt to draw anything out.... This stupid attitude was going out of fashion. A man was taught to use his wits and act with initiative and responsibility, individual instruction was superseding squad drill, and a clear distinction was made between drill pure and simple and field training.(7)

After discarding the venerable Brown Bess (or Tower) muzzle-loading musket in the 1840s, the soldier had to master a bewildering succession of firearms of the percussion type: Brunswick, Minie, Enfield, Lancaster to name a few — all muzzle-loading, and all found wanting in some respect. Then in 1868 came the first breech-loading rifle, the Snider, with its centre-fire round; this was followed, in 1871, by the Martini-Henry, of .45 in. calibre, which was a man-stopper (with a vicious kick) and did yeoman service in the Afghan, Zulu and Egyptian 'small wars'. All these were single-round weapons, but in 1888 the Army adopted a magazine-fed, bolt-action .303 in. weapon, the Lee-Metford, which was finally modified in 1895 as the Lee-Enfield. This rifle, with a few further modifications, outlasted the soldiers themselves, and as the Short Magazine Lee-Enfield, or SMLE, remained in service throughout the two World Wars and down to 1968 when it gave way to the modern automatic weapon. The infantryman's firepower was vastly increased in 1891 by the Maxim gun,[9] the first truly automatic machine gun which ousted the hand-cranked Gatling and Nordenfeldt, and could achieve an unprecedented rate of fire of 600 rounds per minute. Lord Wolseley, as

8. The Army Football Association was founded in 1888. The first Army Boxing Championships were held in 1893. The Army's first swimming pool was opened at Aldershot in 1900.
9. The American-born genius, Sir Hiram Maxim, developed his machine gun in a London basement in 1883. He took out British nationality in 1900 and was knighted the following year. His Maxim Gun Company was taken over by the Vickers armaments group in 1897.

Commander-in-Chief, prophesied that the new weapon 'could not fail to mark a distinctly new epoch, not only in fire-arms, but in warfare.'(8) He was right. In the First World War the Maxim and later its offspring, the Vickers Medium Machine Gun, dominated the battlefield and was influential in the invention of the tank. Like the SMLE rifle, the Vickers machine gun remained familiar to British (and Indian and Colonial) soldiers until superseded in 1968 by the General Purpose Machine Gun. Burgeoning technology had also improved the artilleryman's equipments and all British field gunners now had breech-loading rifled guns which, with the invention of smokeless powder, no longer advertised their position with dense white clouds.

When Queen Victoria succeeded, all British soldiers had to march on their own feet the length and breadth of Britain and India when changing stations. Since the development of the railway system in the 1840s the soldier, and the cavalryman's horse, were moved by special train on long-distance journeys, to their own benefit and that of the railway companies. Perhaps regarded as of little significance by the troops, the first Army motor car made its appearance in Aldershot in 1902, for the use of the G.O.C., General Sir John French, in order that 'it may be tried as to its suitability for aiding, by its capabilities of rapid locomotion, the command of troops in the field.'(9) The soldiers beholding the spectacle of their General mounted in his horseless carriage could have had no inkling that this contraption heralded a revolution in their way of life.

The Victorian age saw significant social reforms and technical innovations, but one feature remained virtually unchanged, and that was the soldier's rates of pay. In 1837 the private received a basic 1s per day. By 1890 this had risen to 1s 2d, before stoppages. A return of the total amount of stoppages from soldiers' pay at Aldershot in the same year showed that out of his annual pay of £18 5d the average man was stopped £7 3s for such items as tailors' and shoemakers' bills, washing, hair cutting, repair of arms and accoutrements and that venerable imposition 'barrack damages'.(10) The Royal Pay Warrant of 1893 generously laid down that after all stoppages had been taken into account 'a residue of at least 1d a day shall be left to the soldier.' Of course higher ranks were commensurately better off: a sergeant-major of cavalry received 5s 4d per day, of infantry, 5s, while the cavalry corporal got 2s, his infantry equivalent 1s 8d.

The Warrant specified certain bonuses allowable to soldiers. One penny a day was granted for each Good Conduct Badge earned: two years' exemplary conduct qualified for the first badge, six years for the second, and twelve for the third. The maximum of six badges could only be earned after 21 years' continuous service. The 1893 regulations for normal pensions were complex, the rates for NCOs and men being divided into five classes, depending on the arm to which the soldier belonged, any special skills or 'trades', and of course total length of service. For example, a Quartermaster Sergeant qualified as Class I and after twelve years' service in that rank could expect a pension of 2s 9d per day. At the bottom of the scale, in Class V, was the private soldier, who was entitled to 1s 1d per day *after 21 years' continuous service*. If he had put in only 18 years, his pension was reduced to 10d.

NCOs and men discharged as unfit for further service on account of wounds or injuries suffered on military duty were entitled to Disability Pensions, the rates again being divided in five Classes. Thus those qualified as Class I (senior NCOs and specialists) received from 1s to 3s per day if partially disabled and from 2s 6d to 3s 6d if totally disabled and incapable of earning a living. The equivalent Class V rates were 6d to 1s 6d for partial disablement, 1s 6d to 2s 6d for total.

The widow of any soldier below Warrant rank killed on service or died of injuries received no pension, but a single gratuity amounting to the yearly rate of pay of her husband (plus any bonuses) when he died. On the other hand, the widows of both commissioned and Warrant Officers got welcome pensions, that of the latter amounting to £20 a year. For any children 'born in lawful wedlock', they received an extra £5 a year 'compassionate allowance'. There was no provision for the offspring of lower ranks' widows.(11)

To us, a hundred years later, all the above figures seem incredibly mean. But as repeatedly observed, monetary values are only relative, and the Army still continued to attract voluntary recruits for the simple reason that, being mostly of the unskilled classes, they had no better prospects in civilian life — if as good. It was calculated that in 1899 nearly half the families in York were living on a combined income of 30s or less per week. The average weekly wage of an unskilled labourer in London was 29s 2d in the same year.(12) Unlike the soldier, the civilian worker had no guarantee of employment, or job security, even though Trade Unions were well established, while he had to meet the entire living costs of himself and his family, including any medical expenses. The long-serving private soldier's pension of 1s 1d a day might seem niggardly, but few civilian workers could expect anything at all. If the soldier fell ill, he did not have to pay the medical officer for treatment.

With the flourishing of such bodies as the National Association for Employment of Regular Soldiers, the Forces Help Society and Lord Roberts Workshops, not to mention the Corps of Commissionaires, the discharged soldier of good character had a fair prospect of securing worthwhile civilian employment to eke out his pension. Speaking at a lecture on Army reforms at the Royal United Services Institution in 1898, Lieut-Colonel G. F. R. Henderson (Staff College) stated that his investigations had shown that most of the larger employers such as the Post Office, the Railway companies and public-service undertakings preferred ex-soldiers as being 'smart, disciplined, honest and hard-working'. At the same meeting Captain G. Le M. Gretton (Royal Warwickshire Regt) said that in consequence of Press reports about destitute old soldiers crowding the casual wards and 'night refuges' of London, he had personally visited these institutions over several weeks, and discovered that the ex-soldiers were of three categories: men dis-charged with bad characters, those addicted to drink who went on the spree after each pension payment and then lived on charity until the next payment, and finally those who had deserted.(13)

As always, Army life was what a man was prepared to make of it. Troop Sergeant-Major Edwin Mole of the 14th (King's) Hussars was discharged in 1888 after twenty-five years' service at home and overseas, and reflected that 'had I my life in front of me instead of behind, I would start again, just as I did when I was a lad of eighteen, and desire nothing better than to live those happy twenty-five years over again in the ranks of the Old 14th as a King's Hussar.'(14)

6

INTO THE
TWENTIETH CENTURY

The Boer War of 1899–1902 marked a turning point in the history of the British Army. Not only was it 'the last of the gentlemen's wars' (and the first large-scale guerrilla campaign), but it exerted a profound influence on the organisation and training of the Army and on the soldier himself. The disturbing revelation that it had taken three years and the loss of 20,700 British lives for 450,000 British soldiers to subdue some 80,000 untrained, irregular Boer 'commandos' indicated that there was something amiss in our military thinking. And a by-product of the campaign was the unprecedented awareness of, and interest in, the soldier aroused among the general public. Previously the 'small wars' of the expanding Empire had made little real impact at home, but now the mobilisation of such vast numbers of Regular, Militia, Yeomanry and Volunteers meant that there were few towns and villages throughout the Kingdom that did not contribute a 'gentleman in khaki ordered South'. Stirred by Kipling's patriotic verses and the jingoism of the popular Press, the British public took Tommy Atkins[1] to their hearts as seldom before.

As a result of the defects in higher command, administration and training shown up by the War, by 1908 Britain had virtually a 'New Model Army', many features of which have survived to the present day. Reforms initiated by St John Brodrick, Secretary of State for War in 1904 and completed by his successor Lord Haldane, commenced with sweeping changes in the military hierarchy. First, the centuries-old office of Commander-in-Chief was abolished (Lord Roberts was the last

1. Said to have been originated by the Duke of Wellington as a specimen name for official forms, 'Thomas Atkins', (or 'Tommy') did not catch on as the popular nickname for the British soldier until the Boer War. Kipling's 'Tommy this an' Tommy that' verses of 1892 did much to popularise it. The sobriquet was never much in vogue among the soldiers themselves, and it died out after the First World War.

incumbent), and in its place was established the Army Council, consisting of four military members (General officers) and two civilians, all
responsible to the Secretary for War. Thus the Army was now controlled
by a committee, which might seem to smack of bureaucracy, but it meant
that the soldiery were no longer subject to the personal whims and foibles
of a single autocrat, as had often been the case in the past. A permanent
General Staff was organised for the first time, and the higher Army
formations — Divisions and Brigades — were also established on a
permanent footing. Previously, these had only been formed on the
outbreak of hostilities, but henceforth all units were allocated to the
peacetime formations with which they would serve in the event of war.

To provide a back-up for the Regular Army, the auxiliary forces were
reorganised. The Militia was converted into a Special Reserve with the
task of providing drafts for the Regulars in wartime. In 1908 the
Yeomanry (part-time cavalry) and the Volunteers (infantry) were
reorganised as the Territorial Force, later to become the Territorial
Army. This provided a second-line force of 14 cavalry brigades and 14
infantry divisions, which in peacetime were liable for service only within
the United Kingdom, but in an emergency they could volunteer for
service abroad. Finally, to form a nucleus of partly-trained officers, the
old 'Volunteer Corps' which had been raised by some public schools and
universities were absorbed by the new Officers Training Corps, which
became familiar as the O.T.C. down to the Second World War.

But these organisational reforms were of no great concern to the
common soldier of the Regular Army. He knew little of the structure of
the Army's Higher Command, and cared less about it. It mattered little to
him that his Regiment now formed part of, say, the 60th Infantry
Brigade, while he might well be ignorant of the fact that this Brigade was a
component of the 6th Infantry Division.

Far more relevant were the revised pay structures and terms of service.
In 1904 Brodrick introduced his contentious ultra-short-service scheme,
whereby a soldier could enlist for only three years with the Colours, after
which he could have the option of discharge to the Reserve for a nine
years' period, or of extending his Colour service. If he chose the latter he
received a bonus of an extra sixpence per day, provided he was of good
character, had gained his Third Class Certificate of Education and was a
Second Class shot.

The short-service scheme attracted recruits, but as critics had forecast,
the vast majority opted for the three-year spell with the Colours, so that

the Army's cadre of trained soldiers dwindled drastically. Statistics given in Parliament in 1905 showed that of 23,500 recruits enlisted for short service only 5,370 had extended; in many infantry battalions the average number of extended-service soldiers was as low as three per cent.(1) As early as 1881 Lord Chelmsford had objected that a soldier 'does not develop into a man you can really trust under three years. . . . I should like to see a man live and die in the Army, so to speak, so long as he conducted himself satisfactorily.' By depriving the Army of men just when they had reached their prime of physical and military fitness, short service deprived it of potential NCOs. Sixty-eight years later similar criticisms were levelled at the National Service scheme. The situation became so serious that in 1905 the Army Council suspended the short-service scheme: in future the soldier would sign on for nine years with the Colours and three on reserve. Lord Haldane had now become Secretary of State, and in the following year he reintroduced the old terms of seven years' Colour service followed by five on the reserve.

The social classes from which recruits were obtained had hardly changed over the centuries. A return by the Army Medical Department in 1903 gave the following statistics on the previous occupations of 84,402 recruits examined prior to enlistment.(2)

Labourers, servants, husbandmen etc.	52,022
Manufacturing artisans	
(cloth-workers, weavers, lace-makers, etc.)	11,971
Mechanics (smiths, carpenters, masons, etc.)	11,201
Shopmen and clerks	5,950
Professional occupations (students, etc.)	827
Boys under 17 years of age	2,431
Total	84,402

It will be seen that, as always, by far the most common sources of recruits were the unskilled classes and agricultural workers. And it is a commentary on the general standard of physique among the humbler strata of the population that of the 84,402 potential recruits examined, no fewer than 23,745 were rejected as being unfit for military service.

Physical standards for recruits had fluctuated widely during the late Victorian period. In 1861 age limits were 17 to 25, while a minimum height of 5 ft 8 in. was demanded. In 1883 the lower age limit was raised to 18, the minimum height reduced to 5 ft 3 in. — the lowest ever recorded. By 1900 this had risen again to 5 ft 4 in. and a minimum weight of 115 lb was specified. Guards regiments of course had their own standards and could accept no recruits under 5 ft 10 in. Before enlistment all potential recruits underwent a searching medical examination by Army doctors, particular attention being paid to heart, lungs and eyesight. According to statistics published in the *Report of the Army Medical Department* in 1901, the most common reasons for rejection were: inadequate chest measurement (6.4 per cent); defective vision (4.2 per cent); under weight (3.4 per cent).

The temporary adoption of khaki service dress during the Boer War became permanent with the issue of khaki serge tunic, trousers and puttees in 1902. For service in hot climates, a lighter, cotton drill material was approved. Six years later the polished leather ammunition pouches and accoutrements gave way to scientifically-designed webbing equipment, including pack and haversack, although the mounted soldier was to retain his leather bandolier down to the day when his horse was superseded by a fighting vehicle. The traditional redcoat and the panoply of Full Dress (or 'Review Order', as it was termed) was now reserved only for ceremonial duties, and henceforth the soldier trained and worked in exactly the same kit he would wear when he went on active service. However, if the days of pipe clay were forgotten, the new uniform did not mean any relief from kit-cleaning chores. In peacetime the webbing equipment had to be laboriously blancoed with the correct shade of green, buttons and badges and all other brasswork to be highly polished with 'Bluebell' or 'Brasso' bought in the Dry Canteen, which also provided the cakes of officially approved blanco. The cavalryman also had to polish his leather bandolier (and its brass pouch studs) and to blanco his breeches strappings and puttee tapes. Puttees (originating in India and derived from *patti*, a bandage) gave excellent protection to the nether limbs, but the soldier regarded them with mixed feelings, for they were irksome to apply correctly. The infantryman started his at the ankle and winding them up his calf, finished below the knee, when the upper part of the trouser legs was folded down over them, to give a sort of plus-four effect. In the cavalry the method was reversed, starting below the knee and finishing at the ankle with precisely two inches of tape showing. Each fold of the puttee had to be exactly the same depth, and there was a nice art in applying the things so that they were not so tight as to constrict the calf muscles, but not so slack as to work loose.

It was not only personal kit that entailed spit-and-polish. Private Stephen Graham recalls the perpetual 'leisure hours' of chores:

The five ration tins have to be shined with bath-brick. . . . we polish the table ends and the metal of our entrenching tools. We burnish the handles of our bayonets with the burnisher. We polish our dummy cartridges, our oil bottles, and the weights of our pull-throughs. For kit inspection we polish the backs of our blacking-brushes, clothes and hair-brushes with 'nutto' or 'soap'. We polish the instep of the soles of our duplicate pair of boots. . . .

Every night we carefully soap the insides of our trouser-creases, wet the outsides, and we obtain smartness by laying the damp garments on our mattresses and sleeping on them. . . . We scrub our equipment, and then paste khaki blanco on it. We wash our kit boxes and bath-brick our shelves.(3)

Graham was soldiering in the Scots Guards, and everyone knows that the Foot Guards were (and are) renowned for their meticulous standards of smartness. Nevertheless the present writer can confirm that the above chores were not exclusive to Guardsmen, but were the common lot of the British soldier in barracks down to the Second World War. Graham might have added that for the Commanding Officer's weekly inspection, barrack-room floors, tables and benches were laboriously scrubbed, coal-buckets burnished, stoves blacked, and tops of kit boxes polished with boot-blacking.

All soldiers were issued with two pairs of hob-nail ankle boots, or 'boots, ammunition'.[2] One pair, the 'best', was kept highly polished and reserved for ceremonial, guard duties and other special parades. The other was dubbined and used for drill and training. The term 'spit-and-polish' had a literal meaning in relation to the best pair. To obtain the mirror-like gloss on toecap and uppers, hours were spent in 'boning' and polishing. First, dabs of blacking mixed with saliva were rubbed into the leather with the bone handle of a toothbrush or knife. Then followed vigorous polishing with a soft duster. The process would be repeated every day until at length a hard, solid layer of reflective blacking had been built up. In some units it was also obligatory for the brass eyelets to be shined with metal polish.

All this is what the soldier termed 'bull', and it seemed to have little bearing on the main purpose of his existence: to train for war. Authority's

2. They were so described because the term 'ammunition' was derived from 'munition' which was applied to all military stores and equipment, not merely to projectiles and explosives.

attitude was, and to a lesser degree still is, that 'bull' was bound up with discipline, and hence morale. Just as unhesitating obedience to orders was essential in action, so a man taught in peacetime to maintain all his kit and arms in pristine, serviceable condition, would be less likely to let everything slide when confronted with the rigours and stresses of the battlefield. Slackness in such details leads to slovenliness, and a slovenly soldier is liable to let himself and his comrades down when up against it. Such, at least, was the theory. But the modern Para and SAS soldier might dispute the value of spit-and-polish.

Although few Edwardian soldiers were totally illiterate, the padres' and schoolmasters' efforts to persuade those who could read to occupy their leisure with improving literature did not bear much fruit. The reading-rooms were well stocked with Shakespeare, Dickens and other classics, and dryly-compiled regimental histories, but when he had finished his kit-cleaning chores in the evening the average soldier preferred the attractions of the canteen or the local pub. If he had any inclination to stretch himself on his cot with a book, the cheap paper-back novelettes and the popular press were more to his taste. Frank Richards tells us that the racing tales of Nat Gould were popular, while he claims that a translation of the *Decameron* of Boccaccio was devoured from cover to cover, 'it was considered very hot stuff', and was probably about the nearest to modern 'porn' that the soldier could get.(4)

But the most popular spare-time diversions in the barrack-rooms were always card games such as 'Pontoon' (*Vingt-et-un*), Nap and Brag. Gambling for money was strictly forbidden, but unless they were unusually 'regimental' (strict disciplinarians) most junior NCOs in the barrack rooms winked an eye at, or even joined in with a card 'school' assembled around a cot in the evening, until 'Lights Out' or the sudden appearance of an Orderly Sergeant broke it up.

The only officially approved form of gambling in the Army was (and is) what the troops termed 'Housey-Housey'. Today it is familiar to the general public as Bingo. In the service Housey-Housey was the most popular form of pastime to while away the long hours of boredom on board troopships bound for the East, and it was properly regulated, often with a senior NCO or Warrant Officer as 'caller'. Exactly when this game originated is not known, but it was certainly well-established after the Boer War, and the familiar cry of 'Look on! — Eyes down for a full house!' echoed from mess decks in the Mediterranean, the Indian Ocean and the China Sea until the demise of the British Empire. It was traditional for the caller to employ rhyming slang or other alternatives for certain numbers, such as 'Kelly's Eye' (one) 'Legs Eleven' (eleven) 'Open the Door' (44), 'Clickety-click' (66) and so on, up to 'Top of the House' (90). Richards relates that some callers would test the players' knowledge of regimental nicknames and ranking by shouting 'Pontius Pilate's Bodyguard' (Royal Scots, 1st of Foot), 'Holy Boys' (Norfolks, 9th) 'Old Brags' (Gloucesters, 28th).

On troopships, but not in barracks, another more venerable game of chance was Crown-and-Anchor, which probably originated in the Navy. It was usually operated by the 'matelots' (sailors) or ship's stewards as 'bankers', and unlike Housey, it was illegal, so that scouts were always posted to warn of prowling authority.

By the end of the Edwardian era sport was well established throughout the Army, at home and overseas. In the larger garrisons such as Aldershot, Tidworth (established 1902) Colchester, the Curragh, spacious areas were set aside for football and cricket fields, not to mention polo grounds and tennis courts for the officers, while there were few single-regiment stations that did not boast facilities for football and cricket, and hockey was also popular in India. As noted earlier, organised soccer had flourished in the Army since the 1870s, and by 1910 regimental and Army teams were regularly competing with civilian clubs in Football Association matches. Rugby was still considered the prerogative of the public schools, and although officers might form their own teams, this sport did not spread to the other ranks until after the First World War. Boxing was actively encouraged as an appropriate sport for the fighting soldier, and regimental teams regularly competed in the Army Boxing Championships held annually in London.

Although the Army's caste system was as rigid as ever, with its social barriers between officers and men, the enthusiasm for all forms of sport generated a certain degree of egalitarianism. Officers and privates could and did play in the same cricket and football teams and, especially in inter-regimental matches, rank could be temporarily forgotten in the interests of team spirit and the honour of the regiment. But the same did not yet apply to mounted sport: polo was strictly an officers' preserve, as of course was hunting, both of which entailed considerable personal expense. However, in the cavalry and gunners the other ranks were encouraged to indulge in mounted skill-at-arms competitions, and to form musical ride teams, which had become such a popular feature of the Royal Tournament. These activities cost the soldiers nothing, for they rode their unit's horses and wore their normal service dress, or for public displays were resplendent in their Full Dress.

The end of the Boer War saw thousands of men discharged, and one result of this was the proliferation of regimental Old Comrades associations. A few had already been established, one of the earliest being that of the Gordon Highlanders formed in 1888, to maintain touch with ex-Gordons, and to raise funds to assist those in need, besides helping them to find employment. These were the objects of the later OCAs, but in 1904 the King's Royal Rifle Corps and The Rifle Brigade clubbed together to do even more. As a memorial to all Riflemen who had fallen in the war, two cottages were acquired at Winchester to provide homes for 'old and infirm Riflemen where they can spend their old age in comfort'. A fund of £6,000 was raised from all serving and ex-Riflemen of all ranks for their furnishing and upkeep. Later the 'Riflemen's Memorial Cottages' expanded to eight in number, and are still maintained by the present Regiment, The Royal Green Jackets.(5)

The military caste system was not confined to that between officers and men, but also prevailed to some extent among the other ranks themselves. Senior NCOs and Warrant Officers had always been creatures apart from the common herd. There was no mixing with the lower ranks in off-duty hours (except on the sports field) while they enjoyed the superior amenities of their own Sergeants' Mess, run on exactly the same lines as the Officers' Mess. Here they took all their meals, and disported themselves in their own bar. Nor did they sleep in the barrack rooms, but had their separate 'bunks' or quarters. The junior NCOs (corporals and lance-corporals) were in a rather more ambivalent position, for although they shared the barrack rooms with the privates, and ate with them in the mens' dining hall, they too had their own Corporals' Club (or 'Mess') wherein, segregated, they took their pints and otherwise occupied their off-duty hours. It was strictly forbidden for a corporal to drink with a private soldier, and he was even discouraged from 'walking out' with one on visits to pubs or music halls. In the barrack room he might muck in with his mates, privates or no, and join in their Pontoon schools, but elsewhere he was expected to maintain his status as a 'superior officer', if only a single-stripe one. It was not easy to be 'popular' and at the same time a good NCO. To quote from Private Richards again, 'It was not wanting to lose touch with my chums that always kept me from putting in for promotion (though a few of them lost touch with me by doing so).'(6)

Touching on Freemasonry in the Army, Richards declares that few soldiers below the rank of sergeant could hope to be elected to the Regimental Lodge. This may have been true in his unit, the Royal Welch Fusiliers, but there is evidence to show that such restrictions were not universal. The first Military Lodge in the British Army was Warranted as early as 1732 in the First Foot (Royal Scots), and by 1910 the number had multiplied to some 500. While the Master was usually the Commanding Officer or the senior Major, the Brothers included many of the lower non-commissioned ranks. In 1910 the Lodge of the 4th (Royal Irish) Dragoon Guards had forty members, thirty-two of whom were NCOs or troopers. At first a newly-admitted trooper must have felt embarrassment at addressing his Commanding Officer as 'Brother' at the meetings, but outside the Lodge 'workings' normal military protocol prevailed, and Freemasonry never endangered discipline.

A curious phenomenon among the soldiery of the Edwardian era, and one which survived until the Second World War, was the prevalence of tattooing. This form of bodily ornamentation (said to have originated among sailors) was particularly popular in India where the bazaar *gudna-wallah* (tattoo artist) was adept in creating the designs favoured by generations of British soldiers, for fees much lower than those demanded in the back streets of London, Liverpool or Woolwich. Most soldiers preferred simple sentimental or patriotic designs, such as pierced hearts and sweethearts' names, Union Flags with 'For King and Country', or regimental badges and insignia. But there were more imaginative and extensive body-murals for those who could afford them and were prepared to undergo hours of painful pricking. The *pièce de résistance*, covering the entire back, depicted a pack of hounds in full cry after a fox about to run to ground in the man's fundament.

With the passing of the Edwardian era and the accession of King George V in 1910, the British Army had been transformed into the force that went to France in 1914, and the soldier, his training, dress and weapons hold living memories for many of the older pensioners of today, for there was to be little radical change until long after the First World War. And not until after the Second did his personal weapon, the Lee-Enfield rifle, give way to modern technology.

The cavalryman received an improved sword in 1908. Previously there had always been dispute between the rival advocates of the 'cutting' and 'thrusting' weapon, but the new sword, known thereafter as the '1908 Pattern' was essentially a thrusting weapon with a straight, 35 in. blade, and was acknowledged as the most effective pattern yet produced. Like the SMLE rifle, it was to remain in service until the cavalryman's horse gave way to the tank and the armoured car.[3]

Both cavalry and infantry now had the Maxim machine gun in their armoury, one section (four guns) being allotted to each unit. But although one Maxim was held to be equivalent to twenty-five riflemen in firepower, the heavy, cumbersome equipments mounted on artillery-type carriages and drawn by two horses were not very popular in the cavalry, being somewhat of a hindrance to cross-country mobility. This type of automatic weapon did not really come into its own until it became the lighter, tripod-mounted Vickers, carried on pack-horses.

By 1910 the British gunner was equipped with a variety of excellent ordnance which reflected the advanced technology of gunnery and ballistics, and with which his successors were to remain familiar until the advent of mechanisation. The Field Artilleryman had the 18 pounder gun and 4.5 in. howitzer, while the Horse Artilleryman fielded the light 13 pounder, which today can be seen bouncing behind the teams of The King's Troop RHA on their musical drives. For long-range and counter-battery work there was the 60 pounder, which had a range of 9,500 yards. The other weapons could fire up to 7,000 yards. All were the QF or Quick-firing type, so-called because they were fitted with hydraulic buffer and recuperator systems which absorbed the recoil, so that the gun remained stable on firing, instead of running back and having to be run up into position again by the detachment numbers. The developed art of gunnery involved the gunner recruit in mastering the intricacies of dial sights, field clinometers, sight clinometers, fuse setting and other mysteries which would enable him to drop a shell on a target he could not see.

The peacetime training of the soldier had evolved into a set annual pattern. It began in the winter with what was aptly termed Individual Training. This was the mastering of the man's basic skills — musketry, arms drill, gun drill, riding school, sword and lance drill, intermixed with lectures on regimental history, Army organisation and general military duties. The cavalryman spent much time on the parade ground sword in hand, squatting on an imaginary horse and obeying commands such as 'On Guard!' 'Infantry lying left-Point!' 'Withdraw!' Perhaps this was slightly more realistic than the stereotyped 'six-cuts' that his prede-

3. The 1908 Pattern sword can still be seen in service with The King's Troop RHA on their ceremonial duties and displays. The Household Cavalry continue to prefer the slightly curved sabre-type weapon.

cessors had practised, but not much. However, more practical training ensued when the trooper was allowed to mount a live horse and gallop at straw-and-sacking dummies.

While the infantry soldier also had to do similar exercises with his bayonet, yelling fearsomely as he plunged it into the dummy, for him there was naturally more emphasis on rifle shooting, or musketry — an anachronistic term perhaps, but one officially used in the training manuals down to modern times. In order to qualify for his proficiency pay he had to fire his annual musketry course at ranges up to 500 yards and obtain certain minimum scores at each range.

When individual training was completed in the spring, there followed squadron and company training or 'collective training' in which the unit worked as a team; then in summer the whole regiment or battalion would go into camp and operate on 'field days' or schemes as a collective unit. Finally in the autumn came the climax in the form of the large-scale annual manoeuvres when whole Divisions would form opposing 'Blue Force' and 'Red Force' and attempt to out-manoeuvre each other in set-piece schemes covering vast areas of southern England, and involving much hard marching, bivouacking, and the expenditure of huge quantities of blank ammunition. If the attack and defence schemes were rather stereotyped, planned in advance, and strictly controlled by officer-umpires galloping about on horseback, they were more realistic than the 'sham battles' organised in Victorian days and attended by concourses of civilian spectators who regarded them as public entertainment. They also gave the soldier a not unwelcome break from the monotonous routine of barrack life, and, especially in bad weather, some introduction to the rigours of active service.

The Boer War, fought against elusive guerrillas over huge expanses of open veldt, had revolutionised tactics and finally dispelled the 'thin red line' mentality. The soldier was now trained to operate in small detachments and was expected to make full use of ground and cover. A lance-corporal in command of his section of eight men was to be capable of leading it on his own and using his initiative, instead of being constantly nursed by his platoon officer. Although the cavalryman still practised the knee-to-knee charge in line, this was no longer the prime object of his existence. The official manual declared: 'If the cavalry learn to think that great precision in drill and in the charge are the highest tests of their efficiency (and that little else is required of them), it will be false training and will only lead to a lamentable waste of the power which this great arm should possess . . . The cavalry soldier should develop a quick eye for country, and his power of quick observation must be highly trained, to enable him to scout and to find his way about a country.'(7)

Before the South African war only officers and senior NCOs were considered capable of mastering the art of map reading and the use of the prismatic compass. Now even the humble private spent regular sessions wrestling with conventional signs, poring over contour lines, measuring heights and distances, and taking bearings and back-bearings. He could not qualify for promotion unless he achieved a pass in his map-reading course.

It would be stating the obvious to declare that the object of all forms of training was to prepare the soldier for war. This is an over-simplification; other factors were involved, such as inculcation of 'the soldierly spirit'. In August 1914, just before war was declared, a new edition of the official manual *Infantry Training* was published, and one of its first paragraphs set forth the desired qualities in terms which could hardly be better expressed. The passage is worth quoting in full:

The objects in view in developing a soldierly spirit are to help the soldier to bear fatigue, privation and danger cheerfully; to imbue him with a sense of honour; to give him confidence in his superiors and comrades; to increase his powers of initiative, of self-confidence, and of self-restraint; to train him to obey orders, or to act in the absence of orders for the advantage of his regiment under all conditions; to produce such a high degree of courage and disregard of self, that in the stress of battle he will use his brains and his weapons coolly and to the best advantage; to impress upon him that, so long as he is physically capable of fighting, surrender to the enemy is a disgraceful act; and finally to teach him how to act in combination with his comrades to defeat the enemy. As soon as the recruit joins he should be brought under influences which will tend to produce and increase such a spirit, and it is the duty of all officers and non-commissioned officers to assist in the attainment of this object by their conversation and example.

The soldier should be instructed in the deeds which have made the British Army and his regiment famous, and as his intelligence develops, this instruction should be extended to simple lessons, drawn from military history in general, illustrating how success depends on the above qualities. The privileges which he inherits as a citizen of a great Empire should be explained to him, and he should be taught to appreciate the honour which is his, as a soldier, of serving his King and country.

The above might seem the prescription for a paragon of a soldier, for VCs and DCMs. Not all could measure up to such a *beau idéal* perhaps, but the passage reflects no more than those desiderata of character and conduct that the British Army has always striven for and so often attained within its ranks. Only the official thinking about initiative, self-reliance and action in the absence of orders is novel.

Although the Edwardian soldier was generally better educated than his Victorian predecessors (in 1912 some 85 per cent of the other ranks were reported to enjoy 'a superior education'), no matter how proficient and ambitious he might be, he had little chance of rising to commissioned rank. There was as yet no provision for the acceptance of serving soldiers as cadets at Sandhurst or Woolwich, and the old practice of granting direct commissions for outstanding gallantry in the field had long since become defunct. With the singular exceptions noted earlier, the only ranker-officers in the Army were those who had risen to Warrant Officer, perhaps after 21 years' service, and had then been granted commissions as Lieutenant and Quartermaster or Riding Master. Few of these could hope to progress beyond Captain, for their age was against them.

Another well-nigh prohibitive barrier to promotion from the ranks was of course the financial one. Quite apart from initial expenses of uniform and accoutrements, even in the least fashionable infantry regiments of the Line an officer could not make his way unembarrassed and pay his Mess bills unless he had private means of at least £150 a year. In most cavalry regiments he needed twice that sum. With the possible exception of the rare 'gentleman-ranker', no soldier could ever aspire to such wealth.(8)

On the eve of the First World War, the Regular Army had assumed the structure that was to remain virtually unchanged until the amalgamations, disbandments and new creations following the war. A young man bent on taking the King's shilling had a bewildering choice of regiments and services. If he were a Londoner, and not less than 5 ft. 10 in. in height, he might opt for the elite of the Household Cavalry with their two Regiments of Life Guards and one of Royal Horse Guards (The Blues). Or if averse to the chores of horsemastership and the terrors of the riding school, he could try for one of the four Foot Guards — Grenadiers, Coldstream, Scots or Irish (the Welsh Guards were not formed until 1915). For many, the attraction of the Household Troops lay in the fact that, except in time of war, they never served in outlandish overseas stations, nor indeed did they soldier outside the capital, apart from periodic forays into Salisbury Plain or the South Downs for annual camps and manoeuvres. A further attraction for Life Guards or Blues recruits was the considerably better pay: a private in these two most senior units of the Army received a basic pay of 1s 9d per day, as opposed to 1s 2d in the cavalry of the Line and 1s. in the infantry. Strangely enough, the Foot Guards private was entitled to less than the Line cavalryman — only 1s 1d. In that other elite corps, the Royal Horse Artillery, a gunner got 1s 4d per day, but a man could not join the RHA direct: he first enlisted in its parent, the Royal Regiment of Artillery, and only if he proved above average in his recruits training course might he be selected for posting to a battery of 'the Right of the Line'.[4]

The recruit for the cavalry of the Line could try for any of 28 regiments: seven of Dragoon Guards (the cavalry's seniors), three of Dragoons, six of Lancers and twelve of Hussars. In 1913 fourteen of these were serving overseas, in India, Egypt or South Africa.

The cavalry had never been associated with any specific county or territorial area (with the exception of the Royal Scots Greys) but as we have seen, since 1881 every infantry regiment had been allotted its 'own' county or recruiting district, and in 1913 there were 70 such 'county regiments', including ten Scottish, eight Irish and three Welsh. As envisaged by Cardwell in his reorganisation of the infantry, a recruit naturally tended to opt for his local regiment where he would be among his pals and acquaintances from 'civvy street'.

If a man wished to become something other than simply a fighting soldier, and perhaps learn a useful trade, he might be accepted in one of the specialist corps: The Royal Engineers, Army Service Corps, Royal Army Medical Corps, Army Veterinary Corps, Army Ordnance Corps. Apart from the highly selective Military Police (Mounted and Foot) and an embryonic Physical Training Corps, these were the only ancillaries until the creation of the Royal Corps of Signals (from the Royal Engineer Signal Service) after the War. Naturally, soldiers in these specialist corps enjoyed better pay: for instance, a Sapper lance-corporal received 1s 10d

4. In 1873 Queen Victoria directed that when on parade with their guns the Royal Horse Artillery should take the Right of the Line, and march at the head of all other troops, including even the Household Cavalry.

a day, while the same rank in the Army Service Corps and the Ordnance Corps got 1s 5d.(9)

In 1908 a new edition of King's Regulations and Orders for the Army was issued, and with some minor amendments in 1914 this remained in force until the 1920s. Since these were the 'KRs' that had regulated the life and conduct of many ex-soldiers alive today, they deserve more than a passing mention.

The subject of Discipline is, predictably, treated at length, but it is significant to find a milder tone adopted. Discipline was still the bedrock of the Army, but it was no longer harsh or brutal. One of the first paragraphs in the relevant section declares that 'admonition is the most suitable treatment. Other punishment should only be resorted to when admonition has failed to have effect.' An officer was to adopt 'such methods of command and treatment as will not only ensure respect for authority, but also foster the feelings of self respect and personal honour essential to military efficiency'. Warrant Officers and NCOs were enjoined to avoid 'intemperate language or an offensive manner' when dealing with private soldiers. And an NCO was not to be reproved by an officer within sight or hearing of private soldiers. If any soldier felt he had been unjustly treated by his superior, whether officer or NCO, he had the right to complain to his commanding officer, and if he were still not satisfied, then he could take his case to a General officer. No soldier could be punished for contracting private debts with civilian tradesmen: if such tradesmen allowed soldiers to run up debts, then 'they will do so at their own risk'.

Soldiers, and officers, were forbidden to attend or take part in 'any meetings, demonstrations, or processions for party or political purposes, either in barracks or elsewhere'. Such an admonition was really unnecessary, for one of the most remarkable and abiding characteristics of the British Army was, and is, its apolitical attitude. Discussion of politics in the Mess was always taboo. While no such taboo existed in the barrack room, the average soldier was simply not interested in party politics. Few could say who was the Prime Minister, and fewer still knew the name of their current M.P. This despite the fact that the majority of the ranks were drawn from the working class, and by 1914 their loyalties in civilian life would probably have been owed to the Labour Party. But when a man joined the Army any political leanings were forgotten, and he transferred his loyalty to his Regiment. While his right to vote was facilitated, whether he was on a home or overseas tour of duty, he tended not to bother.

King's Regulations laid down that if a soldier committed an offence he could be placed either in 'open' or 'close' arrest, pending hearing of his case. Open arrest, for minor misdemeanours (e.g., dirty buttons on parade, and the like), meant simply that he was confined to barracks until his case was dealt with. Close arrest, for more serious offences, such as drunkenness, insubordination or 'offering violence to a superior officer', involved confinement in the Guard Room cell (the 'black hole' of earlier days) under custody of the Guard Commander, who would arrange for periods of exercise under escort. Pending trial he was allowed his normal bedding, and his rations were brought to him.

Minor offences were dealt with by the man's Squadron or Company Commander, who could award up to seven days confinement to barracks ('CB'), extra guards, and fines for drunkenness. More serious cases came before the Commanding Officer and could be dealt with by a Regimental Court Martial. The C.O.'s powers of punishment extended to 28 days' detention in a military prison or the garrison detention barracks. He could also inflict fines up to ten shillings for drunkenness. Every soldier had the right to demand trial by District Court Martial instead of by his Commanding Officer, and certain serious offences, such as sedition, mutiny, striking a superior officer, could only be tried by DCM or General Court Martial. Mutiny and sedition were the gravest military offences, and a General Court Martial could award up to penal servitude for life on any soldier so convicted. For 'gross violence to superiors' the sentence was '1 year and upwards'.

Drunkenness continued to be one of the most prevalent 'crimes' among the lower ranks, and the Regulations laid down a sliding scale of fines. For the first such offence there was no fine, only a caution. For a second offence the fine was 2s 6d, and for the third and subsequent offences, 5s. But if the third or subsequent offences occurred within six months of the preceding one, 7s 6d was the penalty, and if within three months, 10s.

It is noteworthy that nowhere in Kings' Regulations was there any reference to the death penalty. This was provided for in the Army Act, but it could only be inflicted in time of war, and as will be seen in the next chapter, many soldiers were so sentenced and executed during the First World War.

One aspect of military punishment which was considered unjust by several eminent general officers, including Lord Roberts and Lord Wolseley, was the ruling that every conviction for an offence should be recorded in the soldier's Regimental Conduct Sheet, known as AFB 120, where it would be preserved throughout his service. It was objected that a raw young private initially ill-disciplined and perhaps led astray by bad characters, might develop into an excellent soldier, but his prospects of promotion would be prejudiced by the early entries in his Conduct Sheet. Lord Wolseley, and others, suggested that if a man remained innocent of any offence for a period of three years, all former records should be destroyed and he could start afresh with a clean sheet. But the Army Council did not agree, and the ruling remained in the Regulations. A small concession was allowed to senior NCOs and Warrant Officers, whose Conduct Sheets were classed as 'confidential', meaning that they were accessible only to the commanding officer or his deputy, and not to other officers or seniors NCOs, as was the case with the lower ranks' sheets.

The initial periods of service with the Colours laid down in KRs were as under:

Cavalry	7 years
Royal Horse Artillery ⎱ Royal Field Artillery ⎰	6 years
Royal Garrison Artillery	8 years
Foot Guards	7 years
Infantry of the Line	7 years
Royal Engineers	6 years
Other Corps	7 years

After the expiry of these periods, the soldier could either claim his discharge to the Reserve or elect to complete twelve years with the Colours, provided he was efficient and of good conduct. After eleven years' service he could sign on to complete twenty-one years with the Colours, with the same provisos, or take his discharge in the twelfth year. In exceptional cases, service beyond twenty-one years was authorised, but this usually applied only to Warrant Officers, and War Office approval had to be sought.

Any recruit, who, within three months of joining, might decide that the Army was not to his liking, could purchase his discharge on payment of £10. After that, the sum to be paid for discharge by purchase varied according to rank and length of service, reaching a maximum of £30 for a private soldier with seven years' service. The Regulations included provisions for free discharge on compassionate grounds: for example, when a man was needed as the bread-winner for destitute parents or other near relatives. Soldiers could also be discharged at any time for grave misconduct, in which case 'discharge with ignominy' was recorded, and pension was forfeited.

As always, the Army continued to frown on marriage, the attitude being that a soldier's prime loyalty was due to his regiment and his officers, and should not be hazarded by responsibilities to a wife and family. 'The fact is, a soldier has no business to be married,' wrote General Sir Ian Hamilton. 'He is no longer wholehearted in his pursuit of glory.'(10) Marriage was a 'privilege' stressed KRs, which could only be permitted so long as certain regulations were complied with.

Although the limitation on the numbers of married women permitted in a unit had long since expired, a practical limitation existed in the number of married quarters available, which varied from station to station, and a soldier could not be placed on the married establishment unless a vacancy existed. KRs laid down that permission to marry would not be granted unless a number of conditions were fulfilled. First, the prospective wife had to be approved by the commanding officer as 'a woman of good character'. The soldier must have at least seven years' service and two good conduct badges, and if below the rank of sergeant, should have a credit of £5 in the Post Office Savings Bank. Should a married woman be found guilty of 'misconduct' — the interpretation of which can be left to the imagination — the CO could dismiss her from the married quarters. If there were children the husband could continue to live with them in his quarters, but if not, he too would be struck off the married roll.

The accommodation allotted to married soldiers was not over-generous. A man with up to two children was allowed two rooms, 'exclusive of scullery'; three to five children entitled him to three rooms; with six or more he was given four rooms. But at least this was better than the old days when his wife and all offspring had to cram themselves into a blanketed corner of the barrack room.

The system of soldiers' education established in the previous century was virtually unchanged and remained so until after the Second World War. All recruits had to attend the regimental school until they passed their Third Class Certificate of Education, which was necessary for promotion to corporal. To advance to sergeant a corporal needed a Second Class Certificate, and beyond that the First Class Certificate was essential.

An outline for each examination was given in Chapter 4 (p. 69). By 1914 the standards had changed hardly at all in fifty-odd years. The Third Class still demanded no more than the basics of the three Rs and the Second was just about of elementary school rating. The First could have been obtained without difficulty by a bright teenager. There was no competition for a man to progress beyond the Third Class — without which he could not qualify as a trained soldier — only those with ambition for promotion did so, and these were in the minority. In 1913 only 11,000 men out of a total of some 100,000 rank-and-file were reported to have achieved a First Class Certificate, and about 7,000 of these were Warrant Officers.(11)

All instruction was in the hands of the Corps of Army Schoolmasters (and Mistresses) who, as we have seen, were qualified teachers. Within the regiments, selected NCOs with at least Second Class Certificates could teach up to that standard, under supervision of the schoolmasters. Such NCO teachers were classed as 'Soldier Assistants' and received extra-duty pay up to 6d per day (the schoolmasters were paid a maximum of 5s per day).

A feature of the early 1900s was the establishment of London clubs where soldiers on leave in, or passing through, the capital could obtain cheap and comfortable accommodation. Of course officers had enjoyed such amenities (if not 'cheap') from much earlier dates with the founding of the prestigious Guards Club, the Army and Navy, the Cavalry and others during the previous century, but until 1907 there was no equivalent for the other ranks. In that year King Edward VII formally opened the Union Jack Club as a memorial to all servicemen killed during the Boer War. Conveniently sited opposite Waterloo Station, it offered a true club-like atmosphere for the ordinary soldier, with single and double rooms, dining hall, library — and of course, hot baths. It was, and remains, a registered charity. During the First World War more than a million servicemen stayed at the Union Jack on their leave from the Front. The Club still flourishes today, in new premises on the same site. Also in 1907 the Veterans' Club was opened in Holborn. This too was registered as a charity, but as its name implied, membership was limited to ex-servicemen. And, remarkably for the time, it was not exclusively an other-ranks' club, for ex-officers could also join. It claimed to be the only Club in the world to be open to all ranks of the armed forces. Having been renamed the Allenby Club after the First World War (when Field-Marshal Viscount Allenby became president) it later assumed its present name, the Victory Services Club, in new premises near the Marble Arch. Since 1970 it has no longer been restricted to ex-service personnel but is also open to all ranks on the Active List, men and women.

Before closing this chapter mention must be made of a category of soldier so far overlooked — the boy-soldier. Since the earliest days of the Standing Army boys of tender age had served in all arms at home and overseas, in peasce and war, and many had risen to high rank.

Before the nineteenth century there was no minimum age limit for the enlistment of boys, and there are records of infants of seven being attested for drummers, buglers or trumpeters, while ten-year-olds were quite common. An Inspection Return for the 7th Dragoon Guards of 1788 reported that one of the trumpeters was 'too young and little to mount a horse'. By 1844 however, Queen's Regulations were directing that 'no boy is eligible for enlistment under the age of fourteen years, except under very special circumstances.' Such circumstances were not detailed, but they probably related to young orphans in The Duke of York's Royal Military School or The Royal Hibernian, or perhaps to infants 'born in the regiment'. By the time a lad reached the age of sixteen he was judged mature enough to be classed as an adult soldier, and his weapon training began.

The minimum age-limit of fourteen has continued to the present day, but by 1900 the upper limit had been raised to 18 (now 17½). Although juveniles, boy-soldiers were of course subject to normal military discipline, but punishments for misdemeanours were always less harsh than those of their adult comrades. Boys could not be flogged, though they might be caned by the Trumpet-Major or Drum-Major, while they were not to be confined in the Guard Room cells with the men, nor were they to be subjected to punishment drill. They were however liable to fines and confinement to barracks. Officially they were not allowed to smoke, nor to indulge in alcohol. No boy could enter the Wet Canteen, and if seen in a pub he would be 'on the mat' before his commanding officer next morning.

In 1914 a boy on enlistment, in whatever arm of the service, received a basic pay of 8d a day. When fully trained as trumpeter, bugler or drummer, and in possession of a Second Class Certificate of Education, his pay was generously increased as under:(12)

Household Cavalry (trumpeter)	1s 11d
Royal Horse Artillery (trumpeter)	2s 0d
Cavalry of the Line (trumpeter)	1s 4d
Royal Field & Garrison Artillery (trumpeter)	1s 2½d
Royal Engineers (trumpeter)	1s 1½d
Foot Guards (drummer, bugler)	1s 2d
Infantry (drummer, bugler)	1s 1d

It will be seen that these rates are higher than those for private soldiers: even then, boys were regarded as potential NCOs, if not actually termed 'Junior Leaders'. The fact that so many achieved the higher echelons of rank confirmed this view. A chronological leap ignored, in 1979 the Army was reported to boast of two Brigadiers, 54 Colonels and Lieutenant-Colonels and 805 Majors and Captains who had begun their careers as junior soldiers.(13)

It is worth recording that the youngest winner of the Victoria Cross in the British Armed Forces was a boy. Drummer Thomas Flinn of the 64th Foot (later North Staffordshire Regiment) was aged just 15 years 3 months when he gained the supreme award for his gallantry in saving a comrade under fire during the Indian Mutiny, November 28th, 1857. The next youngest was also a juvenile — the better-known Boy 1st Class John Cornwell RN, who earned his VC in HMS *Chester* at Jutland in 1916, aged 16 years 3 months.

7

THE GREAT WAR
AND ITS LEGACY

When the British Expeditionary Force crossed the Channel in August 1914, it was the first time British soldiers had done so under arms since the Waterloo campaign, almost one hundred years earlier. Initially the B.E.F. — the 'Old Contemptibles' — deployed five regular divisions which owed their existence to Haldane's reforms of 1908. The majority of soldiers were long-serving men who had enlisted either during the Boer War or shortly afterwards. But about forty per cent were reservists called up on mobilisation.

Very soon these regulars were joined by floods of volunteers who had answered Lord Kitchener's[1] nation-wide call in their thousands. The euphoria and enthusiasm of the young men who flocked to join 'Kitchener's Army' were astonishing and unprecedented. On a single day in August 30,000 volunteers were enlisted and by July the following year more than two million had joined up. But volunteers were not sufficient to replace the horrific casualties of the next couple of years, while it became obvious that a large reservoir of fit and healthy young men were shirking their duty. And so in January 1916 conscription was introduced with the passing of the Military Service Bill (predictably condemned by the Trade Unions). All able-bodied men between the ages of 18 and 41 became liable for service in the Forces. By March 193,891 had been called up, and conscription remained in force until 1919.

Rarely had the Army's rank-and-file been so truly representative of all classes. The recruits came from every walk of life. Schoolmasters, authors, Oxbridge undergraduates, landed gentry and public school youths, drilled, polished buttons and scrubbed floors with coal miners,

---

1. Field-Marshal Earl Kitchener succeeded Colonel J.E.B. Seely (Lord Mottistone) as Secretary of State for War on August 8th.

bus conductors, shop assistants, publicans, farm labourers. Some had lied brazenly about their age in order to be accepted;[2] some gave false names, for reasons best known to themselves; all were imbued with the exciting spirit of adventure and patriotism.

They donned the grey shirt and ready-made khaki of the new era, and deposited the emblems of class distinction on a common rag-heap . . . It was the formal beginning of a new life, in which men of all classes, starting with something like equality of opportunity, should gain what pre-eminence they might by the merit of their inherent manhood or the seduction of their native tact. Henceforward all fared alike. All ate the same food, slept on the same floor in similar blankets, and in their shirts. Even the pyjama no longer divided them! All took their share of scrubbing floors and washing dixies . . . Gradually all found their level. The plausible were promoted, found wanting, reduced, and replaced by men of real grit and force of character. Mechanics joined the machine-gun section, clerks became orderlies, signallers or telephonists. The dirtiest and most drunken of old soldiers were relegated to the cookhouse.(1)

The 'New Army' was formed into Groups, or *ad hoc* battalions of 1,000 men, commanded by an officer who might be a retired regular recalled to the Active List, or a commandeered Indian Army officer home on leave. The company commanders could also be 'dug-out' regulars, but many of the junior officers were raw young lads who had been corporals or above in their public school OTCs and were granted direct commissions. The Gentlemen Cadets of Sandhurst and Woolwich were likewise immediately commissioned on the outbreak of war: most of these went directly to the regular units. By the end of August 1914 the *ad hoc* 'Groups' had been formally styled battalions and found themselves wearing the cap badges of regular regiments to whom they now owed loyalty.

By September Kitchener's 'First Hundred Thousand' had been organised in six divisions. By next March the number had risen to thirty new divisions, and the first thirteen of them crossed to France in mid-1915.

Conditions at home during training were spartan. Obviously, existing barrack accommodation was nothing like adequate to house the influx, and vast tented camps mushroomed all over England. The tents were the

2. The official age limits were initially from 19 to 30 years, but in 1915 the upper limit was raised to 40.

circular type which were to remain familiar to later generations of regulars, territorials and OTC cadets down to the next War, and were known as Bell tents, though they were more similar to an American Indian tepee, but with a single central pole. Each tent measured twenty feet in diameter, and the regulations laid down a nice distinction in the number of occupants permitted according to rank:(2)

Generals, Colonels and C.O.s	1 to a tent
Other officers	3 ,, ,, ,,
Warrant officers	5 ,, ,, ,,
Sergeants	7 ,, ,, ,,
Men	15 ,, ,, ,,

The men slept like the spokes of a wheel, feet towards the central pole, and fifteen of them with arms and equipment meant literally cheek-by-jowl. Officers, of course, could put up their camp beds, but for the soldiers there were only the ground sheet-cum-cape and blankets. At least the canvas was usually weatherproof.

All cooking was carried out in field kitchens, and the men got three meals a day, the main one being 'dinner' at 1 p.m. This usually consisted of stew with 'plum duff' or rice pudding to follow. Tea at about 5 p.m. was the last official meal: the beverage itself was boiled up together with condensed milk and sugar in huge camp kettles; for solid sustenance there was the inevitable bread-and-margarine and plum jam, or 'pozzy'. Those who could afford it might supplement their rations by visiting neighbouring cafés and pubs: unless a man were on duty, or on 'jankers' (a defaulter) he could usually obtain an evening pass. After twenty weeks' training the soldier was allowed one week's leave, for which a free rail warrant was granted. In addition, when finally detailed for posting overseas all ranks were given up to 72 hours' embarkation leave when, as the saying went, they could indulge in 'a last kiss and cuddle'.

In the prevailing atmosphere in England not much notice was taken of the soldier's morals, or lack thereof; it was accepted as only natural that he should enjoy a little 'square-pushing' with any handy 'bit of skirt' in his off-duty evenings. But once he found himself in a foreign country he was expected to uphold the honour and prestige of the British Army. In 1914 Lord Kitchener issued a cautionary order which was to be pasted in every soldier's paybook before he sailed for France:

Remember that the honour of the British Army depends on your conduct . . . Keep on your guard against excesses. In this new experience you may find temptations both in wine and women. You must entirely resist both, and while treating all women with perfect courtesy, you should avoid any intimacy.(3)

But the British soldier was never a 'plaster saint', and the Secretary of State's pious admonition fell on deaf ears when a lusty youth discovered that the French m'amselles were as willing as he was for a 'spot of jig-a-jig'.

For the first few months in France the euphoria and jingoism prevailed. 'There is a fine heroic feeling about being in France,' wrote Wilfred Owen, 'and I am in perfect spirits. A tinge of excitement is about me.' But with the advent of trench warfare and all its morale-sapping horrors and privations, attitudes changed. Within a year Owen was writing:

> I suppose I can endure cold, and fatigue, and the face-to-face death, as well as another; but extra for me there is the universal pervasion of *Ugliness*. Hideous landscapes, vile noises, foul language and nothing but foul, even from one's own mouth (for all are devil-ridden), everything unnatural, broken, blasted; the distortion of the dead, whose unburiable bodies sit outside the dug-outs all day, all night, the most execrable sights on earth . . . *that* is what saps the 'soldierly spirit'.(4)

Owen of course was a cultured officer, and a poet, but many private soldiers were sickened when they came face to face with the realities of war. Gunner Hiram Sturdy of the Royal Field Artillery recorded his reactions:

> I crouch in behind some infantry holes (I won't call them shelters) and while there one of the infantry is carried in. The top of his head is lifted off, a clean swipe whatever got him. His chum holds his head and I see him die. The first for me to see die as they say, for his country, and it might be glorious, noble, brave, heroic and all the rest of these beautiful words that sound so well on a platform or toasting your toes by the fireside, but it certainly is not a glorious sight to see a young fellow, with his face covered with blood, stiffening out in a hole dug out of clay. It isn't glorious, it's murder, was my thoughts when I saw my first infantrymen die . . .
>
> The chum sits a little while looking at the bloody clay with a uniform on it, then buckles up and goes out to the bloody war.(5)

During the war nearly 678,000 British soldiers died ('gloriously' or not) in performance of their duty and thousands of others endured the years of mud and blood to survive, perhaps disabled, perhaps unscathed, having done all that was demanded of them, sometimes more. But in the testing-time of battle when physical and moral reserves are stretched to the limit it is inevitable that some should reach breaking point.

Until comparatively recent days military discipline made no concessions to individual powers of endurance: any failure was an offence, to be punished 'for the sake of example'. After the retreat from Mons in 1914 when the B.E.F. were mentally and physically exhausted, the C-in-C, Sir John French, issued an Order in which he stressed 'Failure to maintain the highest standard of discipline will result in the infliction of the most severe punishment.'

As already observed, in time of war 'the most severe punishment' could include the death penalty for certain grave offences, such as mutiny, 'shamefully abandoning a post', desertion, sleeping or being drunk while on post, or striking a superior officer.

By 1914 infliction of the death sentence for these offences had become such a rarity, even on active service, that it was considered virtually superseded by the 'such lesser punishments' provided for in the Army Act, e.g. penal servitude. Not a single British soldier was executed during the Crimean War; one was executed for mutiny in India in 1870; two were executed during the Boer War.

On September 6th, 1914, the day after the Mons retreat was halted, a nineteen-year-old private of a Home Counties infantry battalion was court-martialled for desertion and sentenced to be shot by firing squad. The sentence was carried out two days later. On the 27th of the same month another infantry private suffered for a similar offence. Recommending confirmation of the sentence Sir Douglas Haig, the Corps Commander, wrote 'I am of the opinion that it is necessary to make an example to prevent cowardice in the face of the enemy as far as possible.' The official records reveal that by the end of 1915 fifty-nine British soldiers had been sentenced to death. In 1917 104 were shot, and the total for the war years 1914–18 amounted to 304.(6) By far the greatest number, 265, suffered for 'desertion', which could cover shamefully running away in the face of the enemy, or simply disappearing from one's unit.

Compared with the millions of soldiers who served and the thousands who fell in the carnage of the battlefields, the above total may seem insignificant. Nevertheless, it was unprecedented, and was never again approached. What was the reason? The answer may lie in the fact that, on the Western Front where the majority of cases occurred, the conflict was static; with only very brief spells of rest, the troops were continuously subjected to the ordeals of trench warfare and all that implied: not only the hazards of mutilation or death, but the unremitting squalor of mud, rats, lice, wet clothes, the stench of putrefying corpses, by day, by night. Such conditions stretched morale beyond the limit. In his study *Fighting Spirit* Major-General Frank Richardson, late RAMC, seeks to explain the phenomenon of nervous breakdown, or 'shell-shock' as it was termed, by drawing an analogy with a vehicle's battery:

> . . . which recharges properly, but as it ages in use stays at full charge for a shorter period each time it is charged up, and finally will take full charge, but will not hold it. A man's self-control is like that. He responds to rest and goes back to battle apparently normal, but each time his resistance is lowered, and finally if not rested, may break.(7)

A soldier accused of desertion, cowardice or other capital offence was brought before a Field General Court Martial, comprising four officers with a Lieutenant-Colonel, or sometimes Major, as President. The proceedings were conducted strictly in accordance with Military Law. Usually the adjutant of the accused's unit acted as prosecutor, while one of the junior regimental officers was detailed to defend, as 'prisoner's friend'. The soldier was of course allowed to make a statement in his defence, and was also entitled to call witnesses. On several occasions during the war Members of Parliament demanded that a soldier on trial for his life should be defended by a professional lawyer, but as the Under-Secretary of State for War replied in the House in 1916, 'It is obvious that counsel cannot be employed on courts martial which take place in the field.'

If the finding of the court was 'not guilty', the verdict was immediately announced and the prisoner released. But if 'guilty' the formalities were protracted, and the man might be kept in ignorance of his ultimate fate for days, or even weeks. The findings and all relevant documents were forwarded first to the man's commanding officer, then to the Brigade, Division, Corps and Army Commanders, each of whom could recommend either confirmation or commutation of the sentence. The file then passed to the Judge-Advocate's branch for legal checking of the court's proceedings, and finally it went to the Commander-in-Chief for his over-

riding decision. Almost invariably the successive authorities agreed with
the verdict of the court, for it was rare that any additional evidence in
mitigation was forthcoming. In 1915, out of 59 death sentences only four
were commuted to penal servitude. As Judge Babington remarks, the
issue of life or death usually rested on two simple factors: whether the
condemned man might possibly become a good soldier, or whether his
execution would prove beneficial to the maintenance of military
discipline.

When the C-in-C's confirmation was received, the condemned soldier
was subjected to a preliminary ordeal before his execution. When battle
conditions permitted he was paraded before his unit, when the findings of
the court and the confirmation of the sentence were announced. This
usually took place on the eve of execution. During the dreadful hours
before dawn the soldier could, if he wished, be visited by a chaplain of his
denomination, who would offer such words of spiritual comfort as he
could muster.

We have already given an eye-witness account of an execution by a
firing squad in Wellington's day (p. 32); the procedure was much the
same in 1914–18, the only difference being that all the victim's comrades
were not subjected to the trauma of witnessing the shooting. Orders
recommended that it should be carried out in 'a secluded spot'. There
were no regulation numbers for the firing party, but in France and
Flanders the usual composition was one officer and ten men. The latter
were generally detailed from the condemned man's own unit, but again
there was no hard and fast ruling, and they might be ordered from
another unit in the vicinity. Although the officer (usually an unhappy
subaltern) was fully briefed when warned for duty the night before, the
orders usually stated that 'the men need not be informed of the duty for
which they have been detailed until the morning.' But even if they were
not so informed, rumour left little doubt of the macabre task that faced
them. Each hoped that he would be the one whose rifle was loaded with a
blank round: whatever their own views about the victim — who might
have disgraced himself and the Regiment — there was natural abhor-
rence to the killing of a comrade in cold blood.

It had always been the practice for the execution to be carried out
around dawn: various Divisional orders specified 'at daybreak', 'as early as
possible after dawn' or 'at as early an hour as may be convenient'. When
the firing party had assembled and the officer had loaded the rifles (one
with blank), the prisoner was marched to the spot under escort and either

bound to a stake or tree, or, if as sometimes happened, he was in a state of collapse, he would be secured in a chair. Always in attendance was a medical officer, and usually, but not necessarily, a chaplain. The firing party were always ordered to aim at the heart, and to assist them a piece of white cloth or paper was pinned on the victim's chest by a provost NCO, who also bound a cloth round the man's eyes. As a humane consideration, the officer in charge did not give a verbal order to fire: this was done by a prearranged signal.

Immediately after the volley the Medical Officer examined the victim to ascertain whether he was dead or not. If he were still living it was the officer's dreaded duty to administer the *coup de grâce* with a shot in the head from his revolver. It was very rare that trained soldiers firing at pointblank range failed to kill the victim outright, but there are recorded instances when the hapless officer had to do his duty.

The corpse was buried in a temporary grave, recorded by map reference, so that in due course it might be transferred to a permanent war cemetery to lie with those who had met an honourable death in battle. There was, however, a nice distinction in the wording of the inscription on the headstone: instead of the usual 'Killed in Action' or 'Died of Wounds', there was a single word 'Died'. For the first three years of the war there was no attempt to spare the feelings of the next-of-kin of executed soldiers. When Captain Liddell Hart was temporarily posted to the Infantry Records Office in York in 1917, he found 'a nauseating feature' of his duties was the dispatch of formal letters to widows or parents notifying them that their husband or son had been sentenced to death and executed: 'until then I had imagined like most soldiers, that such executions were camouflaged in some way as accidental death.'(8) However, after some questions and exchanges in the House of Commons, in November 1917 Andrew Bonar Law, Chancellor of the Exchequer and Leader of the House, made a statement about capital court-martials and executions, in which he said, 'It has been arranged that in future the communications made to the dependants of the soldiers shot at the front should merely state that they have died on service.'(9) Whether such camouflage succeeded in assuring the bereaved that their son or husband had died honourably is doubtful, for by that time it was well known that executions were taking place, and the subtle variations in wording could only arouse disquiet.

As explained previously, the other disciplinary measure reserved for active service was Field Punishment, which was one of the 'such lesser punishments' allowed by the Army Act in lieu of the death sentence for grave offences, and could also be awarded for less serious offences such as drunkenness or insubordination. In 1914 there were two categories of Field Punishment: FP No. 1 and FP No. 2, the difference being that in the former the prisoner was secured to a fixed object, usually a limber or carriage wheel, while in the latter he was not so secured, but kept in confinement. Robert Graves describes how his own batman, Private 'Tottie' Fry suffered FP 1 behind the lines in 1915:

> On my way to rifle inspection at nine o'clock at the company billet I noticed something unusual at the corner of a farm-yard. It was Field Punishment No. 1 being carried out — my first sight of it. Tottie was the victim. He had been awarded twenty-eight days for 'drunkenness in the field'. He was spread-eagled to the wheel of a company limber, tied by the ankles and wrists in the form of an X. He remained in this position — 'crucifixion', they called it — for several hours a day; I forget how many, but it was a good working-day. The sentence was to be carried out for as long as the battalion remained in billets, and was to be continued after the next spell of trenches.(10)

A commanding officer was empowered to award up to 28 days' FP 1, a company commander up to seven days'. There are no official statistics to show how often this punishment was inflicted, but judging by the reminiscences of soldiers on the Western Front, it was quite common. Captain A. Wright, serving with the 4th Dragoon Guards in 1915, says he saw three instances in two months, one victim being an artillery driver, the other two, infantrymen.(11)

Discipline has to be maintained, and offenders punished — not just for their own good, but for the sake of example. But an army cannot exist in the field unless the soldier's basic needs of food, clothing and medical care are forthcoming, and it is acknowledged that the logistic and medical arrangements in the war were superior to any that a British expeditionary force had enjoyed hitherto. In no small measure this was relevant to the properly organised ancillary services which in previous European wars had been very much *ad hoc* bodies, if not shambles. The Royal Army Medical Corps, Army Service Corps and Army Ordnance Corps (the latter two became 'Royal' in 1918) were now thoroughly geared to performing their essential tasks in the field. Although the fighting soldier in a combatant unit had always tended to look down on such 'tail' elements, he could not subsist without them. To a great extent the static nature of the war on the Western Front rendered medical care and supply of rations, ammunition and other essentials simpler, for it allowed the establishment of more or less permanent bases, field hospitals, and supply depots behind the lines.

Conscripts who declared themselves Conscientious Objectors were assigned to non-combatant duties, which more often than not involved carrying stretchers — indeed the Quakers organised a Friends' Ambulance Unit which did noble work in casualty evacuation. As a rule, the military was less tolerant of the 'conchie' in the First World War than in the Second (see p. 166).

The casualty figures for the First World War battles were horrendous, exceeding anything that the British Army had previously suffered. In a single day's fighting at Thiepval in 1916 more than 57,000 British soldiers were killed or wounded — the highest figure for any one day's combat in the history of the Army. At Passchendaele in October and November 1917 another 300,000 casualties were suffered. It is almost beyond comprehension that the medical services managed to cope with such unprecedented avalanches of mutilated bodies, but thanks to the equally unprecedented organisation and the heroic efforts of the RAMC personnel, cope they did.[3]

To begin at 'the sharp end', each battalion or regiment established its own Regimental Aid Post near the firing line, where the Medical Officer examined and patched up those casualties he could deal with, assisted by the unit orderlies. The more seriously wounded were carried by stretcher-bearers or ambulance (usually horse-drawn) to the Advanced Dressing Station situated behind the lines and staffed by RAMC personnel. Those who could not be treated here were transferred by ambulance to the Casualty Clearing Station, out of range of artillery fire, where the most serious cases were again evacuated to a Field or Base Hospital in a back area. Finally, the 'Blighty' cases were taken by ambulance-train to the waiting hospital ships and evacuated to the general hospitals in England. All this complex organisation, which ran efficiently throughout the war, was in the devoted hands of the RAMC staff, in conjunction with the Movement Control authorities.

A novel feature in the field and base hospitals was the female nursing

3. It should be added that during the four years of the war members of the RAMC were awarded seven VCs and two bars; 499 DSOs, 1484 MCs, 395 DCMs and 3002 MMs.

service, represented by the sisters and nurses of the Queen Alexandra's Imperial Nursing Service, formed in 1902. In addition there was the First Aid Nursing Yeomanry, (or the FANYs) which had been formed in 1909 as a volunteer corps of lady-riders with first aid training, the somewhat romantic idea being that they should gallop about the battlefield to give succour to wounded soldiers. By 1914 of course such gallant activities were deemed impracticable, and the FANYs gave their 'yeoman' service as hospital orderlies and ambulance drivers.[4] Similar duties were performed by the ladies of the Volunteer Aid Detachments (VAD) who took over much of the work of the RAMC orderlies in the hospitals. It can truthfully be said that in no previous war or campaign had the sick or wounded soldier been so well cared for.

In battle the soldier's requirements are many and varied. To remain effective he needs ammunition, rations, water, tools, weapons replacements, RE and ordnance stores, besides creature comforts such as cigarettes, tobacco, to mention only a few. The supply of all these was the responsibility of the Army Service Corps, slightingly dubbed 'Ally Sloper's Cavalry' by the combat troops, but whose duties were as essential and as faithfully carried out as those of the RAMC. From rear railheads the ASC convoys transported supplies through the hazards of shellfire and damaged roads up to a delivery point behind the lines, where they were distributed to individual units' ration and ammunition parties.

The regulations laid down a 'special scale' of daily rations per man on active service, which were to be adhered to 'as far as possible':(12)

Meat	$1\frac{1}{4}$ lb fresh (or 1 lb preserved)
Bread	$1\frac{1}{4}$ lb (or 1 lb biscuit or 1 lb flour)
Bacon	$\frac{1}{4}$ lb
Cheese	3 oz
Tea	$\frac{5}{8}$ oz
Jam	$\frac{1}{4}$ lb
Sugar	3 oz
Salt	$\frac{1}{2}$ oz
Pepper	1/36 oz
Mustard	1/20 oz
Fresh vegetables	$\frac{1}{2}$ lb (or 2 oz dried)
Tobacco	Not exceeding 2 oz per week

4. The FANYs or Women's Transport Service went on to perform equally valuable service (including SOE duties) in the Second World War and as an independent, voluntary organisation are still available for emergency duties.

Naturally, in the turmoil of battle conditions such a precise scale was not always adhered to. And it is doubtful whether any man complained if he did not receive his 1/36 oz of pepper.

Private Harold Horne of the Northumberland Fusiliers describes the normal procedure for collecting rations and cooking them in the field.(13)

Ration parties from each company in the line went to carry back the rations which were tied in sandbags and consisted, usually, of bread, hard biscuits, tinned meat ('bully') in 12 oz tins, tinned jam (Tommy Ticklers plum-and-apple), tinned butter, sugar and tea, pork and beans (baked beans with a piece of pork fat on top) cigarettes and tobacco. Sometimes we got 'Maconochie Rations'. This was a sort of Irish stew in tins which could be quickly heated over a charcoal brazier. . . When it was possible to have a cookhouse within easy reach of the trenches, fresh meat, bacon, vegetables, flour etc. would be sent up and the cooks could produce reasonably good meals, and food and tea was sent along the trenches in dixies (large iron containers the lids of which could be used as a frying pan). In 1916 large containers on the thermos principle, which could be carried on the back, appeared in which hot tea could be carried up to the trenches from Battalion rear HQ where the cooks could work under better conditions.

In winter there was a ration of rum, one or two tablespoons per man; this was a strong, black spirit which was usually issued during the morning 'stand-to'; it was very welcome on a cold winter's morning . . . Water was sent up the line in petrol cans. We were not supposed to use untreated water so each battalion had water carts and the medical officer was responsible for ensuring that it was chlorinated before use.

Each unit had its own cookhouse staff — usually the sloppiest and least efficient soldiers who would not be missed in the firing line. Culinary talent was to come later. (The Mess Call — 'Come to the cookhouse door' — was already a feature of infantry life in 1798.)

The infantry soldier in Field Service Marching Order was laden with a plethora of arms, equipment and ammunition. Besides his rifle and bayonet, 150 rounds of .303 ammunition and entrenching tool, he carried a pack containing holdall with toilet articles, 'housewife' with spare buttons and needle and thread, cap comforter, mess tin, spare socks, shirt, 'drawers woollen', towel. Over it was strapped his bulky greatcoat and his waterproof cape, which also did duty as groundsheet. In his haversack he stowed knife, fork, spoon, a portion of his rations and any other personal items such as cigarettes or pipe and tobacco — but, theoretically, no diary. The total weight of all this burden amounted to something over 61 lb.

This was marching order: once in the trenches, all but essentials was discarded in the dugouts, and when going 'over the top' the men were in Battle Order, carrying only arms, haversack and waterbottle.

It was recognised that the morale of the soldier could be boosted by contact with his family or girl friend at home, and this was seen to by the Army Postal Service, one of the multifarious branches of the Royal Engineers. There were three types of private communication available to both officers and men. The first, and most common, though severely limited in content, was the printed Field Post Card or, in military officialese, Army Form A2042. On the reverse of the address side it had brief stereotyped messages which could be scored out as appropriate: 'I am quite well'; 'I have been admitted into hospital . . . sick . . . wounded . . . '; 'I have received your letter dated —— '. A prominent note cautioned that if anything were added, the postcard would be destroyed. Soldiers could send as many of these as they could obtain, and postage was free. Ordinary letters (also post free) could be sent, in normal envelopes, but these had to be censored by one of the battalion or unit officers deputed for the task. Those who did not care to reveal confidential personal or family details to their own officers might obtain a 'Green Envelope'. Letters so handed in were not scrutinised by the regimental officers but were subject to spot checks by censor staff at the Field Post Offices.

Recreational facilities were entirely *ad hoc*, regimental affairs. There was no Entertainments National Service Association (ENSA) in the First World War. How often units were withdrawn to 'rest areas' obviously depended on the military situation. A battalion might spend a whole month in the trenches, or a week. In the rest areas the only forms of relaxation were the *extempore* concerts and sing-songs, interspersed with soccer and hockey matches and boxing competitions. But very often troops in the rear areas were subjected to such fatigues as road building and repairing, besides regular drill parades and weapon training.

The most coveted privilege for the soldier was of course home leave, but on active service this could be no more than a privilege, and not a right, as was stressed in regimental and other orders. While officers might expect 'Blighty leave' of seven days or more once in six or seven months, the average soldier was lucky if he saw England once in fifteen to twenty months. Many were even less fortunate: those serving in the farther-flung theatres of the war, such as the Middle East, were unlikely to set foot in Britain until repatriated after the end of hostilities.

As always, soldiers permanently disabled by wounds, or illness attributable to active service, received disability pensions on discharge. If totally disabled and incapable of earning a living, a private or equivalent was entitled to a maximum of 2s 6d a day, or £46 9s p.a.; a sergeant could get a maximum of 3s a day or £56 15s 10d. For partial disablement, e.g. loss of one limb or an eye, the rates were 1s 6d a day for a private and 3s a day for a sergeant. Other ranks' pensions varied in proportion. If these figures seem ungenerous, we must again remind ourselves of the relative monetary values between 1914–18 and the present day. Thus, in 1914 a civilian old-age pensioner whose annual income did not exceed £21, received a weekly pension of 5s, or £13 per year. However, in December 1916 a new Ministry of Pensions came into existence, to take over all pensions responsibilities, both Service and civilian. With its formation came a revision of the rates, and a private soldier totally disabled by wounds now received £71 6s per year. This was a flat rate, applicable to men who had no civilian occupation before enlistment. A graded alternative system was introduced to meet the cases of men who had been earning good wages before the war, and thus a totally disabled soldier who had enjoyed an income of £5 a week on enlistment was now entitled to a pension of 75s a week, or £195 a year.

Prior to the war, the treatment of soldiers' widows was mean: the widow of a warrant officer killed on active service or died of wounds received a pension of £20 a year, with £5 a year for each child 'born in lawful wedlock'. Other ranks' widows got no pension, but a single gratuity amounting to one year's pay which her husband was receiving at the time of his death. There was nothing for children. In 1916 the private soldier's widow was given a pension of £35 a year and there was a sliding scale for children.(14)

The new Ministry of Pensions also accepted responsibility for the after-care and retraining of wounded ex-servicemen. Most amputation cases convalesced at the Pavilion Hospital, Brighton, until such time as their artificial limbs could be fitted. This was done at the special remedial centre at Roehampton, where initial training was given. From Roehampton the limbless soldier (and sailor and airman) could complete training in a wide variety of skills and crafts at the Polytechnic or other technical colleges throughout the country. All expenses were paid by the Ministry.

Mention has already been made of several voluntary and charitable organisations formed around the turn of the century to foster the welfare of ex-servicemen. The Great War saw the burgeoning of several others, probably the best-known of which is now the Royal British Legion. This evolved from the merger of four rival organisations, all of them having strong political ties. The earliest was the National Association of Discharged Sailors and Soldiers formed in Blackburn in 1916 and linked to the Trade Union and Labour movements. The following year saw the creation of the National Federation of Discharged and Demobilised Sailors and Soldiers, which, mooted by Liberal MPs, naturally bore the favour of their Party. Also in 1917 emerged the Comrades of the Great War. Sponsored by Lord Derby and several senior officers, this was just as naturally Conservative in outlook, although purporting to be apolitical and democratic. Shortly after the war a fourth society for officers only was formed, with the title Officers' Association. Finally, after intense rivalry, tending to self-destruction, these four bodies agreed to sink their differences and pool their resources, and the resultant amalgam came into being in May 1921 with the title The British Legion, and F-M. Earl Haig as President.[5] Then as now the priorities of the Legion were the welfare of all ex-servicemen, particularly as regards employment, job training, and pensions. After its first year of existence it claimed 116,000 members who had helped to provide financial assistance to nearly a quarter of a million destitute veterans. Later it established special workshops for disabled servicemen, such as the well-known Poppy Factory at Richmond, Surrey and the Cambrian Tweed Factory at Llanwrtyd Wells in Powys. To the general public the most familiar aspect of the Legion's activities is the annual Poppy Day collection, on which its charitable work chiefly relies.(15)

Among other Service charities which owe their origin to the First World War is the Royal Star & Garter Home for Disabled Sailors, Soldiers and Airmen, which opened its doors in 1916 at Richmond, Surrey. This was established with the generous help of the Chartered

5. Later the Officers' Association, which had received its Royal Charter in 1920, became a separate entity, although working in close relationship with the Legion.

Auctioneers and Estate Agents' Institute and was first sited in the old Star & Garter Hotel, hence the name (the 'Royal' prefix was granted in 1982). Here accommodation and rehabilitation were provided for up to 200 ex-servicemen.

In 1915 the blind newspaper magnate, Arthur Pearson, opened a hostel in Bayswater Road, London, for the care and training of blinded ex-servicemen. Shortly afterwards he acquired larger premises in Regents Park, the name of which has been familiar ever since — St Dunstan's. Arthur Pearson was knighted in 1916, when some 500 war-blinded soldiers, sailors and airmen were being cared for by his organisation. In 1984 the number (including servicewomen) was 1,480.

Another wealthy man, who could afford to be generous, was Sir Oswald Stoll, theatrical impresario and music-hall proprietor, whose name was later to become known to the public through the Stoll chain of cinemas. In 1916 Stoll initiated the War Seal Foundation for disabled officers, which after the war became The Sir Oswald Stoll Foundation, open to all ex-servicemen. Today the Foundation runs a block of 138 flats in Fulham Road, London, where disabled ex-servicemen can live with their families at a nominal rent, receiving free medical treatment and physiotherapy.

The aftermath of the war saw yet more Service charities established. In 1920 The 'Not Forgotten' Association began to organise comforts and amenities, including free holidays, for disabled servicemen, and two years later The Ex-Services Mental Welfare Society was set up to provide therapy for sailors, soldiers and airmen suffering from war neuroses.

The First World War was the bloodiest and most costly that the British Army had ever fought, as the dreadful casualty figures of more than 2½ million killed and wounded will testify.[6] But those years of carnage brought not only victory over an enemy more powerful and more menacing than Louis XIV or Napoleon, but left an enduring legacy to the British soldier. With almost every family in the country contributing its members to the armed forces, the 'Tommy this an' Tommy that' mentality of Kipling's day had given way to one of caring and concern. The soldier was recognised for what he was: an ordinary member of society who happened to wear a uniform, his business to preserve

6. The actual breakdown was as under:
   Killed and die of wounds: 677,515
   Wounded: 1,837,613

freedom. As we have just seen, this metamorphosis created those charities and welfare bodies which were to continue their good works throughout another world war, and which have done so down to the present day.

8

BETWEEN THE WARS

With the completion of demobilisation in 1919 the Regular Army settled down to peacetime routine, although there was still a brief campaign to be fought in Afghanistan, as well as almost continuous warlike operations against the troublesome tribes of India's North-West Frontier. And a new commitment was the provision of 403,600 troops for the garrison of occupied Germany — a force soon to be known as the British Army of the Rhine, or BAOR.

The post-war recruit joined an army not markedly changed from that to which his predecessors had flocked in 1914. His uniform, equipment and arms remained the same, drill and training followed the same patterns. But men with a mechanical or technical bent could now opt for one of the new additions to the Army, the Royal Tank Corps and the Royal Corps of Signals.[1] The old prison-like barracks with their draughty 'dormitories' and exterior iron staircases were unaltered, even if they now boasted electric lighting and separate bath-houses with hot water laid on. It is true some new 'barracks' had mushroomed to cope with wartime expansion, but these were merely wooden-hutted camps, like that of Catterick on the wind-swept moors of North Yorkshire, if anything, less inviting than the old blocks of brick-and-mortar. Officially these were classed as 'temporary', yet the spartan Catterick huts continued to house thousands of soldiers until well after the Second World War.

Nevertheless there were developments and innovations welcome to the soldier. The most significant of these were revised rates of pay for all ranks, authorised in 1922. These are reproduced overleaf.

There were benefits, too, for time-expired soldiers. In 1919 Parliament introduced the Land Settlement Bill under which County Councils were

---

1. The Tank Corps was formed from the Heavy Branch, Machine Gun Corps in 1917; it became 'Royal' in 1923. The Royal Corps of Signals emerged in 1920 as the offspring of the Royal Engineers Signal Service.

Basic Daily Rates of Pay

	s	d
Regimental Sergeant-Major and other Warrant Officers Class I	14	0
Regimental Quartermaster-Sergeant	12	0
Squadron, Battery or Company Sergeant-Major	10	0
Squadron, Battery or Company Quartermaster-Sergeant	8	0
Sergeant	6	0
Corporal or Bombardier	4	0
Lance-Corporal or Lance-Bombardier	3	3
Trooper, Gunner, Private (or equivalent)	2	0
Ditto after 3 years' service	2	6
Boy Bugler, Trumpeter, Drummer	1	6
Other Boys	1	0

empowered to purchase land for the provision of small-holdings up to fifty acres each, preference being given to ex-servicemen as tenants. Rents were minimal, and applicants could be given facilities for credit. In 1923 an Army Vocational Training scheme was launched, in which men due for discharge could undergo an intensive six-months training course in a number of trades at various centres throughout the country. In 1922 the railway companies agreed to grant fare concessions to all soldiers in uniform travelling on leave: they could obtain third-class return tickets for the price of a single ticket.

But the most revolutionary innovation came with the publication of Army Order 254 of 1922, authorising the acceptance of selected serving NCOs as cadets at the Royal Military College, Sandhurst. For the first time, the soldier had an opportunity of becoming an officer through the normal channels, alongside the 'Gentleman Cadets'. A candidate for one of these 'Y' Cadetships as they were termed, had to be at least a lance-corporal of not less than six months standing, in possession of a First Class or Special Certificate of Education, and not over 23 years of age. He was to be a British subject 'and of pure European descent', and naturally, needed to be unreservedly recommended by his commanding officer. 'Y' cadets were exempt from the normal fees, and if passing out successfully after the eighteen-month course they were granted an initial outfit allowance of £100. Thirty-two NCOs were accepted for the first course in September 1922, and twenty-seven were ultimately commissioned. At first the 'Y' cadetship scheme was confined to Sandhurst, for potential officers of cavalry, infantry, Royal Army Service Corps and the Indian Army, but in 1928 'Y' cadets for commissions in the Royal Artillery and Royal Engineers were accepted at the Royal Military Academy, Woolwich. Such candidates needed the Army Special Certificate of Education before being considered. In March 1938 Mr Hore-Belisha, Secretary of State for War, stated in the House that 981 NCOs had been commissioned during the past ten years, and the total number of officers who had risen from the ranks was now 2,090, or about 17 per cent of the total officer strength of the Army.(1)

As seen above, the 'Y' cadet (or his parents) paid nothing for obtaining a commission. The maximum fees for the other cadets at Sandhurst and Woolwich during this period amounted to £200 per year for the son of a serving or retired officer or 'a private gentleman', but there were reductions in special cases. Thus the son of a serving soldier, or one who had died while serving, paid £55. The fee for a General's son was £105.(2)

A post-war novelty was the introduction of a uniform system of numbering soldiers. The practice of identifying soldiers by personal numbers had in fact existed since 1829 when every recruit was given a number on enlistment. But these were strictly regimental numbers. Thus a private in, say, the Royal Scots might have the same number as hundreds of other privates in the rest of the cavalry, infantry and artillery. Moreover, a similar system existed in the Militia and the later Territorials. If a man was transferred from one regiment to another he would have to adopt a new number. This led to much confusion in identifying casualties during and after the First World War, when men were frequently transferred. Confusion was worse confounded when, as often happened, two men with identical numbers also bore the same names. In 1920, therefore, the chaos was resolved by Army Orders 338, 520 and 521, which directed that thenceforth regimental numbers should be abolished and there should be a single numbering system throughout the Service. Thus came into being the familiar 'Army Numbers', which are still with us. Numbers were allotted in blocks to each regiment, and the distinction of receiving the first block, Nos 1–294,000 fell to the Royal Army Service Corps. Just to satisfy their idle curiosity, readers may like to know that the soldier who became distinguished as No. 1 in the British Army was Regimental Sergeant-Major (WO1) George James Redman of the RASC. He had enlisted in the Corps as a 14-year old boy in 1888, and took his discharge in 1920 — only a few months after his number had been bestowed.[2]

Although we are concerned primarily with the soldier rather than with the Army as a whole, we cannot omit mention of the 'Geddes Axe' of 1922. Sir Eric Geddes was appointed by Lloyd George as Chairman of a Committee with the task of achieving cuts of some £86 million in public expenditure. Naturally the Armed Forces suffered with the rest, and the Army's strength was to be pared by 50,000 officers and men. A reduction in manpower was inevitable and expected after a war, but consternation, dismay and wounded pride were aroused when the 'Axe' smote the regiments themselves. In April 1922 Army Order 133 announced that sixteen regiments of the cavalry of the Line would be merged in pairs to form eight new regiments, six Irish infantry regiments were to be disbanded,[3] and five English regiments would each lose two of their four regular battalions. Even the elite Household Cavalry were not spared mutilation: the 1st and 2nd Regiments of Life Guards were to sacrifice two squadrons each and combine to form a single regiment, The Life Guards. Redundant officers of amalgamated cavalry regiments were given the option of transferring to other regiments where vacancies existed, or resigning. Similarly the surplus other ranks could either transfer to other units or be discharged to the reserve.

In the cavalry there was much indignation at the roughshod and insensitive manner in which the Army Council directed the amalgamations. The regiments were not consulted about their choice of partners, nor about their new titles, which not only resulted in what one officer described as 'unsightly vulgar fractions' (e.g. '3rd/6th Dragoon Guards'), but in many cases ruthlessly obliterated former cherished distinctions. The most tactless instance was that of the 5th Dragoon Guards (Princess Charlotte of Wales's) and the Inniskillings (6th Dragoons) who were to 'marry' simply as the '5th/6th Dragoons'. The 5th were as deeply affronted by their loss of Dragoon Guards status as were the 6th by the extinction of 'Inniskilling',

2. For this information I am indebted to Major C.W.P. Coan, Curator of the Regimental Museum of the Royal Corps of Transport (Aldershot), who adds that Redman saw service in the Boer War and the First World War.

3. These were: The Royal Irish Regiment, Royal Irish Fusiliers, Connaught Rangers, Prince of Wales's Leinster Regiment, Royal Munster Fusiliers, Royal Dublin Fusiliers. However in November the same year King George V rescinded the disbandment of the Royal Irish Fusiliers and they continued on the establishment, though with the loss of one battalion. They are now represented by The Royal Irish Rangers.

which they had borne for nearly two hundred years. To the civilian — and some senior staff officers long translated from the underworld of regimental soldiering — such trivia as mere names may seem of little import. But a fierce pride in his regiment — The Regiment — has been the abiding characteristic of the British soldier, whether officer or private, and thoughtless tampering with the distinctions and minutiae that set it apart from the other 'mobs' is bad for morale.

Such however is the resilience and sense of duty of the soldier, that all the partners of the 'shotgun marriages' soon settled down in harmony, and today the 17/21st Lancers are as proud of that title as were the original 17th Lancers (Duke of Cambridge's Own) and 21st Lancers (Empress of India's). It should be mentioned that in 1927 the Army Council were persuaded (with some behind-the-scenes approach to the King) to annul that barren '5th/6th Dragoons' title and substitute the happier '5th Inniskilling Dragoon Guards'. Honour was satisfied, and augmented by the 'Royal' distinction in 1935.

The five disbanded Irish regiments of Foot had always been based in southern Ireland, and with the creation of the Irish Free State in 1922 it was perhaps logical that they should be sacrificed. Their Colours were laid up in St George's Chapel, Windsor, and these, together with their published regimental histories are the only tangible reminders of their centuries of service to the Crown.

It was sad, however, that one of these Regiments should have marred its fine record in the final years of its existence. Mutiny, armed or otherwise, has always been the gravest of military crimes. There had been no serious insurrection in the British Army since 1743 when the Black Watch, believing they had been raised solely for services in Scotland, broke into open revolt when ordered to England and (it was rumoured) overseas. Three privates were later executed.[4]

The Connaught Rangers, raised in 1760, displayed hard-earned Battle Honours gained in India, Egypt, the Peninsula, Crimea, South Africa and the Great War. Based in Connaught (Sligo), its ranks had always been almost exclusively Irish Catholics from the south and west — as they were in June 1920. At that date the 1st Battalion was stationed at Jullundur in the Punjab, with one Company on detachment at the hill-station of Solon in the Himalayan foothills. The Battalion was comman-

4. The 'White Mutiny' of 1858 in India detailed in Chapter 5 is discounted, since the soldiers involved, though British, had enlisted in the East India Company's Army, not the British.

ded by Lieut-Colonel H.R.G. Deacon, DSO, who had been commissioned in the Regiment in 1891. Away in Ireland there was turmoil and bloodshed as Michael Collins's Irish Republican Army carried on a guerrilla campaign against the British forces of law and order. The latter included a special auxiliary body known as the 'Black and Tans' whose policy was to combat outrage with outrage. Their methods evoked criticism in the Press and questions in the House, and when rumours of atrocities reached Jullundur there was alarm and indignation among the men of the Connaught Rangers. Matters came to a head on June 28th when a group of NCOs and privates, led by the inevitable 'barrack-room lawyer', staged a 'sit-in' in the guard-room, in protest at the activities of the Black and Tans. So far no show of force or violence had been offered, and the men merely refused to do duty. They were eventually arrested and confined in an outlying camp under guard. But in Solon itself, the situation took a more serious turn. On June 30th a young private named James Daly marched men of C Company to the Officers' Mess and, in a perfectly respectful manner, informed the Company Commander that they were in sympathy with their arrested comrades and intended to do no duty until the outrages of the Black and Tans had been curbed and British 'oppression' in southern Ireland had ceased. The Captain's warning of the gravity of such action was received in silence; then Daly marched off his followers to their bungalow, over which they hoisted the Irish tricolour. The mutineers were next visited by the Regimental Chaplain, who persuaded them to allow their rifles and ammunition to be collected and secured in the magazine. Surprisingly, they were left in possession of their sidearms (bayonets). Meanwhile, the forty-seven mutineers at Jullundur had been transferred to the military prison at Dagshai, not far from Solon. Private Daly had promised the Chaplain that there would be no more than passive resistance; but during the night rumours began to circulate that the Jullundur rebels had been ruthlessly 'mowed down' by machine guns of an English regiment. These of course, were totally unfounded, but the more fanatical of Daly's men, himself included, were by now only too susceptible to rumour, and they resolved on stronger action.

At midnight on July 1st Daly led twenty-seven of his men, armed with their bayonets, in a reckless attempt to rush the magazine and recover their rifles. After challenging, the guard opened fire, killing two of the attackers and injuring a third. At this, Daly surrendered. The mutiny was over.

The 75 mutineers were tried in three groups at General Courts Martial held at Dagshai over a period of three weeks from August 23rd. The accused were mostly private soldiers, but included several corporals and lance-corporals, and two band-boys. All were from southern Ireland. Fourteen, including the two boys, were acquitted; 52 were awarded prison sentences varying from one year to fifteen years; the remaining nine, Daly among them, were sentenced to death. All sentences were of course subject to confirmation by the Commander-in-Chief, India, General Lord Rawlinson, and on reviewing the evidence he commuted eight of the death sentences to life imprisonment. The exception was Private James Daly, who was duly executed by a firing party from the Royal Fusiliers in Dagshai prison on November 2nd, 1920.

It has been asserted that Daly was the last British soldier to suffer capital punishment for a military offence, in peace or war, but this is not true. In 1946 a private of the RASC was hanged for treacherous conduct on active service. In November 1970 a Parliamentary Question elicited the fact that 51 soldiers had been executed since the beginning of the Second World War, the last sentence being carried out in Malaya in 1953. There were three cases of mutiny, including the one quoted above, the remainder being convictions for murder.(3)

As events turned out, none of the other convicted Connaught Rangers served more than three years' imprisonment. In 1923 all were released under an amnesty agreed upon between the British and Irish Free State governments. And, as a curious piece of Irish logic, all were later awarded pensions by the Dail — based on length of service in the British Army.(4)

The tragedy of the Connaught mutiny is not so much that a misguided 21-year-old soldier destroyed his own life and the lives of two of his comrades, but that he and his fellow-mutineers cast an opprobrious slur on the name of one of the British Army's finest infantry regiments. In all justice to the memory of the Connaught Rangers it must be stressed that only seventy-five out of nearly 900 of the 1st Battalion were involved, while the 2nd Battalion in England and the 3rd and 4th (reserves) in southern Ireland itself remained loyal and completely untainted.

Despite the official Thirty Years Rule, the complete proceedings of the courts martial have not yet been released, and without the evidence presented it is difficult to categorise about the true motives of the mutinous soldiers. For his book, *Mutiny for the Cause*, Pollock interviewed some survivors, among them ex-Private Joseph Hawes, who had been the real instigator. Unlike the executed Daly, and most of the others, this man had joined as a regular soldier in 1914 and had fought throughout the war. Until that June of 1920 his character had been exemplary. According to Pollock he said: 'When I joined the British Army in 1914, they told us we were going out to fight for the liberation of small nations. But when the war was over I found that so far as one small nation was concerned — my own — these were just words.' Other mutineers had more domestic motives for reaction. One told how his home had been burned by the Black and Tans and his aged father had died after being left shelterless on a freezing winter's night. Another's sister had been wantonly shot. These and many more similar stories, some true, some inflated rumour, were sufficient to sow the seeds of mutiny among a naturally volatile race of soldiers whose native land was then in the birth-pangs of independence. All this is not to condone their actions for, whatever the provocation, rebellion in an armed force cannot be tolerated. As already observed, one of the strongest pillars of the British Army has always been its aloofness from any form of political involvement. Strangely, one of the mutineers was no susceptible Irishman, but an English sergeant who had won the DCM during the war. Why he should have thrown in his lot with the others, to ruin his career, cannot be explained. And without the courts martial proceedings one cannot level any charge of slackness against the Battalion commander or his officers, though it is difficult to believe that rumours of impending trouble could not have reached their ears well before the explosion. It is a fact, however, that Colonel Deacon was allowed to remain in command until his regiment was disbanded, two years after the Mutiny.

During the 1920s there was much agitation in the House — chiefly from Labour members — for abolition of capital punishment in the Army, or failing that, its limitation to the gravest offences such as mutiny and treachery. The abolitionists, led by Ernest Thurtle, Labour MP and ex-wartime soldier, urged the substitution of penal servitude as the maximum sentence for certain offences on active service. This was contested by several eminent generals, including Field-Marshal Viscount Allenby who put forward the consensus of military views in Committee in the House of Lords:

> I say most emphatically that in my opinion penal servitude is not a deterrent. It means safety. The only deterrent for the man who will wilfully behave in such a way as to endanger the lives of his own comrades in order to avoid the risk to his own life, is the knowledge that

while his comrades may possibly incur death at the hands of the enemy, which will be a glorious and honourable death, he, if convicted of one of these offences . . . will die a death which is dishonourable and shameful.(5)

Finally in April 1930 a new Bill was passed, and henceforth the only offences for which a British soldier could suffer death were mutiny and treachery.(6) Treachery was defined as 'treacherously holds correspondence with or gives intelligence to the enemy, or treacherously or through cowardice sends a flag of truce to the enemy'.(7) But of course, a soldier was not above the criminal law of the land and could still be hanged for murder.

Although the conception of totally mechanised warfare was as yet merely the dream of such revolutionary military thinkers as Fuller and Liddell Hart, the Army of the post-war years had become increasingly technical and reliant on the machine. Apart from specialists such as the Royal Engineers, Royal Army Ordnance Corps and Royal Corps of Signals, the Royal Tank Corps was established in permanent form. The motor vehicle was rapidly ousting the horse for transport purposes. Wireless communication was still an art peculiar to the Signals, but before long it would supersede the helios and semaphore flags in the non-technical arms. In 1927 an 'Experimental Mechanised Force' of tanks and armoured cars was formed on Salisbury Plain, only to be disbanded after a year, victim of Government defence cuts. In 1928 all dedicated cavalrymen were alarmed when two of the Army's most distinguished regiments, the 11th Hussars and the 12th Lancers, were ordered to give up their horses and take to armoured cars (at least they gained the further distinction of being the first British cavalry to be mechanised).

All this march of technology meant that the Army had to seek recruits capable of learning higher skills than firing a rifle and sticking dummies with sword or bayonet. Since such recruits were not readily forthcoming, in 1924 the War Office instituted a training scheme for boys, initially at Chepstow, Woolwich and Maresfield, later at other centres. Here boy-recruits between the ages of fourteen and fifteen were taught the elements of such Army 'trades' as those of armourers, artificers, electricians, vehicle mechanics, instrument-makers and wireless operators. They were paid 7s per week on joining and could receive 12s 3d per week on reaching the age of eighteen. At this age, like all other boys in the Army, they commenced their 'man service' and were required to serve for twelve years from the same date. By August 1924 more than 700 boy apprentices were in training at the several centres.(8)

Increased attention was given to the general education of the rank-and-file. In 1931 a new *Educational Training* manual was issued, and its preamble contained some enlightened observations, such as the following:

> One of the chief characteristics of modern war is the necessity for decentralising responsibility and for encouraging junior ranks to exercise initiative. Discipline is no less important than it was formerly, but the rigid discipline of the past, which consisted mainly of control imposed on the individual from without, must be reinforced and made elastic by individual self-discipline. The well educated and intelligent soldier who can think and act rightly without constant supervision is essential in a modern army. . . .
>
> Educational training aims primarily at the development of these individual qualities for the purposes of war, but they are equally important in the citizen, and by promoting them in the soldier a valuable contribution to national life will be made. To this end every effort should be made to enable the serving officer and soldier to keep in touch with the activities of civil life.

Further, it was to be borne in mind that improving the soldier's education while serving would give him better prospects of employment on return to civil life.(9)

The four Army Certificates of Education mentioned in Chapter 5, *viz.*, Third, Second, First and Special, were retained, but the syllabus of each was upgraded. In the Third Class the arithmetic paper now included vulgar fractions, elementary geometry and 'some skill in practical measurement' besides applications of the four rules applied to money. Normally the candidate was expected to pass (with a minimum of 50 per cent) before he completed his recruits' training. The Second Class Certificate demanded more advanced mathematics, essay writing and questions on a set book, written and practical map reading and a paper on 'Army and Empire', involving questions on the development of the British Empire from the Elizabethan era down to contemporary times. As an alternative to the mathematics paper, a soldier could offer one of the approved modern languages, European or oriental.

The Second Class Certificate was the obligatory standard for all soldiers, and school attendance was compulsory until it was obtained. Without the Second Class, they were not eligible either for proficiency pay or promotion to corporal. The Certificate was held to be equivalent to the civilian School Certificate, and any soldier in possession of the latter before enlistment was required to qualify only in the map-reading paper to be granted the Second Class.

As previously, there was no compulsion for further study, but a First Class Certificate was essential for promotion to higher ranks beyond sergeant. 'It is most desirable' stressed the Manual, 'that general education should be continued throughout a soldier's Colour service, so that he may prepare himself for further advancement in the army and for his return to civil life.' The syllabus for the First Class embraced the same four subjects as for the Second, with the addition of Geography, but of course the standard was higher. The English paper included grammar as well as set books, both prose and poetry, while the mathematics posed problems with equations, graphical solutions, and construction and properties of areas. Geography demanded knowledge of the earth's land-forms, climate, vegetation, animal life and human occupations and activities in relation to such physical conditions. A candidate for the First Class could sit all four papers at one examination or could take them singly. Once in possession of his First Class Certificate the way was open for a soldier towards the rank of Warrant Officer Class I — or to a 'Y' cadetship at Sandhurst.

The Army Special Certificate was the ultimate in military education. It was accepted as the equivalent of Matriculation by all British Universities except Oxford and Cambridge, and by several professional bodies. The syllabus comprised advanced papers on English grammar and literature, mathematics, map reading, an ancient or modern language, and one optional subject which could be history (ancient or modern), mechanics, physics, physiology, biology, geology, another language, or (with potential Bandmasters in view) theory of music and musical history. Unless a man was studiously inclined, there was no great stimulus to achieve a Special Certificate, for the First Class was the highest standard needed for promotion to Warrant rank, or admission to Sandhurst, but of course a Special enhanced his prospects, and would stand him in good stead on return to civilian status.

Within the regiments educational training was organised thus. Candidates for the 3rd and 2nd Class Certificates were taught by their own suitably qualified NCOs — i.e., those with at least 2nd Class Certificates. Instruction for the First Class and Special Certificates was the responsibility of sergeants of the Army Educational Corps, though in the case of the Special they acted more in an advisory capacity, recommending literature and sources, since they could not be expected to be qualified in all the highly specialised subjects. Since the First and Special were voluntary examinations, all study for them was officially to be done in the man's spare time, usually in the evenings; but the Manual urged Commanding Officers to 'do all in their power' to encourage study, and in practice certain parades or fatigues might be excused.

Statistics for higher education throughout the Army in the 1930s are not forthcoming, but those for the present writer's Battalion of a county regiment serving in India in 1935 might be taken as typical. Out of 860 rank-and-file, 56 men held the First Class Certificate, 28 of these being warrant officers and sergeants. Only two had achieved the Special Certificate: one was a corporal who was commissioned later; the other was an exceptional private soldier who had also passed the Indian Government Higher Standard Urdu Examination and who subsequently transferred to one of the Indian military grass farms with the rank of Conductor (equivalent to Warrant Officer Class I).(10)

In addition to the prescribed educational examinations, all ranks in India could study for the Indian Government language examination in Urdu (*lingua franca* of the Indian Army) and Pashtu (language of the Pathan tribesmen on the N.W. Frontier). Not many soldiers did so, for few had any urge to progress beyond the bastardised '*bazaar bat*' they employed with the Indian menials and shop-keepers, while all such study had to be done in their own time, at their own expense, which involved the engagement of a *munshi* or Indian language teacher. However, there were worthwhile rewards for success in examinations — 100 rupees for the Lower Standard and 200 for the Higher. Candidates for both examinations had to master either the Perso-Arabic or Nagri (Hindi) scripts, and to study set books in the script. In the author's battalion only two soldiers undertook all this effort and expense. One was the private mentioned above and the other was the author himself who had his sights on a commission in the Indian Army.

India was still garrisoned by some 60,000 British troops in addition to those of the Indian Army, and most regular soldiers spent four or more years in 'the Shiny'. Conditions there had not altered greatly since before the 1914–18 war, although new barracks had been built in many of the major stations such as Peshawar, Rawalpindi, Meerut, Delhi and

Secunderabad. And of course all now boasted electric lighting, electric fans (vast improvement on the old punkahs) and proper ablution and sanitary facilities. Despite the ever-present hazards of Frontier 'incidents' or even large-scale operations against the recalcitrant tribesmen, and despite the recurring, distasteful duties 'in aid of the Civil Power' or in other words, quelling communal riots in the cities, the soldier's life was still easier than at home. He was still a 'sahib', still had bearers and other servants to relieve him of much of the chores of kit-cleaning and menial tasks. In the hot weather there were no duties during the sweltering afternoons, while all units that could be spared spent at least a month in the pine-scented coolness of the hill-stations. And of course, Thursday was still sacrosanct as a 'free day'. Moreover, an Indian posting no longer meant separation from his family for the married soldier: all families accompanied the regiment, and were housed in well-appointed married quarters. And some of the wives could afford a luxury undreamed of in England — servants to do the dirty work and fetching and carrying. Most cantonments boasted a cinema where for about eight annas (sixpence) soldiers could lose themselves in the latest offerings from Hollywood.

In the old days a change of station for a regiment in India meant slogging it for sometimes weeks and hundreds of miles, bag-and-baggage and 'followers' lumbering in bullock-carts. Now, organised by the Movement Section of the QMG's Branch, special troop trains carried whole battalions and their families. The khaki-painted military carriages were familiar to British soldiers from the time of the 1914–18 war down to the demise of the Raj in 1947. Accommodation for the troops was a good deal more spartan than that of the 3rd class compartments in which soldiers travelled at home. Each 70-foot carriage was supposed to hold 66 men and all their arms and equipment, in compartments of six men each, connected by a corridor. The 'compartments' were not completely enclosed, merely separated by iron stanchions (so that air would circulate freely), and the facing bench seats had only wooden slats. Arms and equipment were stowed on overhead racks. Officers of course enjoyed the luxury of first-class carriages with all conveniences, while soldiers' families travelled Second Class. Even these compartments were self-contained, with wash-room and toilet, and electric fans. In the hot weather, when the temperature could soar over 100°, large blocks of ice were provided in trays for each compartment. These not only reduced the temperature but came in useful for cooling the infants' milk and mothers' lime-juice (apart from tea, *nimbu pani* was the favoured thirst-quencher). The complete troop train was made up with a kitchen car, so that cooked meals could be served at regular intervals.

Apart from the over-crowding, the ordinary soldier's grouse about troop trains was the seemingly interminable time it took them to travel from A to B. This was because they usually exceeded the weight and length limits for civilian traffic, while they might have to spend hours shunted into sidings to allow such prestigious trains as the 'Bombay Mail' or 'Frontier Express' to thunder past. And there were obligatory halts two or three times a day to allow the men to stretch their legs and eat their meals. A week's journey in a troop train was nothing unusual. Since the train steamed through the night, the men had to 'kip down' as best they could on folding slatted bunks. All this was certainly not luxury travel, but perhaps it was less demanding than a march of say 1,000 miles, with full pack, arms and equipment.(11)

Until well after the Second World War the smart white-painted troopship with blue waist-line and yellow funnel was a familiar sight in Southampton docks, and in the shipping lanes to the Far East. The post-World War I troopers were purpose-built vessels, chartered by the Government and operated by such well-known passenger lines as Bibby and British India. They were capable of carrying up to 1,600 troops with all weapons, ammunition and heavy baggage. Officers, warrant officers and families enjoyed comfortable cabins, but the soldiers who were officially termed '3rd Class Government passengers' were exactly that, for they slept, ate and in bad weather were confined to, the two or three troop-decks below the main deck. On each deck the soldiers were divided into messes of twenty men each who ate their meals, ten a-side of a collapsible deal table, seated on deal benches. All arms and ammunition were centrally stowed in racks on the troop-deck, as were also the rolled hammocks in daytime. At night, hammocks were slung, and the whole deck became a swaying mass of ghostly forms as the ship rolled in a swell. Few soldiers had ever been to sea before embarking in a troopship. A nocturnal dash to the latrines (or 'heads' as the sailors termed them) involved stumbling between swinging hammocks and down seemingly endless, dimly-lit gangways. The ordeal was too much for some afflicted stomachs, and after a stormy night the odour in a troop-deck did not encourage breakfast appetites, while there was much unpleasant cleaning up to be endured by the unfortunate sanitary orderlies.

Although of course the ship's Captain exercised overall authority, the actual responsibility for the troops' discipline and administration was in the hands of a military officer (usually an ageing Lieutenant-Colonel) appointed OC Troops, with his staff of Adjutant, RSM, Medical Officer and Quartermaster.

In the 1930s the voyage to India could take up to three weeks and there was an unvarying routine for each day. It usually went thus:

0600 *hours*	Reveille (Hammocks rolled and stowed. Wash and shave)
0630	Draw rations (Mess orderlies from each deck)
0700	Troops' Breakfast. After which clean up troop decks
0900	Guard mounting
1000	Boat stations
1030	Ship's Inspection (by Captain and OC Troops)
1130	OC Troops' Orderly Room
1230	Troops' Dinners
1600	Draw rations
1700	Troops' Teas
2100	Cocoa and biscuits (or bread-and-jam)
2130	Sling hammocks
2200	Last Post (All troops in hammocks)
2215	Lights Out

The most important item of the routine was Boat Stations, when the whole of the ship's complement of passengers (including families) and men not otherwise on duty or watch, fell in alongside their allotted lifeboats and were inspected by the Master or Chief Officer to ensure that lifejackets were properly adjusted and everyone knew the drill if the order 'Abandon ship' had to be given. The Ship's Inspection, immediately following, was much the same as the weekly CO's Inspection in barracks, all troops parading on their mess-decks with tables and benches scoured, everything polishable polished and spruced, including the soldiers themselves. Unless the OC Troops was unusually 'regimental', there were few other parades save some PT (Physical Training) sessions, or a mile's jogging round and round the boat deck. But the boredom of a long voyage was relieved by the inevitable 'housey-housey' sessions (and the furtive Crown-and-Anchor schools), while regular ships' concerts were organised in the evenings when surprising musical talents might be revealed. Otherwise there was plenty of opportunity to laze on the upper deck when warm climes were reached, and to attempt to gain some 'old sweats' tan'. Sea trooping continued until RAF Transport Command took over in the 1960s; today names such as *Somersetshire*, *Oxfordshire*,

Nevasa, Dilwara, are memories only for grey-haired ex-soldiers who steamed East of Suez in those once-familiar troopships.

Prior to the First World War all soldiers were supposed to wear uniform at all times, even when on leave, though of course officers could and did slip into 'mufti' when not on duty. In 1920, however, the privilege of wearing civilian clothes on leave or when 'walking out' was officially extended to Warrant Officers and senior NCOs. It was left to the discretion of Commanding Officers to grant the same privilege to the lower ranks, provided they were of good character. Oddly enough, there were mixed feelings about such privilege. Some keen soldiers were proud to wear their regimental uniform in the streets, especially the cavalryman with smartly-cut breeches, spurs glinting and jingling on heels. But those who welcomed the privilege — probably the majority — had their enthusiasm tempered when they found they had to pay for their 'civvies' out of their own pockets, and just as with uniform, sartorial standards had to be met. No soldier would be allowed past the guardroom in suiting out of the rag-bag. The wearing of plain clothes was only permissible at home. In India and other overseas stations the soldier still had to appear in uniform at all times, on or off duty. In the Indian hot weather the day-time walking-out dress was shirt-sleeve order, sleeves of the khaki drill shirts neatly rolled to just above the elbow, shorts and puttees for dismounted units, slacks for mounted — and of course topis. After dusk, sleeves were rolled down and all units wore slacks — a precaution against mosquito bites.

The decade preceding the Second World War saw the Army constantly short of the manpower needed to fulfil its role of Imperial gendarmerie. As late as 1937 the strength was reported to be 980 officers and 20,000 soldiers short of establishment: recruits were simply not forthcoming. Apart from the prevailing atmosphere of pacifism fostered by the League of Nations and the anti-military lobbies, there were other more pragmatic factors put forward to account for the reluctance of young men to enlist. Some of these were cogently expressed by Lieut-Colonel A.F. Lambert MC, of the Royal Artillery, in a paper published in the Journal of the Royal United Services Institute for August 1935.

The modern young man, it seemed, was naturally averse to military discipline. Outside his working hours he wanted freedom to come and go as he pleased, but in the Army he had to sacrifice that freedom. The soldier might have leisure time, but except when on leave he was never really off duty and could be summoned at any hour of the twenty-four.

Then there was pay. Fourteen shillings a week, the recruiting sergeant had told him. But he found he got only ten or twelve shillings on pay-day. Often the recruit had not the reasoning power to understand that the deductions were indirectly for his own benefit (perhaps they hadn't been clearly explained), and on his first furlough he might tell his pals that the Army swindled you.

Barrack accommodation was another deterrent to recruiting, lack of privacy and home amenities being the chief criticisms. Admittedly, new barracks were being built to replace the Victorian 'prisons' and temporary wartime huts, but at the same time comfortable modern housing estates were springing up all over the country for the civilian worker, and even the newest barracks could not bear comparison with these. In Victorian times the transference from a back-street slum dwelling to a barrack room was an upward step. The same could not be said of a similar move from a modern Council house to a barrack quarter. Finally, thought Colonel Lambert, terms of service did not encourage recruits. Those who were not bent on a long-service career, knew that after their six or seven years in the Army they would return to civilian life that much older but no better qualified for employment, while the chances were that most of them would spend the greater part of their service life abroad. It was true that the Vocational Training scheme was fully operating, but only a very small proportion of soldiers could take advantage of it. Other military pundits, greater and lesser, expressed their views about the problem. Writing in *The Army Quarterly* for January 1937, Major-General J.F.C. Fuller (armoured warfare proponent) roundly declared that inadequate pay, restrictive conditions and terms of service were the basic deterrents. The private soldier, he claimed, should receive at least one pound a week, free of all deductions: 'this may seem a heavy increase, but when it is considered that many recruits send up to five shillings a week to their parents, after the normal deductions are made, little remains over for themselves.' Like Colonel Lambert, Fuller demanded more freedom for the off-duty soldier. 'Where in civil life is a man compelled to go to church? the negation of true religion. Where is he compelled, once his day's work is ended, to be in his house at a fixed hour or to continue to wear his working garments?' The idea that relaxation in these matters would undermine discipline was archaic: modern soldiers were not the drunken rabbles of a dead military age '— animals to be perpetually caged up'. Turning to terms of service, Fuller advocated that a recruit should initially sign on for three years when, if he found Army life uncongenial, he could be discharged to the Reserve; but if he wished to soldier on he could re-engage for successive periods of three years, up to a maximum of thirty. A more startling suggestion was that long-serving men should be periodically transferred from one arm of the Service to another, Infantry to Tanks, Tanks to Gunners and so on. This would obviate the 'dullness' of unvarying training, year in and year out. 'If this is done, interest will never be lacking and the soldier will be kept mentally young.' As with his views on mechanisation, General Fuller was a man ahead of his time. Although such a radical scheme as inter-arm 'swapping' could never be practicable, others of his far-sighted ideas came to pass within his lifetime.

The Government, no less than the Army Council, was seriously concerned about the recruiting problem, especially as by now there was ominous sabre-rattling by Hitler and his Axis friends. In May 1937 the Secretary of State for War (Duff Cooper) introduced certain reforms designed to make the Army more attractive. Some of these, such as the inclusion of butter instead of margarine in the soldiers' rations, and an increased kit allowance for recruits, seemed only to nibble at the problem; but there were more realistic incentives.

The private soldier's basic rate of pay was now raised from 2s a day to 2s 9d. In addition, he received an extra 6d a day if he passed his Second Class Certificate of Education and qualified as a 2nd Class shot on his musketry course, while after three years' service he was entitled to an increment of 9d a day. Thus the fully-trained soldier could expect a total pay of 4s a day.(12) Messing was improved. Hitherto the Army had provided only three meals a day — breakfast, dinner and tea — but in future the soldier would be given a supper as well (in practice this usually amounted to no more than cocoa and bread-and-jam). Soldiers on leave had been entitled to a ration allowance of 1s 11d over and above their pay: this was now raised to 2s 2d. Cookhouse equipment was to be upgraded and machines for potato-peeling, bread-slicing and other tasks would be provided, relieving the soldier of much of his former 'cookhouse fatigues'. Regimental institutes and reading rooms were to be better furnished with carpets, curtains and more comfortable chairs, to give a homely atmosphere.

The new Army Estimates also allowed for the acceleration of the barrack-building programme. All hutted camps were to be replaced by the latest type of 'Sandhurst' barracks, with full amenities for recreation and sport (but alas, the War intervened before this programme could be implemented). Overseas barracks were not allowed to lag behind. The new barrack complex in Changi (Singapore) with its generous recreation areas, bathing pools, children's schools, was claimed to represent 'the highest standard of living accommodation ever provided by any nation for its military forces stationed in the tropics'.(13) In 1936 an entirely novel design of married families accommodation was erected in St John's Wood, London. Known as 'Jubilee Buildings', the five-storey premises consisted of self-contained flats on civilian lines, accommodating 68 families. Each flat included gas cooker, fitted wardrobes, bathroom, balcony, 'pram garage' and rubbish chutes, besides fitted carpets and furnishing. In the design stage the advice and suggestions of soldiers' wives were freely adopted, and the Jubilee Buildings were held to be a model for future married quarters. The rent for each flat was fixed at seven shillings per week.[5]

Prior to 1938 the marriage allowance for soldiers on the Married Quarters Roll of their units varied from seven shillings to ten shillings per week, according to the man's rate of pay and length of service. The Defence budget now allowed an increase to a flat rate of 17s per week for all married soldiers above the age of twenty-six. In addition, 5s 6d per week was granted for the first child, 3s 6d for the second, and lower rates for any subsequent children.

Until 1938 there were only two classes of Warrant Officers in the Army: In Class I were the Regimental Sergeant-Major or his equivalents (including Bandmasters); Class II included Regimental Quartermaster-Sergeants and Squadron or Company Sergeant-Majors (and equivalent). In October 1938 however, the new rank of Warrant Officer Class III was introduced, to enable selected NCOs of exceptional character and ability to be given command of sub-units such as Troops and Platoons formerly commanded by junior subalterns. Thus came into being the rank of Troop (or Platoon) Sergeant-Major. To be eligible for such promotion the NCO (usually sergeant) had of course to possess his First Class Certificate of Education besides being otherwise qualified. The first batch of some 1,000 senior NCOs were promoted WOs III on October 1st, 1938.

Twenty years of peace had brought the usual apathy towards the Services on the part of the public. 'The danger past and all things

5. The flats (in Queen's Terrace) are adjacent to the barracks of The King's Troop RHA, whose soldiers' families still enjoy their amenities.

righted . . . ' meant that the soldier, if not slighted, once more tended to be forgotten. Not surprising, perhaps, for the Army had always moved in a world of its own, within its own barrack complexes and reserved training areas, and with the increasing privilege of civilian clothes off duty, the man in uniform was rarely seen. The British public still delighted in the ceremonial and panache of such events as Trooping the Colour and the stirring spectacles of the Aldershot Tattoo and the Royal Tournament, but they had little real understanding of, or interest in, the Army as a profession, while as always some sections of the Press, and Left-Wing MPs, were only too ready to decry it, and the money spent on it. In the November 1935 issue of the RUSI Journal a Highland Light Infantry officer complained that the Army did little or nothing to protect its public image, and that adverse comments in the Press and elsewhere usually went unanswered. The typical officer was at heart everything he should be and was genuinely concerned for the care and welfare of his men '— yet sometimes he fails to see the necessity for keeping up the prestige of the soldier as a class.'

In an effort to redress the balance by making the Army more accessible to the public (and thereby stimulating recruiting), in 1937 the Army Council took the unprecedented step of creating a Directorate of Public Relations. Headed by a Brigadier with a selected staff of officers (some ex-journalists), the new organisation was directly responsible to the Secretary of State. Its stated aims were to promote a better mutual understanding between the Army and the public and to present the Service as 'a more attractive profession, well able to stand comparison with the alternative careers open to young men'. But before much headway could be achieved the Second World War intervened, relegating public relations to a low priority. After the War, however, the Directorate, or DPR as it is known, was greatly expanded to include all three Services, with civilian as well as military staffing. Today, under the Ministry of Defence banner, its functions fall into two main categories: keeping the Servicemen themselves informed about relevant developments, and disseminating news stories and other information to the Press and television — not to mention countering shots from sniping media men.

9

1939–1945

As seen in the previous chapter, when the soldier enlisted immediately after the First World War his way of life, his weapons, dress, and the Army itself, were not greatly changed from those of his predecessors in the Boer War. Just twenty years later, when general mobilisation was ordered in August 1939, the Army had undergone a metamorphosis that would have made it virtually unrecognisable to the men of 1914-1918.

The most radical change was seen by the cavalry soldier. After centuries of service the horse, that 'warrior without enmity', had virtually disappeared from the ranks, superseded by the tank and the armoured car. In 1937 all but the Household Cavalry, the Royal Dragoons and the Royal Scots Greys were ordered to mechanise, and in April 1939 the Royal Armoured Corps was formed, consisting of the eighteen mechanised regiments plus the Royal Tank Corps. Since it would have offended against designation to have a Corps within a Corps, the latter was renamed Royal Tank Regiment.

The armoured cavalry soldier of today, with all his technological and mechanical expertise that would have boggled the mind of the horse-soldier, can have no conception of the traumatic impact of mechanisation. Even the Secretary for War (Duff Cooper) when announcing the conversions in the House, apologised for 'the great sacrifice' demanded of the regiments, adding 'it is like asking a great musical performer to throw away his violin and to devote himself in future to the gramophone.' Most recruits had opted for the cavalry because they had a genuine feeling for the horse; many had been country lads, born and bred to the world of livestock; not a few were ex-jockeys or hunt servants. And there was the matter of prestige. Although the infantry had other ideas, the cavalry, descendants of the prestigious regiments of Horse, had always been the aristocrats of the Army, just as the horseman had always been, literally and metaphorically, a cut above the plodding footman. While both officers and men accepted their fate with a loyal sense of duty, conceding that evolution was inevitable, there were sad 'Farewell Mounted Parades' when regiments obeyed the venerable command 'Prepare to dismount: Dismount!' for the last time in two hundred and fifty years or so. Both on and off duty, the horse had been an intrinsic part of the cavalryman's life, almost an extension of his own being. It was not easy for a trooper to transfer any regard to a lifeless mass of metal. However, if mechanisation was a wrench, it brought its compensations. Previously the unremitting demands of horse-management had spelt much extra toil for the mounted soldier; his horse had to be watered, fed, hayed-up, bedded down, mucked out, groomed, exercised, any ailments attended to, day in, day out, for 365 days a year. Even at night, men had to be detailed for stable-picket duty. And while the infantryman might grouse about his kit-cleaning chores, the cavalryman was additionally burdened with saddlery to be cleaned, soaped, polished, not to mention the perpetual humping of straw and fodder. Of course vehicles and their armament demanded attention. The daily maintenance parade replaced the old 'Stables', but in off-duty hours and at weekends tanks and armoured cars could be locked away in hangars and, if not forgotten, at least they did not need attention.

Except for the cavalry regiments mentioned above, and six Yeomanry regiments (all of whom were mechanised by 1942) the Army of 1939 was dependent on petrol rather than on hay and oats for its mobility. The infantry now had their Bren carriers and a variety of 'soft-skinned' transport vehicles from 15 cwt trucks to 3 ton lorries; since 1938 the field gunners had been equipped with the excellent 25-pounder gun-howitzer drawn by a 4 × 4 tractor termed 'Quad' (from 'quadruped', or gun-team horse).[1] All the supporting arms and services were fully mechanised. The infantryman still relied on the veteran .303 in. Lee-Enfield rifle and Vickers Medium Machine Gun (the latter now transported in the tracked carriers), but his close-support firepower was improved by the Bren Light Machine Gun which had replaced the obsolete Lewis gun in 1936, and by the 2 in. and 3 in. mortars which could lob out some thirty projectiles a minute with a well-trained crew. The infantry itself was reorganised into 'rifle battalions' and 'machine-gun battalions'. The former were much as they always had been, but the latter were each armed with 48 Vickers machine guns, the idea being that, like artillery, they would be

1. With their unerring sense of epithet, the soldiers soon dubbed this bulky, bloated-looking vehicle 'pregnant frog'.

allotted to brigades and corps as reserve firepower. In effect, this was a revival of the old Machine Gun Corps of the First World War, although the battalions retained their regimental identities.

There were other novelties. For the first time in history the soldier was given a specifically-designed active service dress. Soon to become familiar as 'Battledress', this was the outcome of trials carried out as early as 1933-34 with a two-piece suit of blouse and trousers and short ankle-puttees for infantrymen. At first the material was Denim, but as might have been foreseen, this was not warm enough for field service in European winters, and so the serge of the existing service dress was substituted. In 1938 the final pattern was authorised for all arms, except the few remaining horsed cavalry regiments. The waist-length blouse, based on the skier's attire, had two patch-pockets on the chest, with one inner pocket, and was buttoned up to the neck for soldiers, the officer's worn open to expose collar and tie. The trousers, buttoned on to the blouse at the waist, were buttoned round the ankles, which were further protected by short puttees, later replaced by canvas gaiters. They were generously fitted with side and hip pockets plus an awkwardly-placed one on the front thigh to contain a field dressing. The original head-dress was a very unmilitary, floppy deerstalker's hat but this was replaced by the 'cap, field service' or sidehat. The mechanised cavalry were allowed to adopt the Tank Corps pattern black beret, worn by the tankmen since 1924.[2]

Although Battledress was acknowledged as a more practical attire than the old Service Dress for the fighting soldier in the field, it came in for much criticism. The traditionalists complained of its sloppy appearance: it was difficult for a man to look smart and soldierlike in such essentially working garb. But more seriously, there was general condemnation of the short blouse, which gave no protection to the most vulnerable part of the anatomy around the loins. If, as frequently happened, buttons flew off at the back, the soldier was left with a chilling gap just where he needed warmth. The khaki sidehat, too, was regarded as an abomination: it afforded no protection against rain or sun, and was apt to fall off in energetic activity. With their genius for descriptive terminology, the soldiers commonly referred to the vulvar-shaped thing by a term which cannot be reproduced here. However, it was only intended for drill and

2. After the war, the Royal Tank Regiment claimed exclusive right to their black beret and the rest of the Royal Armoured Corps adopted dark blue.

walking-out: on active service it was replaced by the steel helmet (except for tank crews who wore the beret). Of course, all articles of clothing were issued free, and these included such items as 'shirts angola drab', 'drawers cellular', 'drawers woollen', 'vests woollen' and 'jerseys, pullover', besides toilet necessities. Among the latter were 'razor, safety' and 'brush, shaving': it was expected that the soldier should appear clean-shaven, even before the enemy (when practicable), although he was permitted to sport a moustache.

With war looming imminent, in May 1939 Parliament introduced a limited form of conscription in an eleventh-hour effort to augment the under-strength Army. Predictably opposed by Labour members, a Bill was passed requiring every man on reaching the age of twenty to register for two years' compulsory service. It was estimated that this would bring in 300,000 recruits during the first twelve months. There were no exemptions on any grounds. It was a tribute to the general health standards of the country's youth that on medical examination 93 per cent of the initial intake were found to be fit for active service. This 'militia scheme' as it was known, soon had to be implemented, through *force majeure*. On 2nd September, 1939 the National Service (Armed Forces) Bill was introduced in Parliament, under which all able-bodied men between the ages of eighteen and forty-one were rendered liable for military service 'for the duration of the hostilities'. By December 1939 the Army's strength was 1,128,000, of whom some 726,000 had been called up since September.(1) Thus, unlike the soldiers at the outbreak of the Great War, who were entirely volunteers, those who confronted the Nazi menace of 1939 were more than 50 per cent conscripts. If the professional soldier may have inclined to look askance at the newly recruited civilian, the hazards of war saw to it that each was soon bonded in a common loyalty to the unit in which they served.

Although inevitably some square pegs found themselves in round holes, the manpower organisation was such that men were channelled into the specific arms and services most suited to their individual aptitudes and skills. The days when the generality of recruits were unskilled, semi-literate labourers or farm-workers were long since passed, and the Army that mobilised in 1939 included a large proportion of skilled tradesmen; electricians, mechanics, engineers, power-tool operators and the like. There was pressing demand for such skills in the specialist arms and services such as the Royal Engineers, Royal Army Ordnance Corps and Royal Corps of Signals. The Second World War saw the establishment of radio communication as the dominant factor in tactical control, not only in armoured units, but throughout the fighting formations and the services. Even the humblest infantry private was expected to be familiar with the jargon of radio traffic and with the elements of operating the portable sets with which his platoon was equipped. In higher formations there was ever-increasing demand for Royal Signals specialists, both for communication, and for repair and maintenance of sets. In 1939 the Corps' strength was 34,000 all ranks; by the end of the war it had risen to more than 154,000.

Mechanisation and the widespread use of highly complex equipment and weaponry created the need for an entirely new specialist corps. In the pre-war years individual units were usually capable of dealing with the repair and maintenance of their own vehicles and equipment, but by 1942 it became clear that the tasks of recovery, repair and maintenance in the field had surpassed the potentials of non-technical unit personnel, and in May of that year the specialist corps of Royal Electrical and Mechanical Engineers was formed. Its highly-skilled Craftsmen personnel were not only responsible for the recovery of damaged fighting vehicles from the battlefield and their repair in field work-shops, but attended to problems with guns, small arms and the wide diversity of electronic and optical instruments, even medical and dental equipment.

The soldier in the non-technical fighting arms may not have been a specialist, but the variety of skills required of him far outstripped those of his previous generation. Take the tank crew: if the driver were knocked out, one of his comrades must immediately take over, and the same applied to the gunner, the loader-radio operator, not to mention the tank commander himself. All were interdependent; all had to know the other's job and all had to be able to maintain the vehicle in the field and carry out minor running repairs. Anything beyond their skills was seen to by the Light Aid Detachments of the REME who accompanied each armoured regiment in the battle zone. If much was demanded of a young soldier in his combat duties, so his other responsibilities had increased. It was not unusual for a 22-year-old corporal with perhaps four years' service to find himself in command of a fighting vehicle with all its armament, equipment and ammunition worth about £80,000. In the old days his command might have been limited to a section of eight soldiers with rifles.

During the first couple of years of war men on enlistment were posted direct to arms and services as required, though they were allowed to express a choice. In 1942, however, the General Service Corps was formed, to which all recruits (and newly-commissioned officers) were initially posted. Here they underwent tests to determine their individual aptitudes and skills, and were then directed to the most suitable arm or service.

Hitherto the infantryman had used his feet to get himself to the battlefield. Now he could be dropped out of the sky. The formation of the Parachute Regiment in 1942[3] created a new élite infantry which demanded men of high moral and physical calibre. Even more exacting were the standards required of officers and soldiers of the Special Air Service Regiment which had been formed as an *ad hoc*, almost private army, by Colonel David Stirling in 1942. This highly select force of two British regiments had grown into a Brigade by 1944 with the addition of French and Belgian units. There was never any shortage of volunteers for the Paras or the SAS, but the standards were such that no more than thirty per cent ever made the grade. Airborne infantry were also carried into action in towed gliders, which could be an even more hazardous way of making contact with a landing zone than floating gently down by parachute. By May 1943 two complete Airborne Divisions were ready for action, and as is well known, the 1st Airborne suffered severely in their heroic stand at Arnhem.[4]

Not all those who wore uniform were combatant soldiers. During the War some 60,000 young men claimed exemption from military service on religious or moral grounds. The tribunals granted unconditional exemption to 3,500 of these; 29,000 were put to work in agriculture, 12,500 had their claims dismissed, and 15,000 were conscripted in the specially-formed Non-Combatant Corps.(2) The combatant soldier understandably regarded all 'conchies' as contemptible shirkers, if not cowards: whether their pacifist/religious scruples were genuine or not, they were happy to let others defend their freedom and way of life. Many of the conscientious objectors, such as Quakers and Jehovah's Witnesses, were genuine in their religious beliefs: others had less high-minded 'conscientious' motives for avoiding military service. In 1943 one

3. The first battalion of parachutists was raised on Churchill's orders in June 1940. Three more battalions were raised subsequently, and the four were regimented as The Parachute Regiment in August 1942.
4. Commanded by Major-General Urquhart, the 1st Airborne Division comprised two Parachute Brigades, one Airlanding Brigade (glider-borne) and a Polish Parachute Brigade.

Michael Tippett, music teacher and budding composer, had his claim for unconditional exemption dismissed by a tribunal who ordered him to do full-time work in the ARP, or the Fire Service, or on the land. He refused, and was sent to Wormwood Scrubs prison for three months. On the other hand, the 26-year-old Benjamin Britten was granted total exemption, and thereupon betook himself to the United States.

Meanwhile, in 1940 the Non-Combatant Corps had been formed specifically for those objectors who refused to bear arms but were willing to perform non-combatant duties, either at home or overseas. Some 6,700 men were immediately enlisted in the Corps. They were given normal battledress uniform and a simple badge (merely the letters NCC), and underwent basic training in drill (without arms), passive air defence, anti-gas measures, and other non-combatant tasks. There were no promotion prospects for the NCC ranks: officers and NCOs were attached to the companies from the (combatant) Pioneer Corps, but in 1941 deserving men could be appointed 'Section Leaders' equivalent to lance-corporal, though without any increase of pay.

Throughout the war the NCC were employed on multifarious duties of non-offensive nature, from the building and maintenance of hospitals, barracks and roads, to quarrying, timber-felling, filling-in of trenches and care of burial grounds. Some, however, volunteered for more hazardous duties. During the Blitz of 1940-41 many companies were engaged in rescue work in Bristol, Coventry, Liverpool and London, while later on 162 NCC men voluntarily transferred to the Parachute Field Ambulance as medical orderlies, and were among the first to be dropped in France on D-Day. The fighting soldier may have had a healthy contempt for the conscientious objector; but, if not prepared to take the lives of others, many of the Non-Combatant Corps were willing to face danger and hardship, and if necessary, to risk their own lives.(3)

The Army of the Second World War was more democratic than it had ever been in respect of commissioned ranks. Its huge expansion demanded a corresponding expansion in the officer corps (more than 200,000 men received commissions during the six years of war), and the net was spread wide. The normal method of officer entry from Woolwich and Sandhurst was abolished. These two establishments closed for the duration and in their place were formed thirty-five Officer Cadet Training Units, catering for all the arms and services. All candidates for commissions were now selected from the ranks, so that any soldier of promising potential had an opportunity of becoming an officer. The initial selection was in the hands of Commanding Officers who, if satisfied that an applicant was a proficient soldier of adequate education and likely 'officer material', recommended him to an interview board. If he passed this hurdle, the man was duly appointed Officer Cadet at one of the OCTUs. There was no form of entrance examination or other test, and the intensive course of training at the OCTU, lasting on average about six months, was entirely free, the cadets dropping whatever rank they had held in their units and receiving a flat rate of pay.

The method of selection of OCTU cadets soon aroused contention. Many Commanding Officers complained of the poor quality of their newly-commissioned subalterns who were not up to the standards of the old Woolwich or Sandhurst cadets. The selection merely by recommendation and brief interview, by boards whose members were co-opted for the day, was also criticised, while predictably, some sections of the Press, and left-wing MPs, alleged that an applicant's social class and background exerted more influence on the interview boards than any fundamental military qualities he might possess.

In the face of the growing criticism the Army Council introduced an entirely new system with the establishment, in 1942, of War Office Selection Boards. These were staffed by permanent members, including officers and civilians (and a psychiatrist), and imposed in-depth interviews lasting three days, with personality, initiative and intelligence tests. An accepted candidate was then sent on a pre-OCTU course of up to six weeks, in which there were more searching tests of character and leadership potential. This weeded out any not up to standard, who were returned to their units. Successful candidates were passed to the OCTUs proper, where they underwent further training, which varied in length from seventeen weeks for the infantry cadets to thirty weeks for those aspiring to the Royal Engineers and other technical corps. On passing out, the cadet was promptly gazetted 2nd Lieutenant and posted to his unit.

With the extension of the catchment area for officers, there was a significant decrease in what was once termed the 'officer class', or the Public School youth. In 1939 it was estimated that some 84 per cent of Sandhurst cadets were of this category. By 1946 the proportion had sunk to 15 per cent.(4) The writer himself was training at an OCTU in 1940, and out of the thirty cadets in his Troop no more than eight were products of public schools. But whatever their social class, all wartime officers had served in the ranks.

Between 1939 and 1945 the British Army lost 144,000 all ranks killed or died of wounds, while 239,500 were wounded and survived. These figures may seem tragic enough, but they represent only about one-fifth of the First World War casualties. While there were many factors accounting for the decrease, two were paramount — the greatly improved methods of casualty evacuation and the medical care of wounded and sick. Despite the highly mobile nature of the warfare, as in the Western Desert, and in Europe after D-Day, casualty clearance and evacuation was speeded up by the use of all forms of mechanical transport, from Bren carrier and Jeep to motor ambulance and aircraft. Air evacuation was a novel feature, limited at first by shortage of aircraft. But with the co-operation of the RAF an efficient organisation was developed, which in difficult terrain such as Burma, resulted in casualties reaching base hospitals within a few hours over distances which would have involved days or even weeks of painful transport by normal methods. Official statistics show that during the fighting in South-East Asia in 1944 and 1945 more than 178,000 wounded were speedily evacuated to India by air.(5)

Until the twentieth century, active service usually saw more soldiers incapacitated through disease than through enemy action. In the Boer War, for example, some 8,000 British soldiers were killed in action while about 14,000 succumbed to sickness. Despite the fact that in the Second World War troops fought and subsisted for long periods in fever-infested regions of the South-East Asia theatre, the more advanced medical precautions and therapy kept mortality to a minimum. Deaths from the two tropical scourges, malaria and dysentery were only .05 and .07 per thousand respectively; in 1945 both had sunk to .01.(6) Anti-malaria measures were strictly enforced and regimental officers were held responsible: 'It is they who see that the daily dose of mepacrine is taken, that shorts are never worn, that shirts are put on and sleeves turned down before sunset...'(7) The drug mepacrine (a form of atebrin) had superseded quinine as a more effective suppressive, but many soldiers were averse to taking it: a jaundiced yellow hue of the skin was one of the side effects, and somehow the totally unfounded rumour got around that it rendered men impotent. In Burma, General Slim was insistent that his 14th Army commanding officers should be personally responsible for seeing that no man evaded his mepacrine tablets. He even went so far as to sack three COs who had defaulted in this respect. But, as the official history makes clear, the strict anti-malaria discipline was a paramount factor in maintaining fighting fitness. 'One important reason why the Allies were able to defeat the Japanese was that they were able to hold the malaria parasite in check, while the Japanese were not.'(8)

Compared with the First World War, the Second saw increased attention to the general welfare of the troops. In 1941 the War Office published a booklet entitled *The Soldier's Welfare. Notes for Officers* (a second edition appeared in 1943). The Foreword contained some pertinent observations and comments which reveal the enlightened attitudes of authority. The following are extracts:

> An officer cannot provide properly for his men's welfare unless he first knows and understands them as human beings. It is his job to learn to know and understand them in this way, as without such knowledge the best welfare intentions are of no avail.... The care of his men is an officer's duty which he puts before his own comfort....'Care of men', properly understood, is opposed to any form of pampering; on the contrary it fosters self-reliance.
>
> Discontent seldom arises from hardship, provided that the men feel the hardship is reasonable, i.e., that it is a necessary part of the business of winning the war. They are ready to endure cheerfully anything which they believe to be unavoidable, but they are easily disgruntled if they feel that the hardships are caused by red tape or by inefficiency. . . .
>
> Every man is entitled to be treated as a reasonable human being, unless he has shown himself unworthy of such treatment. Whenever possible, therefore, the reason for irksome orders or restrictions should be explained to him, and in most matters affecting his own welfare the man's point of view should be obtained and considered.

With the onset of Luftwaffe raids over Britain, the fighting soldier overseas was afflicted with an anxiety not experienced in any previous war — the safety of his family at home. This was recognised by the authorities, and the above pamphlet devoted an entire Appendix to 'Soldiers' Air Raid Problems'. Apart from the normal means of communication from relatives or friends, a soldier worried about his family after air raids could ('with the help of his officer') seek information by reply-paid telegram to the civil authorities or to the Soldiers' Sailors' and Airmens' Families Association. Should his wife, children or parents have been killed or seriously injured, or his house destroyed, he could be granted compassionate leave, 'provided the military situation permits'. Like all civilians, the soldier was entitled to claim compensation for air-raid damage: if a householder, he could get £200 plus £100 for wife and £25 for each child under sixteen. If not a householder the limits were £50, £50 for wife and £25 per child. In 1943 an organisation known as The Services Air Raid Enquiry Scheme was set up to alleviate the soldier's air-raid worries by relaying prompt information about damage and casualties, assisting him to obtain compassionate leave, and arranging for any necessary advances of pay and ration allowances.

Normally soldiers serving in overseas theatres of war were not granted home leave until September 1944, and then only from the European theatre. It was obviously impracticable to transport leave men back and forth from such far-flung battle zones as Burma, even if the military situation allowed it.

The official troops' welfare organisation provided entertainment in rest areas at home and overseas, and included cinema shows and live concert parties. In 1940 the latter were organised as the body which became familiar as ENSA (Entertainments National Service Association) which functioned under the auspices of NAAFI. Including professional music hall entertainers, vocalists, jazz bands and mobile cinema crews, ENSA's activities were at first confined to the UK, but later its artists travelled far and wide. In 1944 the soldiers in Burma were able to applaud their own 'Forces' Sweetheart', Vera Lynn, while such top-rating favourites as Gracie Fields, George Formby and Tommy Trinder were also to be seen in the field. After D-Day ENSA had 4,000 artists on its rolls, and in a single month put on 13,500 stage shows and 20,000 films.(9)

No such forms of relaxation had been available to the soldiers of 'the Kaiser's War', who had to improvise their own entertainment when practicable. But whereas they wallowed in nostalgic songs such as 'Tipperary' and 'There's a Long Long Trail A-Winding', the men of the Second World War remained virtually mute — perhaps because they did less foot-slogging. In an effort to boost morale (if not musical talent), in 1942 General Auchinleck, C-in-C Middle East, offered a cash prize for anyone who could produce a song which would be to the Eighth Army what 'Tipperary' was to the Old Contemptibles. The entries were minimal, and no classic emerged. Instead, and to the initial disapproval of Authority, the soldiers seized upon an amorous German ditty picked up from Rommel's Afrika Korps. Its name was 'Lilli Marlene', and ironically it became almost the *leitmotif* of the British Army for the rest of the war.[5]

The official *Soldier's Welfare* pamphlet quoted above stressed the importance of pay and allowances as an adjunct to morale, and urged that every effort should be made to issue pay as promptly as possible in the field. By 1944 the basic pay of the private soldier had been increased to 4s a day, which rose to 4s 9d after three years' service; a corporal received 6s, a sergeant 7s, and a Warrant Officer 13s (these are exclusive of any additional pay for tradesmen and specialists). A married soldier was entitled to Family Allowance, amounting to £1 1s 6d for his wife plus 12s 6d per week for each child. These sums were paid direct to the wife.

Prior to 1944 a soldier discharged from the Army or transferred to the Reserve received a cash allowance for the purchase of civilian clothes, but in that year the allowance was abolished and actual clothing was issued in lieu. This was the origin of the familiar (or notorious) 'demob suits' handed out to all ex-servicemen discharged after the war. The man could opt for a single or double-breasted suit, in blue, grey or brown, or sports jacket and flannels, or hacking jacket and flannels. For raincoat he could also choose between the single or double-breasted style or the trenchcoat type. The issue was completed with one pair of shoes (black or brown), a hat, one shirt with two collars, two pairs of socks, tie, and even studs and cuff links. As the order ran, this free issue was approved 'in order to ensure that the discharged soldier is adequately clothed for his return to civilian life.'

The subjects of discipline and morale (the two are interdependent) have been extensively dealt with in several post-war works by soldier-writers and psychiatrists.(10) Figures published after the war showed that of all offences committed by British soldiers, by far the most prevalent was that of desertion, which meant an absence without leave extending beyond 21 days. The annual rate of desertion rose from 6,889 in 1940 to a peak of 20,248 in 1941 and then declined slightly to 17,663 in 1944-45.(11) The death penalty for desertion on active service had been abolished by Parliament in 1930, though not without strong opposition by the military authorities. During the war there was a revival of feeling, both among senior staff officers and regimental commanders, who were of the opinion that a soldier who ran away and deserted his comrades in

5. 'Lilli Marlene' was first heard in a Hamburg nightclub in 1938. Its lilting tune and mawkish words immediately caught on with the German troops.

action forfeited humane consideration and should suffer the extreme penalty. General Sir David Fraser:

> It was by no means difficult for a man to disappear before an operation, leaving his comrades to suffer proportionately greater losses; and where the choice lay only between the risk of death or mutilation on the battlefield and the security of a prison cell for a period... it was too easy to choose the latter. In other words it was contended by the fighting soldiers that the absence of the death penalty for desertion in the face of the enemy placed an intolerable burden on men's courage and determination by removing any comparable fear of the consequences of failure. To those who argued against the death penalty . . . they countered, bitterly, that the bullets of the enemy had no mercy on those who did not choose to abandon the field.(12)

In May 1942 General Auchinleck was so concerned about the incidence of desertion that he cabled the War Office urging the immediate reintroduction of the death penalty. The authorities refused, their contention being that it would antagonise public opinion. In the First World War desertion in the field was branded as cowardice, or in the words of the *Manual of Military Law* 'an unsoldierlike regard for his personal safety in the presence of the enemy'. With the advent of the psychiatrist and the general softening of penal attitudes, there arose the view that the soldier who cracked under stress was a case for psychiatric investigation and medical treatment.

It was recognised, both by psychiatrists and medical officers, that in many instances the soldier who 'disappeared' from the battlefield was not deliberately deserting his comrades but had suffered a complete nervous breakdown. As Colonel R. H. Ahrenfeldt observed in the official history, *Medical Services in War*,

> In the light of experience in the Second World War it is certain that modern mechanised warfare imposes on the individual a strain so great that men involved in active fighting, however basically stable they may be, will ultimately break down, in direct relation to the intensity and duration of their exposure to the stress of battle.... thus psychiatric casualties of the type described as 'campaign exhaustion' are as inevitable as gunshot and shrapnel wounds in modern warfare.

Similar views had been expressed in the First World War (see Chap. 7), but the problem had been forgotten in the intervening years of peace.

Ahrenfeldt records that between 1939 and 1945 such psychiatric casualties amounted on average to some ten per cent of total battle casualties. There was now a proper organisation for military rehabilitation of genuine psychiatric cases. Those needing skilled treatment were evacuated to special hospitals run by the Emergency Medical Services in the UK. Ahrenfeldt reveals that as a result of this organisation some sixty per cent of neurosis cases who would otherwise have been unfit for further service were enabled to be retained in the Army.

For deserters not judged to be suffering from neurosis, discipline had to prevail. In the First World War they would have been liable to the death penalty. Now penal servitude was the punishment on conviction. Officially the maximum sentence was three years, but few men actually served this term: six months was the average.

Field Punishment for offences less serious than desertion was still in force, as specified in the Army Act. But the former practice of pinioning the offender to a gun or carriage wheel had been abolished by the 1923 Act, and he was now merely to be secured, by handcuffs or straps, to prevent his escape. 'He may be subjected to the like labour, employment and restraint, and dealt with in like manner as if he were under sentence of imprisonment with hard labour.' A Field Court Martial could award up to three months' Field Punishment, a commanding officer, 28 days'. When the prisoner's unit was actually on the move, he had to march with it and carry out all his normal military duties: the punishment sentence was to be continued whenever the stituation allowed.

The soldier's strong 'tribal' loyalty to his regiment, on which we have already had occasion to dwell, is vividly illustrated by an incident in September 1943 in the Mediterranean theatre, which became known as 'the Salerno Mutiny', the most serious — and controversial — incident of its kind during the whole War. The Allied landing at Salerno, southern Italy, met with heavy German opposition and General Alexander wired to Cairo for 1500 infantry reinforcements from the Eighth Army in North Africa. After these arrived at the Salerno beachhead, General McCreery, Corps Commander, was shocked to learn that 700 of the soldiers had staged a 'sit-down' and were refusing to move up to the front-line units. Immediately visiting them, he found their main complaint was that they had been promised they would be rejoining their own units, but at the last minute, without explanation, had been switched to other units in the Fifth Army. He warned them of the gravity of wilful disobedience of military orders, and assured them that just as soon as the situation allowed they would be posted back to their own units. If the men retracted and obeyed orders, he promised that the incident would be forgotten, without prejudice to any. His words had some effect: 508 of the mutineers responded and were moved up to the battle zone. But the remaining 192 stubbornly resisted. They were accordingly placed under arrest and confined in a prisoner-of-war cage next to German captives, who, learning the trouble, jeered at them as cowards. They were then shipped back to North Africa and tried by court martial at Constantine, Algeria. All but one were convicted of mutiny. The private soldiers were sentenced to seven years' penal servitude, the corporals to ten years. The only three sergeants among them received the death penalty. Then it was announced that all sentences would be suspended on condition that the men would continue to soldier with no further trouble and fight on with whatever unit they were sent to. This they did, although a few subsequently deserted, were picked up, and served prison sentences in England.

On learning of the mutiny, Field-Marshal Montgomery said that although the mutineers' action was quite inexcusable and could not be condoned in any way, 'where soldiers get into trouble of this nature, it is nearly always the fault of some officer who has failed in his duty.'(13)

Although the official documents, including the court martial proceedings, are still unreleased, in February 1982 the BBC transmitted a television documentary on the incident, which included interviews with surviving ex-mutineers and certain of the officers involved.[6] From these and other unofficial sources(14) certain facts emerge. First, the convicted soldiers were not cowards or shirkers. All of them had fought valiantly throughout the North African campaign with fine regiments such as The Cameronians, Argyll and Sutherland Highlanders, The Black Watch, Gordon Highlanders. All were imbued with that fierce 'tribal' spirit, loyalty to their units and their comrades, and a justifiable pride in belonging to their 51st Highland Division. Lieut-Colonel T. F. Main, Montgomery's chief psychiatrist, stated in the BBC programme, 'It's difficult to explain today the intensity of the family loyalties that existed in these units at that time. They were the only people in the world and the rest of the world were rubbish.' Major-General Douglas Wimberley, commanding the 51st Division, often told his men that if wounded and

6. *Mutiny* ('Forty Minutes' Series) BBC2, February 25th, 1982. An article, 'Mutiny at Salerno', by the Producer, Alan Patient, appeared in *The Listener* for the same date.

sent back to base, they should do all they could to rejoin the 51st when fit.

There was unfortunate staff bungling from the first. The reinforcements were to be sent from Philippeville in Algeria, but the orders, and the ships, turned up in Tripoli, some 450 miles away, where the troops were expecting to be posted back to their units in the Eighth Army. Not until the draft was well at sea did a curt ship's tannoy announcement reveal that they were being posted to strange units and strange divisions in Italy.

When the mutineers were confined at the beachhead, it was curious misjudgement to place them in immediate proximity to German prisoners-of-war, from whom they were subjected to insults and catcalls. The three sergeants sentenced to death were first told that there was no recommendation to mercy. Only several days later was it revealed that their sentences were suspended on the same conditions as the rest. On the troopship returning the men to Italy, they were segregated in a separate mess deck and again had to endure insulting remarks from the other troops.

The great majority of the mutineers went on to fight bravely with their new units and were pardoned in 1944. There was never any suggestion that these men were cowards, seeking to evade their duty as fighting soldiers. It was claimed that their action was motivated solely by the regimental loyalty that has always been the virtue of the British soldier. However, it must be added that General McCreery later told the historian, Hugh Pond, that prior to the mutiny a decision had been taken by the Second Front planners to return the 51st Highland Division and other Eighth Army units to England, to reorganise and train for the Normandy landings. Slack security allowed rumours of this move to filter down to the troops, and after three years' fighting in the desert, the prospect of seeing 'Blighty' again prompted them to do their utmost to remain with their units, rather than be drafted to some others for retention in the Mediterranean theatre. If this is true, there was no mention by officers or soldiers interviewed in the BBC documentary, nor is there in the other literature.

Obedience to orders is fundamental to military discipline. Unlike his civilian counterpart, a soldier who goes 'on strike' commits a crime, and must suffer the consequences. There can be no denying that whatever their motives, the Salerno mutineers committed a crime. But equally it must be admitted that the Army's principle of good 'man-management' was sadly disregarded. Writing in 1968 Colonel Ahrenfeldt summed up the Salerno incident thus:

> There was, on the part of the local military authorities at the time, a total disregard... of those well-established group loyalties in attempting to draft these men as reinforcements to other divisions, in the complete absence of any clear direction, precise information or firm leadership throughout... The effect of these serious errors in man-management and leadership was a gradual disintegration, first of carefully built-up and well tried group morale, and then of individual morale.(15)

The British soldier can endure the slings and arrows of his profession with fortitude and stoicism, but one thing that gets him down is bad man-management, or, as he terms it, being 'buggered about' for no apparent reason. When this happens, trouble can start.

The other side of the picture can be seen in some illuminating remarks from the Chief Military Censor in a report of October 1942:

> The fact that General Montgomery, GOC-in-C Eighth Army, took the whole Army into his confidence, right down to the last man, and stated exactly what he hoped to do and how he was going to do it.... brought the spirit of the troops to a new high level and intensified their assurance and grim determination, which was to be fully tested and proved to the hilt in the historic days which followed.... No Army ever went into battle with higher morale.(16)

10

THE PROFESSIONALS

The radical reforms that have taken place in the British Army and its soldiers' way of life in the decades following the Second World War would be sufficient to fill a book — and in fact, have done so. Henry Stanhope's masterly study, *The Soldiers. An Anatomy of the British Army* (Hamish Hamilton, 1979) deals in depth with this transformation. In this concluding chapter only an outline is possible.

When the War ended in August 1945 the Army boasted a strength of 2,900,000 all ranks. By 1984 the figure had dwindled to 164,212. The demolition of the Empire with its demand for thousands of troops to garrison far-flung possessions, and the constant slashing of the Defence budget resulted in the small, highly mobile amd multi-skilled Army of today, in which virtually every soldier is a specialist. 'Join the Professionals', says the recruiting publicity. The bewildering variety of skills which the modern soldier has to master means that he no longer spends hours 'square-bashing' on the parade ground (at least, not after he has completed his basic recruits' training), nor is his spare time taken up with the chores of blancoing and polishing. Anodised buttons and badges stay bright without manual labour. In many respects he has become almost a civilian in uniform. Often he may live out of barracks and drive to work in his own car. If in barracks ('modular suites' in the current terminology), he will usually share a centrally-heated, adequately furnished room with three of his mates, instead of the old cheerless barrack room for thirty or more. His pay is now termed 'salary', and is commensurate with what he might earn on the shop floor. And like the civilian, he pays for his board and lodging, though less than the average worker would have to find, while most of his clothing is free. Facilities for recreation are beyond the scope of most civilian youths. Apart from the usual organised sports of football, cricket, hockey, the soldier is now encouraged to indulge in mountaineering, ski-ing, hang-gliding, orienteering, riding, while Adventure Training sees him join expeditions to remote parts of the world. In 1976 two NCOs of the SAS reached the summit of Everest in a joint British-Nepalese Army assault. In 1969 a platoon of The Queen's Own Highlanders drove by Land-Rover from Edinburgh to the Persian Gulf, and in 1984 eight soldiers of The Royal Green Jackets retraced (on foot) the 300-mile route of Sir John Moore's historic withdrawal to Corunna.

No army can function without discipline, and this is still an essential part of the machinery. No doubt a more relaxed relationship between officers and other ranks subsists in extra-mural activities such as 'adventure training', though even today the soldier and officer on duty are not on first-name terms, and parade-ground protocol has remained traditionally strict. But with better educated, intelligent soldiers, discipline is now based more on understanding than on blind obedience to orders. As a recruiting pamphlet puts it: 'It's all designed to help you work as an efficient member of a team. When you're relying on your mates, and they're relying on you, there's no room for slackness or sloppiness. If you're not prepared to accept the rules, you're better off where you are.'

The transformation into the 'Professional' Army was gradual. What some regarded as a setback was the introduction of National Service in 1949, whereby all youths of eighteen were called up for eighteen months' service, later extended to two years. Many of the conscripts were unenthusiastic recruits who viewed their compulsory term in the Forces as a sheer waste of time, resenting the interruption in their civilian studies or careers. They had no will to become soldiers, good or otherwise. There were of course exceptions who went on to achieve Regular status and senior rank. One young man called up in 1959 underwent a change of outlook, was commissioned, and by 1981 was commanding the same Regiment of Dragoon Guards that had trained him when a bolshie recruit.

For the Regular Army, National Service meant recurring floods of reluctant youths on its doorstep every fortnight, twenty-three times a year, all to be documented, kitted, drilled and transformed into something resembling soldiers. In 1958 there were 170,000 conscripts in the Army, compared with only 70,000 Regulars. The regiments themselves were hard-pressed to cope with all the time and effort spent on training men who, by the time they were reasonably efficient, would depart back to civilian life.

The contrasting attitudes of National Servicemen themselves are revealed in the following recollections.(1)

I did not think. I came in, was more broken by basic training than made a man of by it, and thereafter settled into a sullen policy of minimal contribution for the remainder of my service. I resolved to myself that I would accept no rank other than the honest one of private. I even had some misgivings about taking an extra three shillings a week for having passed a trade test....

It was a good training.... it taught me always to be smartly dressed, not only when the occasion arises, but always to keep myself in a decent manner. Basic training taught me, apart from the whole of my service, to respect other human beings. Just because a bloke's got two stripes, and he's a bit nasty, doesn't mean he's always nasty; more than likely he's doing it for my own good, he's got his job to do. Drill instructors and officers get people out of civilian life without the slightest conception of what a military force is about, and they have to try and turn them into professional soldiers.... they have a really hard job.

The above are extremes. Perhaps the norm is that remembered by a retired General who was commanding a squadron of Hussars in 1958: 'I think I said goodbye to every NS man who served in my Squadron as he left the Regiment. Almost without exception, each said: "I'm glad to go, Sir, but I'm very glad I came." One can't say fairer than that.'(2)

National Service was abolished in 1963, when some 1,132,000 young men had been introduced to the realities of service life. Many had fought valiantly in Malaya, Korea, Kenya and elsewhere: some had not returned. Most were the better, morally and physically, for their experience.

The subject of pay naturally looms large in the soldier's priorities, though never so large as among some sections of the civilian workforce. During the post-war period the pay structure has become increasingly complex, based not only on the initial terms of service for which the soldier has opted, but on length of completed service, trade or other qualifications, marital status, and of course, rank. Taking the unmarried private soldier on the lowest rates, a simplified review of his basic receipts can be given thus: In 1948 he was paid £2 per week; in 1956 this had risen to £3 10s; in 1972 it had soared (with inflation) to £19 53, and in 1984 it had reached £90 09. To give a detailed breakdown of the successive rates would require most of this chapter: suffice it to reproduce the revised rates of 1985:(3)

Soldiers' Daily Rates of Pay, April 1985
 (Minimum and maximum depending on applicable Scale and Band)

Warrant Officer Class 1	£29.93/£38.59
Warrant Officer Class 2	£27.96/£36.62
Staff Sergeant	£26.16/£34.82
Sergeant	£24.60/£30.42
Corporal Class 1	£22.48/£27.84
Corporal Class 2	£20.99/£23.96
Lance Corporal Class 1	£19.60/£24.96
Lance Corporal Class 2	£18.30/£21.27
Lance Corporal Class 3	£17.08/£20.05
Private Class 1	£17.08/£22.44
Private Class 2	£15.91/£18.88
Private Class 3	£14.50/£17.47
Private Class 4	£13.40/£14.15

As already noted, all soldiers pay for their accommodation and meals, a system introduced with the 'military salary' scheme in 1970. In 1984 a single soldier in barracks paid a total of £19.81 per week out of his pay, being £14.42 for meals and £5.39 for accommodation. Married men paid rent for their quarters: from £11.06 for a single-bedroom apartment to £17.99 for a three-bedroom. These charges included rates, but did not cover heating, electricity or gas. On discharge to the Reserve the soldier received a tax-free gratuity, scaled according to length of service, and varying from £305 after twelve years to £1,250 after twenty-one. To qualify for the (non-contributory) pension, a man had to serve for at least twenty-two years. In the unlikely event of a soldier being discharged as private after such a period, his annual pension would be £2,241. A corporal with the same service was entitled to £2,829; a sergeant £3,127 and a Warrant Officer Class I, £3,998.

Serving soldiers are eligible for certain fringe benefits. All ranks from private to Brigadier on duty in terrorist-infested Northern Ireland receive an extra £15.05 per week. 'Local Overseas Allowance' is paid to offset any additional cost of living in foreign stations, while married soldiers posted away from their families can claim separation allowance. This is currently £1.60 per day within North-West Europe and £2.05 outside Europe.

As in former days, the soldier of the 1980s needs to pass educational examinations if he is ambitious for promotion. But in 1971 the old Army Certificates of Education — Third, Second, First and Special — were phased out and replaced by two EPCs, or Education Promotion Certificates. The lower, necessary for promotion up to sergeant, covers English (or what the Army terms 'communication skills'), mathematics (anything from geometrical problems to the balancing of accounts), military organisation and administration, and current affairs. For promotion to Warrant Officer the EPC (advanced) is necessary, the syllabus being similar but of a higher standard. Before enlistment all potential recruits undergo written and oral tests. Those aiming at certain tradesmen jobs in the technical corps must produce civilian GCE or CSE qualifications, in some cases up to a number of A-levels.

The adult recruit, between $17\frac{1}{2}$ and 25 years of age, must sign on for a minimum period of three years, after which he may re-engage for periods up to six, nine or a maximum of 22 years. If he initially opts for the longer terms, he immediately receives a correspondingly higher rate of pay. In 1972 the Ministry of Defence introduced the Notice of Engagement scheme under which soldiers with at least eighteen months' service from the age of 18 might give eighteen months' notice of their intention to leave the Army. Those who enlist as Junior Soldiers (under $17\frac{1}{2}$) may leave at any time within their first six months if they find Army life is not to their liking.

Technically-minded youngsters with aspirations for commissions in such Corps as the Royal Engineers, REME, RAOC or Royal Signals can now receive pre-Sandhurst education at the Army's own 'sixth-form College' near Worksop, Nottinghamshire. Welbeck College was founded in 1953 on the recommendation of Committees set up by the then War Office, who were concerned at the dearth of suitably qualified potential officers for the increasingly technical specialist corps. Funded by the Ministry of Defence, the college offers a sixth-form education to A-level standard for boys between the ages of 16 and $17\frac{1}{2}$. Competition for places has always been keen; in addition to producing the required academic qualifications of a number of O-levels, all applicants are assessed by the Selection Board for general character and potential as future leaders. Welbeck is not a military unit; its pupils do not wear uniforms, and the atmosphere is little different from that of the Sixth Form in any normal boarding school. Tuition is free, but parents are required to make 'contributions' towards the cost of board and lodging. These are based on a sliding scale according to the parents' basic income. Thus those with £6,000 per year or less pay nothing; those enjoying £19,000 must contribute £950 per year. The social background of

Welbexian boys covers a wide spectrum. The present Headmaster reports: 'I always feel the archetypal Services parent at Welbeck is a Major (QM), but having said that, we have had sons of Brigadiers and Corporals. The percentage from public schools is small... eighty-five per cent of our boys are normally from comprehensive schools.' Surprisingly, only about twenty per cent come from Services families.

The course at Welbeck lasts two years and, provided the pupil has achieved at least two A-levels, he can then be recommended by the Headmaster for direct admission to Sandhurst as a cadet. Unlike the normal applicants for cadetships, he does not have to undergo the ordeal of searching character and initiative tests at the Regular Army Commissions Board. Rightly, Welbeck standards are high, and not all pupils measure up to them. To date some 2,500 boys have entered the College: 1,800 have been commissioned. The vast majority naturally go to the technical corps, REME topping the list with thirty-four per cent.(4)

According to the Directorate of Army Recruiting, there are three main factors governing what it terms the recruiting climate. These are: the Army's public image, pay rates, and civilian unemployment figures. While the first two have always exerted some constant influence, increases in the last-named predictably see corresponding increases in would-be recruits. Thus with unemployment soaring to unprecedented heights during the past five years, the numbers of young men queueing up to join the Service have been the highest recorded in a decade. But the slim 'Professional' Army of today cannot take all who come forward. With fewer vacancies and the demand for quality rather than quantity, it has to be very selective about its recruits. Gone are the days when a young man could become a soldier merely by passing a medical examination and taking the Oath. In 1971 a Recruit Selection Centre was established at Sutton Coldfield and since then other centres have been set up. These are staffed by Regular officers and senior NCOs, and all would-be recruits have to attend for three days of in-depth interviews, intelligence tests and character assessment. The scheme works both ways: not only does the Army decide whether it likes the potential private, but equally important, the latter is given every chance to decide whether he will really like the Army. In addition to the interviews, when he can question the interviewer as well as be questioned, he is shown films and given honest talks on Army life. If at the end of all this he changes his mind about soldiering, he is free to return whence he came, all expenses paid. Most candidates have already expressed a choice of regiment or corps, but the

Army does not want square pegs in round holes. If a youth keen on the Royal Engineers or the REME proves to lack any mechanical or technical bents he is gently persuaded that he would be happier in the infantry. On the other hand, it might be suggested to an academic lad with mathematical leanings that the Royal Army Pay Corps would offer him better prospects than the Royal Green Jackets.

Previously, regiments had been able to pick and choose their own recruits, and there was some initial suspicion that the RSCs would foist on them types they did not care for, or channel away those they sought. But the scheme has worked smoothly, to the benefit of regiments, recruits and the Army itself.

Post-war years have seen many minor (but to the soldier, significant) ameliorations in the military lifestyle. In 1946 that bone of contention, the compulsory Church Parade, was abolished in the revised King's Regulations, and all ranks became free to attend divine worship or not, as the spirit moved them. Also, the privilege of wearing plain clothes out of barracks was confirmed for private soldiers and junior NCOs as well as more senior ranks. During the past few years, the soldier's tonsorial style has changed. Although he has no need of a hairnet, as in certain foreign armies, the cropped 'short back and sides' rule is out. A recruiting pamphlet of 1981 declared: 'The rules have relaxed to the point that you don't stick out like a sore thumb when you're wearing civvies but you still look smart in uniform. But you can forget any ideas of hair being shoulder-length.'

Soldiers have always groused about Army 'grub'. They may still do so, but surely with little justification. As reported in *The Daily Telegraph*, in 1984 Services catering earned the accolade of unreserved praise in the Egon Ronay *Lucas Guide*. After touring Army barracks, at home and overseas, Egon Ronay found that, after applying his normal exacting criteria, 'the food is of unexpectedly high quality, the variety of choice truly amazing almost everywhere. The food is infinitely better than in civilian mass catering, the management more conscientious, efficient and concerned to please.' The days of monotonous bangers-and-mash, soggy cabbage, glutinous porridge, are now only 'old sweats'' memories. Naturally, as the soldier pays for his meals out of his own pocket, he expects and usually gets, more appetising menus. The credit for this culinary revolution is due to the Army Catering Corps, formed at Aldershot in 1941. Before that, regimental cooks were merely given some basic instruction and then let loose in the cookhouses, often to become the butts of the suffering soldiery. Now the Corps runs its own Army School of Catering, in which both Army specialists and civilian chefs put student cooks through an intensive course embracing every aspect of dietary and food preparation. The bulky official 'cook's bible', the *Army Manual of Catering*, contains hundreds of recipes and is greatly sought after by civilian catering concerns. When Princess Anne was married in 1973 it was the Army Catering Corps who made the wedding cake, at Aldershot.

Mention has been made in previous chapters of the several Services charities founded to look after the welfare of soldiers and their families. Today the Army's central charity is the Army Benevolent Fund, first registered in 1944. Its stated aim is 'to give help where State assistance is either inapplicable or inadequate. Any man or woman who is serving or has served in the British Army and their families are eligible.' During 1983-84 a total of nearly £2¼ million was paid out to 21,000 serving and ex-soldiers and their dependents. More than £100,000 was devoted to handicapped Services children, and to the provision of educational bursaries. Nearly £1 million was loaned to ex-soldiers to assist them in securing civilian occupations. By 1984 £450,000 had been paid to victims of IRA terrorist outrages in Northern Ireland.(5)

The ABF funds are derived from many sources. Some come from the public as donations or legacies, others from sponsored military displays, such as the musical rides of the Household Cavalry and The King's Troop RHA. But the largest contribution comes from serving soldiers themselves. In 1965 a Day's Pay Scheme was initiated, under which every soldier was encouraged (but not compelled) to give one day's pay per year to his Regimental Association, which then passed on a generous proportion to the ABF. These sums naturally vary with the strengths of regiments or corps. A single-battalion infantry regiment might donate a few hundred pounds. In 1977 the Royal Corps of Signals produced £23,000, the REME £27,000.

Traditionally, soldiering has been a man's business, or as current recruiting publicity stresses, 'a man-sized job'. However, since the Second World War it has become increasingly a woman-sized job as well. Apart from the Queen Alexandra's Royal Army Nursing Corps, who are of course nurses rather than soldiers, there are now nearly 5,000 members of the Women's Royal Army Corps who, when duty demands, wear combat dress and carry arms. These women-soldiers, or Servicewomen, are the descendants of the ATS (Auxiliary Territorial Service) who performed non-combatant duties in most theatres of the Second World War.

WRAC personnel have replaced male soldiers in a wide variety of jobs ranging from chauffering, clerical and administrative duties to communications and computer programming. Never combatant soldiers, until 1981 they were not allowed to bear arms. But in that year the Defence Secretary (Francis Pym) announced that the WRAC were to fall into line with other NATO forces and undergo weapon training with small arms. In certain situations they would carry submachine guns or pistols. This was no attempt to turn the WRAC into a bunch of tough Amazons: it was stressed that the object was purely 'for limited self-defence on bases in emergencies'. The WRAC would not carry arms at all times, and would never be employed in a combat role. Nevertheless, the vision of gun-toting girls raised some eyebrows, military and civilian. Among the WRAC themselves there were mixed reactions. Interviewed by a *Soldier* journalist, some took a realistic, soldierlike view. A staff-sergeant declared 'On the whole I think women in the Army have got to be able to defend themselves in the situations suggested, and be capable of standing by their male counterparts.' An eighteen-year-old lance-corporal admitted: 'I couldn't kill anyone... I think I would refuse to carry a gun. I didn't join the Army to carry guns, and I don't think girls are built for them anyway, although I've done Battle Camp training with competition shooting on the ranges.'(6)

Pay rates for women-soldiers are slightly lower than men's. For example, in 1984 a WRAC Private Class III received £94.78 per week, her male counterpart, £97.02. The WRAC Warrant Officer Class I could reach a maximum of £246.12, compared with £251.79 for the male RSM or equivalent.

This book has been concerned with the British soldier, but by extension that adjective covers all members of the British Army. Since 1947 these have included those cheery little hillmen from Nepal, the Gurkhas, whose qualities have always been acknowledged by the indigenous British soldier as equal to his own (British officers of the Gurkha Rifle Regiments will dispute this: better, they claim).

On the granting of Independence to India in 1947, four of the ten Gurkha Rifle Regiments on the strength of the former (British) Indian Army were transferred to the British service, and for the first time since the disbandment of The King's German Legion after Waterloo, the British Army included foreign mercenaries in its establishment. The

British soldier of today, with no personal experience of the splendid combat qualities, and comradeship, of the Gurkha riflemen in two World Wars and in countless other far-flung fields, may not regard them with quite the same degree of affection and camaraderie as hitherto. Normally, he has little contact, and tends to view them as strange little aliens with odd customs, unpronounceable names and incomprehensible speech. But he ungrudgingly respects their professionalism, as he did in the Falklands, and was probably aware, until 1985, that the Army's only serving holder of the Victoria Cross was a Gurkha.[1]

Gurkha soldiers, 'Bravest of the Brave', have loyally served the Crown since 1815, and are still recruited in their native Nepal. Such is their inherited enthusiasm for soldiering under the British flag, that there are always more young hopefuls than the recruiting officers can accept. To all intents and purposes they are 'British' soldiers, under exactly the same regulations and code of discipline. But, resulting from a tripartite agreement between Britain, India and Nepal, their basic rates of pay are lower than their British comrades', being linked to those of their compatriots in India's Army. However, the difference can be made up by Local Overseas Allowance payable to all serving outside their homeland. In effect, therefore, Gurkhas serving in England and Hong Kong (Headquarters of the Brigade of Gurkhas) can earn almost as much as the British soldiers. The vast majority of officers in Gurkha regiments are still British, but since 1958 suitably qualified Gurkha candidates have been admitted to Sandhurst, to obtain the Queen's Commission. Such commissioned Gurkhas, however, can serve only in Gurkha regiments.

The Gurkha recruit signs on for four years and can then extend up to fifteen years, when he qualifies for a pension. If he has risen no higher than corporal after that period, discharge is obligatory, but if he has reached sergeant he may continue up to eighteen years. A Warrant Officer can remain up to twenty years.

The welfare of Gurkha soldiers is generously provided for. Since 1967 when the Gurkha Welfare Appeal was launched, more than £1½ million has been raised, producing an annual investment income of some £100,000. The British Government pays all administrative costs, so that

---

1. In March 1985 Captain Rambahadur Limbu VC, MVO, (10th Princess Mary's Own Gurkha Rifles) was ceremonially retired from the Army on a special Farewell Parade at Church Crookham, Hampshire. He had won his Cross as a Lance-Corporal in Borneo, in 1965.

95 per cent of the funds can be devoted directly to the aims of the Appeal. In addition, like the British soldier, serving Gurkhas surrender one day's pay annually. Concern for Gurkha welfare is not confined to Britain. In 1968 a fund was initiated by Canadian ex-soldiers who had fought alongside 'Johnnie Gurkha', and the Canadian Government magnanimously agreed to contribute two dollars for every one raised by the organisers. All this largesse is devoted mainly to helping Gurkha ex-soldiers, and their families, in need, and to major projects such as the building of schools and hospitals in the remote recruiting areas of Nepal. By British Army standards, the Gurkha's pension may seem minimal — only about £96 a year on the lower scale. But in a primitive mountain village, that is almost affluence, being as much as the average peasant could expect to earn by the sweat of his brow. Quite apart from the monetary aspect, the long-standing service tradition among these loyal hillmen is still honoured and cherished. An ex-soldier, particularly if NCO or officer, is respected as a man of integrity education and experience.(7)

While Army discipline has long ceased to be a subject arousing questions in the House, the erring soldier must be punished (or 'corrected'). Normally, minor offences incur fines from his pay, but for more serious crimes such as 'offering violence to his superior officer' he may still have to undergo detention. Formerly in addition to the dreaded 'Glasshouse' at Aldershot, there were detention barracks, or military prisons, in most garrisons. Today there is only one, and indicative of changed attitudes, it is designated not 'prison', but Military Corrective Training Centre. It is located near the ancient garrison town of Colchester (where Roman soldiers probably underwent 'corrective training') and is staffed by officers and NCOs of the Military Provost Staff Corps. This body, equivalent to the civilian Prison Service, is no relation to the Corps of Royal Military Police — although they may be instrumental in providing its clients. The latter are no longer referred to as 'prisoners', but as SUS: Servicemen Under Sentence. As in civilian life, the treatment of offenders has become more liberal, if not softer.

> Everything we do here has a purpose. There is no question of men shifting heaps of sand just to keep them occupied. Our aims are simple: to improve their efficiency, discipline and morale, and establish in them the will to be better Servicemen; and for those leaving the Service on discharge, to help them prepare for their return to civilian life....

They're not bad lads, but mostly young soldiers who have gone off the military rails a bit and need some guidance. We're here to provide that guidance in a humane but disciplined fashion.(8)

Depending on the gravity of his offence, the soldier can be sentenced to anything from 28 days to two years at the Colchester MCTC.

Since 1945 soldiers have had their own fortnightly magazine, entitled appropriately enough, *Soldier* and styling itself 'The Magazine of the British Army'. This originated in Brussels in March 1945 as a news (and morale-boosting) sheet for the troops of the British Liberation Army, and the first issue carried a typical 'good hunting' message from Monty. In 1950 it acquired an office in London, but in 1971 it moved to its present location in Aldershot. The editorial staff are civilian and the contents are produced exclusively by staff journalists and photographers (though some are ex-soldiers). *Soldier* has become a glossy, profusely illustrated and brightly written magazine which is probably glanced through, if not digested, by every member of the Army. More orientated to the soldier rather than the officer, it is a Ministry of Defence organ and thus eschews controversial matters, to concentrate on newsy stories about the Army's doings, personalities, and straight facts, such as revisions in pay rates, changes in dress, and so forth.

The Army boasts another strictly official ('Restricted') journal, *The British Army Review*, founded in the 1960s and appearing only three times a year. This describes itself as 'the house journal of the Army', and is more serious and professional in its contents, which are slanted more to the officer. Unlike *Soldier*, its columns are open to contributions 'on all matters of professional interest' from serving ranks, commissioned or not, for which modest payment is made. However, all offerings have first to be vetted by the author's commanding officer, and are then subject to final clearance by the Editor, who is a member of the Ministry of Defence staff at Whitehall, where the journal is published. There is nothing unusual in such restrictions. In Victorian times officers (and other ranks if literate) could and did pen controversial letters to *The Times* or the RUSI *Journal*, hiding under pseudonyms. Not so today. No serving member of the forces is allowed to publish anything without prior clearance by Authority.

This book has attempted to survey the lifestyle of the British soldier over more than three centuries. During this span the Army and human society have undergone revolutionary transformations which would have seemed sheer lunatic fantasy could they have been foreseen by General George Monck and his regiment when they marched from Coldstream to London, there to lay down their arms and take them up again as soldiers of King Charkes II.

The soldier of our modern 'professional' Army is as different from his prototype of the first Standing Army as is the Challenger tank from the crude musket and cannon of Stuart days. He is an intelligent, educated being, taught to think for himself and display initiative, and expecting to be housed, fed and cared for much as any other member of society. If he still has to submit to discipline and irksome restrictions, he realises that such are essential to the proper functioning of his chosen way of life. And he is ready to accept the hardships and hazards of that life as part and parcel of a military career.

Some would aver that the modern soldier is softer than his predecessors of, say, Victoria's army. Perhaps there may be a modicum of truth in this. In peacetime at any rate, he is not subjected to the harsh discipline, brutal punishments and uncaring attitudes that afflicted the 'common soldier' of other days. It might be thought that a society that is cossetted from cradle to grave by a Welfare State is unlikely to breed the stuff of which thin red lines were made. But anyone holding such views should have been confounded when the Task Force went into action in the Falklands. In Northern Ireland, bombs, bullets and booby-traps are confronted with the same stoic courage that the British soldier has always displayed. He even endures with contemptuous stoicism the snide jibes and caricatures from trendy journalists and TV producers, some of whom do not yet seem to have realised that the Army is not a rabble of loutish oafs and blimpish officers.

The soldier and his attitudes may have changed, but there is one characteristic that has abided through the centuries, and that is his instinctive loyalty. Loyalty not so much, perhaps, to the monarch to whom he formally swears allegience, but more immediately to his 'family', the regiment or corps in which he serves. This unique feature of the British Army is sometimes regarded with bemused envy by foreign military. There is a story that a German officer visiting the Camberley Staff College once remarked to his British host 'All you people seem to belong to independent regiments: I've never met anyone who says he's in the British Army.'

What is it that induces the *esprit de corps* and sense of duty that is so markedly lacking in civilian life? Perhaps in the first place it may be that the young man who elects to become a soldier enjoys basically different values and motivations from his pal in civvy street who clocks in on the shop floor, or at the pithead every day, or is content to draw his unemployment benefits while waiting for the State to bring a worthwhile job to his doorstep. Once enlisted, the recruit lives by a very special code of ethics. This not only encourages self-discipline, respect for authority and regard for duties rather than 'rights', but imbues in him the sense of belonging and comradeship that he does not find elsewhere. To put it simply, he enjoys job satisfaction.

Although he himself would probably be reluctant to admit it, the soldier is not as other men are. He is a member of an élite that holds steadfastly to virtues and values which are constantly eroded outside the Services.

The final words of this book can come from a leader who understood the British soldier and his make-up better than most, and appreciated his true worth. On retiring after fifty years in the Army, Monty wrote:

I shall take away many impressions into the evening of life. But the one I shall treasure above all is the picture of the British soldier — staunch and tenacious in adversity — kind and gentle in victory — the man to whom the nation has again and again in the hour of peril owed its safety and its honour.(9)

REFERENCES

CHAPTER 1

1. The prime sources for the raising of the British Army are:
   CLODE, Charles M., *The Military Forces of the Crown* (1869)
   DALTON, Charles, *English Army Lists and Commission Registers 1661–1714*
   (Vol. 1, 1892)
   FORTESCUE, Hon. (Sir) J. W., *A History of the British Army* (Vol. 1, 1899)
   WALTON, Colonel Clifford, *History of the British Standing Army A.D. 1660
   to 1700* (1894)
2. Walton, *op. cit.*
3. The original Mutiny Act of 1689 is quoted in full in Clode, *op. cit.*
4. Defoe, *An Argument for a Standing Army* (1698)
5. Walton, *op. cit.*
6. J. Deprepetit to Lieut-Colonel John Coke. Quoted in *The Manuscripts of the
   Earl of Cowper KG.* (Historical Manuscripts Commission)
7. Public Record Office. Wo24/844
8. Howell, John (Ed.), *The Life of Alexander Alexander* (Royal Artillery)
   written by himself (Edinburgh, 1830)
9. Unpublished letter from Private James Sharloe to brother, 28th March 1698.
   (Regimental Museum, The Queen's Own Hussars, Warwick)
10. *An English Military Dictionary* by an officer who has served several years
    abroad (1702)
11. Singer, S. W. (Ed.), *Correspondence of Henry Hyde, Earl of Clarendon and
    his Brother Lawrence Hyde, Earl of Rochester 1687 to 1690.* (London, 1828)
12. Clode, *op. cit.*
13. Walton, *op. cit.*
14. *Rules and Orders for this Summers Encampment upon Hounslow-Heath...*
    Public Record Office, Wo26/6
15. *The Diary of John Evelyn* (entry for January 27th, 1682)
16. Dean, Captain C. G. T., *The Royal Chelsea Hospital* (1950)
17. Dean, *op. cit.*
18. *Advice to a Soldier, in Two Letters, written to an Officer in the English Army*
    (Printed by John Shadd, London, 1680)

REFERENCES

CHAPTER 2

1. Walton, Colonel Clifford, *History of the British Standing Army* (1894)
2. Dalton, Charles, *George The First's Army* (Vol. II, 1912)
3. MS letter, Regimental Museum, 4th/7th Royal Dragoon Guards
4. Millner, Sergeant John, *A Compendious Journal of Marches, Famous Battles and Sieges...* (London, 1733)
5. Murray, General The Rt. Hon. Sir George, *The Letters and Dispatches of John Churchill, First Duke of Marlborough, from 1702 to 1712,* (1845)
6. Millner, *op. cit.*
7. Parker, Captain Robert, *Memories of the Most Memorable Military Transactions* (Dublin, 1746)
8. Trevelyan, G. M., *England Under Queen Anne. Blenheim* (1930)
9. Letter, Captain Richard Pope to Thomas Coke, M.P., in *The Manuscripts of the Earl of Cowper KG preserved at Melbourne Hall, Derbyshire* (Historical Manuscripts Commission)
10. Luttrell, Narcissus, *A Brief Historical Relation of State Affairs from 1680 to 1716* (Oxford, 1857)
11. Quoted in Murray, Robert H., *The History of The VIII King's Royal Irish Hussars* (Cambridge, 1928)
12. The most reliable outline for the life of 'Mother Ross' is that in the *Dictionary of National Biography,* which is partly based on the anonymous work *The Life and Adventures of Mrs Christian Davies, commonly called Mother Ross* (1740). Authorship has been attributed to Daniel Defoe, but this is disputed by the *DNB.*
13. Grose, Francis, *Military Antiquities respecting a History of the English Army* (1786)
14. This well-authenticated case is quoted by *inter alia*, Fortescue, *A History of the British Army* (Vol. I), and Trevelyan, *op. cit.*
15. Hamilton, Robert, *The Duties of a Regimental Surgeon Considered* (1787)
16. Somerville, Alexander, *The Autobiography of a Working Man* (Ed. J. Carswell, 1848. Reprinted 1967)
17. Marshall, Henry, *A Historical Sketch of Military Punishments* (1840)
18. (Quoted in) Claver, Scott, *Under The Lash: A History of Corporal Punishment in the British Armed Forces* (1954)
19. Curling, Henry (Ed.), *Recollections of Rifleman Harris* (1929. Reprinted 1966)
20. Fortescue, J. W., *A History of the British Army* (Vol. IV, Part II, 1906)
21. Clode, Charles M., *The Military Forces of the Crown* (1869)
22. Clode, *op. cit.*
23. Spiers, Edward M., *The Army and Society* (1980)
24. Jervis, Patrick, *From Ensign to Ship's Captain* (Dublin, 1812)
25. Cobbett, William, *The Autobiography of William Cobbett* (Ed. W. Beitzel, 1967)
26. Fortescue, Sir John W., *A Short Account of Canteens in the British Army* (Cambridge, 1928)
27. De Watteville, Colonel H., *The British Soldier* (1954)

28. Shipp, John, *Memoirs of the Extraordinary Military Career of John Shipp, late a Lieutenant in His Majesty's 87th Regiment* (1829)
29. Quoted in Strachan, Hew, *British Military Uniforms 1768–1796* (1975)
30. Hinde, Captain R., *The Discipline of the Light Horse* (London, 1778)
31. Cuthbertson, Bennett, *A System for the Compleat Interior Management and Oeconomy of a Battalion of Infantry* (Dublin, 1768 and 1776) Quoted in Strachan, *op. cit.*
32. *Regulations for the Colours, Cloathing &c of the Marching Regiments of Foot and for the Uniform Cloathing of the Cavalry, their Standards, Guidons, Banners &c.* (Public Record Office W.O. 7/25)
33. Clode, *op. cit.*

CHAPTER 3

1. Wellington, 2nd Duke of (Ed.), *Supplementary Despatches & Memoranda of Field Marshal The Duke of Wellington* (14 Vols, 1858–72)
2. Hart, Captain B. H. Liddell (Ed.), *The Letters of Private Wheeler 1809–1828* (1951)
3. Memoirs of a Serjeant, late of the 43rd Light Infantry Regiment (1835)
4. Sir John Moore. Quoted in J. C. Moore, *Life of Sir John Moore* (2 Vols, 1834)
5. Glover, Michael, *Wellington's Army in the Peninsula 1808–1814* (1977)
6. Statistics of civilian wages over three centuries are given in Lipson, E., *The Economic History of England* (1956)
7. Parliamentary Proceedings, quoted in *United Service Journal* (April, 1834)
8. Stanhope, Philip Henry, 5th Earl, *Notes of Conversations with the Duke of Wellington 1831–1851* (1888)
9. Oman, C. W., *Wellington's Army 1809–1814* (1912)
10. General Order, Horse Guards, March 18th, 1829
11. State Papers, Domestic: Military. PRO SP41
12. *The Standing Orders of the 15th (or King's) Regiment of Hussars.* Compiled by Lieut-Colonel Joseph Thackwell (1832) (Northamptonshire Record Office. XV.17)
13. *Report on the Regimental and Garrison Schools of the Army* by Bt. Colonel J. H. Lefroy (1859), quoted in Skelley, A. R., *The Victorian Army at Home* (1977)
14. Spiers, Edward M., *The Army and Society 1815–1914* (1980)
15. Farwell, Byron, *For Queen and Country. A Social History of The Victorian and Edwardian Army* (1981)
16. *The Autobiography and Services of Sir James McGrigor, Bart.* (1861)
17. Jackson, Thomas, *Narrative of the Eventful Life of Thomas Jackson, late Sergeant of the Coldstream Guards* (Birmingham, 1847)
18. Fortescue, Sir John W, *A History of the British Army* (Vol. IV — Part I)
19. Heathcote, T. A. *The Indian Army. The Garrison of British Imperial India, 1822–1922* (1974)
20. Sheppard, Major E. W., *The Ninth Queen's Royal Lancers 1715–1936* (1939)

21. Richards, Frank, *Old Soldier Sahib* (1936)
22. *Royal Commission on the Sanitary State of the Army in India. Report of the Commissioners* (1865)
23. *Standing Orders for the Seventh or Princess Royal's Dragoon Guards, issued by Colonel Francis Dunne* (1823) (National Army Museum)
24. *United Service Journal* (April, 1834)
25. *Report from His Majesty's Commissioners for Inquiring into the System of Military Punishment in the Army* (1836)
26. The case of Private White is recorded in C. R. B. Barrett's *The 7th (Queen's Own) Hussars* (Vol. II, 1914), but a more detailed (if slanted) account is that of H. Hopkins in his book *The Strange Death of Private White* (1977). The subsequent debate will be found in *Parliamentary Debates* 3rd Series, Vol. 91, April 26th, 1847.

CHAPTER 4

1. Fitzherbert, C. (Ed.), *Henry Clifford V.C. his letters and sketches from the Crimea* (1956)
2. *Medical Memorandum* by Dr John Hall, quoted in *Illustrated London News*, September 23rd, 1854, p. 289
3. Lieutenant (Later Major-General) Godman, 5th Dragoon Guards. Quoted in *The Fields of War: A Young Cavalryman's Crimea Campaign*, Ed. Philip Warner (1977)
4. For a valuable study of medical mismanagement in the Crimea, and the origins of the Medical Staff Corps see: Sweetman, John, 'The Crimean War and the Formation of The Medical Staff Corps' *Journal of the Society for Army Historical Research*, L111, 214 (Summer, 1975)
5. Barthorp, Michael, *The Armies of Britain 1485–1980* (National Army Museum, 1980)
6. *Report of the Army Sanitary Commission* (1857–58)
7. *The Sanitary Reform of the British Army* (1859). Pamphlet, *anon.*, but ascribed to Sir Duncan MacDougall.
8. *General Report of the Commission appointed for Improving the Sanitary Condition of Barracks and Hospitals* (1861) Quoted in Spiers, Edward M., *The Army and Society* (1980)
9. *J. Royal United Service Institution* (May, 1861) Letter by 'Medicus'
10. Anon. (John E. Acland), *Through the Ranks to a Commission* (1881)
11. Skelley, A. R., *The Victorian Army at Home* (McGill-Queen's University, 1977)
12. Grenville Murray, E. C., *Six Months in the Ranks* (1882)
13. *Anon.* Acland, *op. cit.*
14. Skelley, *op. cit.*
15. *Selections from the Diary of the Rev. Francis Kilvert*, Ed. William Plomer (3 Vols, 1977)
16. Trevelyan, G. M., *English Social History* (1944)
17. *Parliamentary Debates* 3rd Series, Vol. 191, March 28th, 1868

18. Claver, Scott, *Under the Lash: A History of Corporal Punishment in the British Armed Forces* (1954)
19. *Mutiny Act* (1860)
20. Spiers, Edward M., *The Army and Society 1815–1914* (1980)
21. Cardwell: Memorandum on Military Organisation, 1870. Quoted in 'The Late Victorian Army' by Brian Bond (*History Today* XI, 9. September, 1961)
22. Robertson, Field-Marshal Sir William, *From Private to Field-Marshal* (1921)
23. Smyth, Sir John, V.C., *Sandhurst* (1961)
24. Skelley, *op. cit.*
25. *Report of Royal Commission on Army Promotion and Retirement* (1876)

CHAPTER 5

1. Surprisingly, there is no book devoted specifically to 'the White Mutiny'. Facts and figures have been culled from the following sources: *Parliamentary Papers* H.C., 169 and 471 of 1860 and H.C. 77 of 1861; Maclagan, M., *'Clemency' Canning* (1962); Shadwell, Lt-General, *The Life of Colin Campbell, Lord Clyde* (1881); Elsmie, G. R., *Thirty-Five Years in the Punjab* (1908); Steele, Capt. Russell, '1st Bengal European Light Cavalry 1858–61' — *J. Society for Army Historical Research* XX, 80 (Winter 1941) A more detailed account of the whole episode is given in the present author's 'The White Mutiny', *History Today* XXIX (April 1979).
2. Shadwell, *op. cit.*
3. Letter by 'A Retired Officer' in *J. Royal United Service Institution* (May, 1891)
4. Robertson, F-M. Sir William, *From Private to Field-Marshal* (1921)
5. Acland, John E., *Through the Ranks to a Commission* (1881)
6. A complete history of The Royal Tournament (to 1951) is given in Lieut-Colonel P. L. Binns, *The Story of The Royal Tournament* (1952)
7. Hay, Ian, *Arms and the Men* (1950)
8. Maxim, Sir Hiram, *My Life* (1915)
9. Letter, War Office to G.O.C. Aldershot Command, January 21st, 1902. (Quoted in Cole, Lieut-Colonel H. N., *The Story of Aldershot* (1951))
10. *Return on the Total Amount of Stoppages from the Pay of Privates Stationed at Aldershot*, 1890. (Parliamentary Papers, L [c209] 1890–91)
11. Details of rates of pay etc. and pensions are taken from *Royal Warrant for the Pay, Appointment, Promotion and Non-Effective Pay of the Army 1893* (H.M.S.O. 1893)
12. Beveridge, Sir William, *Prices and Wages in England from the Twelfth to the Nineteenth Century* (1939)
13. *J. Royal United Services Institution* (June, 1898)
14. Mole, TSM Edwin, *A King's Hussar* (Ed. Compton, H., 1893)

CHAPTER 6

1. Dunlop, Colonel John, *The Development of the British Army 1899–1914* (1938)
2. *J. Royal United Services Institution* (August, 1903)
3. Graham, Stephen, *A Private in the Guards* (1919)
4. Richards, Frank, *Old Soldier Sahib* (1936)
5. *The King's Royal Rifle Corps Chronicle* (1961)
6. Richards, *op. cit.*
7. *Cavalry Training* (1908)
8. Writing in *The Cavalry Journal* for March 1910, Field-Marshal Sir Evelyn Wood VC declared, 'Eight years ago most commanding officers recommended an annual allowance of from £500 to £600 (for a cavalry subaltern). Now, it is alleged, a very careful officer may join the cavalry at an initial expense of £400 and either hunt or play polo on an allowance of £300.'
9. *Royal Warrant for the Pay... of The Army* (1913)
10. Hamilton, General Sir Ian, *The Soul and Body of an Army* (1921)
11. Bonham-Carter, Maj-General G., 'Recent Developments in Education in the Army': *The Army Quarterly* (January, 1931)
12. *Royal Warrant for the Pay... of the Army* (1914)
13. Stanhope, Henry, *The Soldiers: An Anatomy of the British Army* (1979)

CHAPTER 7

1. Hankey, 2nd Lieut Donald, *A Student in Arms* (1916)
2. *Field Service Pocket Book* (1914) Exactly the same scales for tented accommodation were being specified in the 1939 issue of the *FSPB*.
3. Special Army Order, August 1914.
4. Owen, Wilfred. Letter to his brother, quoted in *Wilfred Owen: War Poems and Others*, ed. by Dominic Hibberd (1973)
5. Quoted in Brown, Malcolm, *Tommy Goes to War* (1978)
6. These and subsequent details are taken from Judge Anthony Babington's book, *For the Sake of Example* (1983), which is a detailed study of all the capital courts martial convened between 1914 and 1920.
7. Richardson, Major-General F. M., *Fighting Spirit: Psychological Factors in War* (1978)
8. Liddell Hart, Captain Basil, *The Memoirs of Captain Liddell Hart*, Vol. I (1965)
9. House of Commons Oral Answers, November 26th, 1917, quoted in Babington, *op. cit.*
10. Graves, Robert, *Goodbye to All That* (1929)
11. Unpublished diaries of Captain Archibald Wright, 4th Royal Irish Dragoon Guards, 1914–15 (Regimental Museum, 4th/7th Royal Dragoon Guards)
12. *Field Service Pocket Book* (1914)
13. Quoted in Brown, *op. cit.*

14. Facts and figures for pensions and welfare are taken from *The War Cabinet Report for the Year 1917* (Government Blue Paper. HMSO, 1918)
15. For a detailed survey of The Royal British Legion's origins and development see Wootton, Graham, *The Official History of The British Legion* (1956)

CHAPTER 8

1. *Journal of the RUSI* (Army Notes) May, 1938
2. *Regulations respecting Admission to the Royal Military Academy Woolwich and the Royal Military College Sandhurst...* (War Office, 1931)
3. *Hansard* Vol. 806, Friday November 20th, 1970. (Written Answers to Questions)
4. A detailed, if somewhat coloured and slanted, account of the Connaught Rangers mutiny is given in Pollock, Sam, *Mutiny for the Cause* (1969). It is also referred to in Judge Anthony Babington's book on capital courts martial, *For the Sake of Example* (1983)
5. Quoted in Babington, *op. cit.*
6. *House of Commons, Army and Air Force (Annual) Bill*, April 16th, 1930
7. Manual of Military Law (1929)
8. *Journal of the R.U.S.I.*, August 1924
9. *Educational Training 1931* (HMSO). The syllabuses for the various Certificates are taken from the same source.
10. From personal notes made while serving with 2nd Bn. The Border Regiment, Ferozepur, 1935
11. While the author was one of those soldiers very familiar with troop trains, some details are taken from 'Troop Trains in India' by Captain R. M. Hall, in *Journal of the Royal United Services Institution* (November, 1935)
12. Royal Warrant for the Pay... of the Army (HMSO, 1937)
13. *J. Royal United Services Institution* (May, 1937)

CHAPTER 9

1. Details of conscription schemes and statistics are taken from Hay, Ian, *The Second World War 1939–1945: Arms and the Men* (HMSO, 1950)
2. Central Statistical Office: *Statistical Digest of the War* (HMSO, 1947)
3. A detailed study of conscientious objectors and the Non-Combatant Corps in the Second World War will be found in Hayes, Denis, *Challenge of Conscience* (1949)
4. Central Statistical Office, *op. cit.*
5. Macnalty, Sir A. S. and Mellor, W. F. (Eds.) *Medical Services in War* (HMSO, 1968)
6. Macnalty and Mellor, *op. cit.*
7. Slim, Field-Marshal Sir William, *Defeat into Victory* (1956)
8. Macnalty and Mellor, *op. cit.*
9. Ellis, John, *The Sharp End of War: The Fighting Man in World War II* (1980)

10. A comprehensive study will be found in Colonel R. H. Ahrenfeldt's *Psychiatry in the British Army in the Second World War* (1958). The subject is also examined in Macnalty and Mellor *op. cit.* and Ellis, *op. cit.*, while there are percipient passages in General Sir David Fraser's *And We Shall Shock Them: The British Army in the Second World War* (1983)
11. Ahrenfeldt, *op. cit.*
12. Fraser, *op. cit.*
13. Quoted in Ahrenfeldt, *op. cit.*
14. The Salerno Mutiny is referred to in: Pond, Hugh, *Salerno* (1961); Ellis, *op. cit.*; Fraser, *op. cit.*
15. Ahrenfeldt, R. H., in Macnalty and Mellor, *op. cit.*
16. McPherson, Brigadier A. B. (Ed.), *The Second World War 1939–1945: Army Discipline* (War Office, 1950)

CHAPTER 10

1. Quoted in Johnson, B. S. (Ed.), *All Bull: The National Servicemen* (1973)
2. Private communication from General Sir Patrick Howard-Dobson, GCB.
3. *Soldier* magazine (July 1st, 1985)
4. Private communication from M. J. Maloney, Headmaster Welbeck College, February, 1985.
5. Report by Major-General E. Fursdon, *The Daily Telegraph*, July 14th, 1984
6. *Soldier* magazine (February, 1981)
7. Readers seeking an in-depth study of the Gurkha, his history, training and conditions down to modern times, should refer to Farwell, Byron, *The Gurkhas* (1984)
8. Lieut-Colonel J. Robinson, MPSC, reported in *Soldier* (January 30th, 1984)
9. Field-Marshal Viscount Montgomery, *Memoirs* (1958)

INDEX

Individual units, etc. are listed under Regiments and Corps.
Wars and Campaigns will be found under that heading.